P9-DIY-164

CAKE BOSS

ɕ

Stories and Recipes from Mia Famiglia

BUDDY VALASTRO

FREE PRESS

New York   London   Toronto   Sydney

*f*P

FREE PRESS
A Division of Simon & Schuster, Inc.
1230 Avenue of the Americas
New York, NY 10020

Copyright © 2010 Discovery Communications, LLC. TLC and related logos are trademarks
of Discovery Communications, LLC, used under license. All rights reserved. tlc.com

All rights reserved, including the right to reproduce this book or portions thereof
in any form whatsoever. For information address Free Press Subsidiary Rights Department,
1230 Avenue of the Americas, New York, NY 10020.

First Free Press hardcover edition November 2010

FREE PRESS and colophon are trademarks of Simon & Schuster, Inc.

For information about special discounts for bulk purchases,
please contact Simon & Schuster Special Sales at 1-866-506-1949
or business@simonandschuster.com.

The Simon & Schuster Speakers Bureau can bring authors to your live event.
For more information or to book an event, contact the Simon & Schuster Speakers Bureau
at 1-866-248-3049 or visit our website at www.simonspeakers.com.

DESIGNED BY ERICH HOBBING

Manufactured in the United States of America

11   13   15   17   19   20   18   16   14   12

Library of Congress Cataloging-in-Publication Data
Valastro, Buddy.
Cake boss: stories and recipes from *mia famiglia* / by Buddy Valastro.
p. cm.
Includes bibliographical references and index
1. Valastro, Buddy.   2. Bakers—New Jersey—Hoboken—Biography.   3. Cake decorating—
New Jersey—Hoboken—Biography.   4. Carlo's Bakery (Hoboken, N.J.)   5. Hoboken (N.J.)—
Biography.   6. Baking—United States.   7. Cake—United States.   8. Pastry—United
States.   9. Cookery, Italian.   I. Title.
HD9058.P372V35 2010
664'.752092—dc22
[B]   2010009760
ISBN 978-1-4391-8351-9
ISBN 978-1-4516-0924-0 (ebook)

*I dedicate this book
to the memory of my father,
Bartolo "Buddy" Valastro,
whose love, talent, and legacy
continue to inspire me every day.*

Contents

Introduction   3

1:   Coming to America   9

2:   The Prince of Pastry   21

3:   Education of a Cake Boss   41

4:   Calling Saint Anthony   69

5:   Big Shoes   77

6:   Making My Mark   89

7:   Polishing the Diamond   101

8:   Brides and Grooms and Sweet Little Things   117

9:   Ready for Our Close-up   135

10:   Recipes from *Mia Famiglia*   153

Sources   239

Acknowledgments   241

Index   245

CAKE BOSS

My hands were crumbling, falling apart, disintegrating, turning to dust.

It was the summer of 1994, and I was experiencing an unfamiliar sensation—failure.

My hands had finally met their match, something that had previously been unthinkable to me. From the time I was a kid, my hands had been able to master anything related to baking. Anything. Forming pasticiotti *(small, custard-filled pastries), rolling* taralles *(vanilla cookies), icing a cake.*

The lobster tails were something else altogether. They begin with a clam-shaped shell made from sfogliatelle *dough.* Sfogliatelle *means "many layers," and is the Italian answer to puff pastry. It's the hardest Italian dough to make, and is used in a few classic desserts. The original Neapolitan pastry, also called* sfogliatelle, *is filled with orange-infused ricotta cheese and baked. The lobster tails created in the United States are filled with cream puff dough before baking, then the finished shells are piped full of a rich pastry cream. Lobster tails are one of the signature offerings of my family's business, Carlo's Bake Shop.*

Making sfogliatelle *is like going for your PhD in pastry. You may have other degrees, but this will take it to a whole new level. There are guys who have been baking for thirty or forty years who can't do it. It's not their fault. Baking is like any other craft; you either have it or you don't. Really, when it comes to* sfogliatelle, *it's not you that's doing the hard work. It's your fingers. Once the dough is rolled out—and we're talking a lot of dough, about sixteen feet long by three feet*

1

wide—you massage it from beneath, stretching it until it's almost transparent. Then, you roll the sheet up tightly, greasing it with shortening and pulling it taut after each turn, until it's coiled into a thick spool that we call the salami. *You cut cross sections of it, then it's up to your fingers to push the layers out into a cone, opening it up, to give them room to breathe, so that when the pastry is baked, it'll unfurl, each layer as thin and delicate as parchment. Doing all of this requires incredible finesse, as the dough can tear, or the salami can be uneven or too loosely packed. It's not just a matter of understanding this; the bottom line is that some fingers can do it and some can't. Simple as that.*

The only thing was that I didn't have the luxury of being one of those who couldn't do it. I should have been able to make that sfogliatelle. *Because I had my father's hands. And his name. And his bakery.*

Day after day, I'd tussle with the dough, trying to get it to come out right, but it was hopeless. Every attempt ended the same way, with me standing over the bench, looking down at a mound of mangled dough, ready to put my fist through a wall. My Uncle Dominic, a stocky hard worker in his mid-forties then, with an echo of Italy in his voice, would be standing over me.

"You should be able to do this," he would say, shaking his head, confounded. "You're Buddy's son."

I'd be thinking the exact same thing: I'm Buddy's son. And that had always been enough. I was born for baking, but my crisis with the sfogliatelle *left me doubtful.*

Did I have what it took?

Would I be able to succeed?

Could I ever, truly, be the Boss?

Introduction

THE DECORATING ROOM on the second floor of Carlo's Bake Shop, my family's business in Hoboken, New Jersey, is like heaven on Earth to me. It's where my comrades in arms and I work our magic, turning out wedding cakes, birthday cakes, and theme cakes for every occasion imaginable.

Every day is a new adventure in that decorating room: On Monday, the big challenge might be a ten-tier wedding cake draped with rolled fondant and showered with delicate, lifelike sugar flowers; on Tuesday, it could be a birthday cake shaped like a soccer field, complete with figurines of the players; by Wednesday, we might be replicating a pop star's new CD cover in icing and gum paste for a television show; and Thursday and Friday . . . well, we'll cross those bridges when we get to them.

I used to spend all my time in the decorating room, but now I have other responsibilities as well, because I'm not just a decorator; I'm the Boss. A portion of each day is spent in my office, down the hall from that grown-up playpen. When I'm in my office, the hallway outside its door is always crowded. It's a narrow passageway on the second floor, and half of its width is taken up with steel utility shelving. On a normal day, there's a line outside made up of family and other employees waiting to come in and see me. Some of them need me to sign off on something, like the design and baking of a cake for fifty people for a special event by *tomorrow*, even though our production schedule is maxed out. Others have a question that only I can answer,

Mia famiglia.

like what we should charge a local rock band for a sheet cake with modeling-chocolate figurines of themselves on top, accurate right down to their facial hair and earrings. Billing issues, vendor screwups, Web site glitches . . . it all comes to my door.

On a normal day, inside my office, there's no telling what I might be up to. I might be having a consultation with a couple planning their wedding, describing the cake they dreamed up the night they got engaged, and wondering if I can bring it to life for them. The look in the eyes of a bride as she describes her dream cake is like nothing you've ever seen, a constant reminder that although I may be just a baker, my responsibility is awesome. Our customers entrust their dreams to us, and we have the power to make or break memories. That might not be the same as being a surgeon or a fireman, but you feel the weight of expectations every time somebody new walks through that door.

If I'm not immersed in a consultation, I might be meeting with my assistants, going over phone calls and meetings, or with one of my four sisters—Grace, Madeline, Mary, and Lisa—talking through a problem that's cropped up with the pastry counter they manage downstairs.

My life isn't just about baking, decorating, and consultations: We're a family business, so, sometimes, there are family squabbles. It's just as likely that a voice that comes crackling through the intercom will shout out, "Buddy, where do you want the new mixer installed?" as it is, "Buddy, Mary and Grace are fighting again." I hear *that*, and it's a code-blue situation because it means that two of my sisters are going at it. I drop whatever I'm doing and hustle downstairs, because breaking up those arguments is part of my job, too.

Just like the counter is run by my sisters, the top dogs in the back are my brothers-in-law. Upstairs in the decorating room is Mauro Castano, my right-hand man, husband to my sister Madeline, and one of my best decorators. There's also Little Frankie Amato, the son of my Uncle Frankie and

I love to meet our customers. These people came all the way from Canada!

my father's godson, who's been around the bakery since he started hanging around there as a kid, and has been working with us since he left Wall Street in 2006. There's Danny Dragone, a mustachioed Italian who we call "the Mule," a jack of all trades who helps out wherever he's needed—the baking equivalent of a utility player. And, of course, there are the designers, our own little team of magical elves, like Stephanie "Sunshine" Fernandez, who was the first woman to ever work in the back with the bakers, in 2004, which was no small thing, because in addition to the long, grueling days, it can get a little bit like a frat house back there. She and the other designers can make anything at all out of fondant, modeling chocolate, and gum paste: people, animals, palm trees, cars, boats, footballs . . . you name it, they can sculpt it.

Downstairs, in the bakery, there's Joey Faugno, another brother-in-law, who's married to my sister Grace, and is one of our top bakers and another utility player; in addition to being a champion mixer and oven guy, he's a fine decorator. And there's Sal Pininch, who's been with the bakery since the 1960s, and is my most trusted baker because, beyond baking, he's somebody who I can go to for fatherly advice.

Whether we're related by blood or marriage or not at all, these people are my family, and most of them have been at Carlo's for years. They are also my co-stars, because, starting in 2009, our family and our bakery became the subject of a television show, *Cake Boss*. The show depicts who we are and how we do what we do and how sometimes things get a little crazy at Carlo's. The funny thing is that the show itself has made things crazier than ever: A team of producers and directors and camera people and sound technicians and production assistants have practically moved in with us. I spend the day doing everything I just described, but I do it wearing a microphone, like the informant in a crime movie. There's a camera and light aimed down at my desk from the ceiling, and my every move and conversation in the bakery and decorating room is tracked. That hallway outside my office is twice as crowded as usual, with as many people wearing walkie talkies as wearing aprons.

Since the show hit TLC, whenever I visit the retail floor, the customers burst into applause, and I stop and pose for pictures with them. I'm flattered by the attention, but it's also a little funny to me, because all I do on television is what I've been doing since I was a teenager.

That same attention has made the bakery busier than it's ever been before. There's a line out the door most days, filled with people who have come from all over the country just to pay us a visit and taste the pastries they've seen on television. It's been quite a ride, and it just gets more exciting and more gratifying all the time. My only regret is that sometimes things move so quickly that we don't have time to stop and take them in. But, at the end of the day, before I change into my street clothes and pull my black, varsity-style Carlo's Bake Shop jacket on, I sometimes stop and savor the silence. I look out the window of my office onto Washington Street, one of Hoboken's main thoroughfares, and I remember.

I remember all the things that brought my family and me to this moment.

1

Coming to America

MY STORY ISN'T just my own. No real baker's is.

I am the fourth generation of baker in the Valastro family, and all that I am, personally and professionally, can be traced back to the homes and bakeries that my ancestors lived and worked in, both in the United States, and back in Italy. Baking is one of the last great artisanal culinary pursuits and, with all the technology that's come into my profession in the last twenty-five years, I am an endangered species—the pure-bred baker, one who can do it all, armed with nothing but his hands, a rolling pin, a mixer, and the knowledge passed down to him by patient, nurturing elders.

Most people like me are the sons of bakers and the grandsons of bakers, and it's not just knowledge that we inherited from them; it's their *hands*. Ask a second- or third-generation baker if he thinks he has his father's hands and he'll tell you that there's no doubt. When you visit an authentic Italian bakery and look across the shelves of pastries behind the glass—cannoli, cream puffs, napoleons, lobster tails, and on down the line—you are looking at a direct link to the past, to recipes that were likely first taught by one generation to another somewhere back in Italy.

More than anything, I am my father's son, and so I need

Carlo's on Adams Street. We actually don't know the date of this old photo as a kind fan gave me this as a gift.

to begin telling my story by telling *his* story, and the story of my mother, and of their romance, and of the family bakery they ran together, because it's the world my sisters and I, and our families, continue to inhabit today. It's where we spend our days, and how we make our living.

My father was born on December 31, 1939, in the town of Lipari, Sicily. His father, Antonio, had been born in America, but relocated to his ancestral home, where his father owned a bakery. Antonio married a woman named Grace, and they had three daughters: Franny, Josie, and Anna. Times were hard. It was the dawn of World War II and poverty was an epidemic in Italy, and particularly rampant in Sicily. So, while Grace was pregnant with a fourth child, Antonio, familiar with the prosperity and possibility there in America, returned, going to work as a baker in Hoboken. He said he was going for the family, and would send them money regularly, but they scarcely heard from him, and the money never came.

Grace was hurt, incensed, but life went on. She gave birth to a son, my father, Bartolo Valastro. There's a faded, tattered, sepia-toned, naked picture of my father when he was a baby that my grandmother mailed to America to show her husband that she had delivered a boy. It sounds like something out of the movies, but it's still an important thing in many Italian families to have a boy in the mix; it ensures that the family name will survive for at least another generation. I think she sent him that picture mostly for spite, so he'd know that he'd miss out on raising the heir to his name.

I don't know much about the old days in Sicily, but there's a story that's become mythic in my family: When he was just a year old, a helpless infant born to an impoverished, fatherless family, my father became very, very ill. Nobody can remember quite what was wrong with him, but it had to do with an extremely delicate digestive system that required him to drink goat's milk. Something made him lapse into a frighteningly deep sleep, almost a coma.

A doctor was summoned, who determined that the end was near, and a priest was called to the house to say the last rites and prepare a death certificate.

Grace, normally a strong, proud woman, cracked under this news. She dropped to her knees and began sobbing and tearing her hair out in a spectacle of anguish.

"Please!" she cried to the heavens. "Please, Saint Anthony, give me my son back. If you bring him back, I will make a novena for you every year." Saint Anthony is the saint to whom we pray for help recovering lost things; according to a Paduan legend, the mother of a drowned child once promised Saint Anthony the boy's weight in grain, to be given to the poor, if he would bring her child back to life. Of course, the legend continues, the boy soon revived, and that's what happened in the Valastro family, as well. Moments after Grace's fervent prayer, she heard a cry from the table where her son lay: "Mama?"

My grandmother took her baby in her arms and squeezed him tight, still sobbing. She made good on her promise: To honor Saint Anthony, she had a special brown Franciscan-style robe made and, every year, on June 13, Saint Anthony's feast day, she wore it to church and prayed in his name. (As an adult, my father honored the legend of Saint Anthony in his own way: Though he wasn't a bread baker, every year, on June 13, he baked bread for a local church. I carry on his tradition: I bake two hundred pounds of dough to make 1,000 loaves, and we deliver them to Saint Francis Church, where the priest blesses them and distributes them to people in need.)

That story might sound incredible, but it's accepted as fact in our family. We're religious, and we believe in miracles and that God does things for a reason. We believe that our ancestors are looking over us from heaven, and we believe that if you're a good person, goodness will come back to you. We believe in all of those things as surely as we believe the sun will rise in the east and set in the west.

Things were tough for my grandmother and her children. They'd often go to bed hungry, or turn to other people's garbage for sustenance; as an adult, my dad occasionally ate fish heads, because he'd developed a taste for them as a little boy.

By the time he was seven, my father had become the bread earner for his family, literally. He went to work as a delivery boy for his grandfather's bakery, and his daily compensation was a loaf of the family product. Sometimes, he'd sneak extra loaves out the door to feed his mother and sisters, before my grandmother, realizing she couldn't take care of the entire family, made the painful decision to send her two oldest daughters, Franny and Josie, to live with their grandparents, keeping her youngest daughter, Anna, and her son, Bartolo, at home.

When Antonio realized that his two eldest daughters, Franny and Josie, were old enough to work, he sent for them to come to America, finding them jobs at the bakery where he worked. The girls discovered that he had become a playboy, a womanizer, and had a main squeeze whom he introduced them to as "your new mother." The girls were horrified, not just because they didn't like this strange young woman, but because the house they shared was a pig-sty. Grace may have been poor, but she had never lost the pride she took in keeping an immaculate home.

For a year, Franny and Josie chipped away at their father, begging him to send for Grace, Anna, and Bartolo. They appealed to Antonio's selfish-ness, pointing out that his girlfriend didn't cook and clean the way their real mommy did. Finally, their dad relented and invited Grace and the kids to come to America, to Hoboken.

Young Bartolo, as the baby of the bunch, had a tough time settling in, largely because of the language difference. In school, as if it wasn't enough that my dad didn't speak English, the other kids couldn't even pronounce his name. They'd butcher it, Americanize it, strip it of its accents and poetry. Eventually, they said, "We are going to give you an American name. We are going to call you *Buddy*."

I wasn't there, of course, but I'm quite sure that those kids didn't just call him Buddy because it started with a B, like Bartolo. I'm positive that even though he was just learning the language, they had picked up on something that everybody who knew him came to realize about my father: that despite everything he'd been through at such a young age, he had an absolutely win-ning disposition, a warm and genuine smile, and a generous soul. In other words, he was a buddy, *everybody's* buddy.

My paternal grandfather may have been a ne'er-do-well in his personal life, but he had the opposite standing in his profession and was reputed to be a tal-ented bread baker. "One of the best," the old timers still say. Despite all that he didn't do for my dad, he did give him what the men of the Valastro family think of as the Gift: hands touched by God, made for massaging dough and getting it to do what you want it to. Once the family was reconstituted in America, Antonio also gave my father some advice: Bread bakers work the graveyard shift because their product is delivered to restaurants and shops at the crack of dawn, so he urged him to go another route, to apprentice in cakes and pastries.

It was some of the last advice he'd ever give his son, because Grace sim-ply couldn't get over what he'd done to them by leaving Sicily. "I will never forgive you," she promised him. They lived together for about a year, then split up. Grace and the kids stayed in Hoboken and my grandfather deserted them again, crossing a river this time instead of an ocean, and settling in the Coney Island section of Brooklyn.

Although Grace had found work in a skirt factory, once again, it was up to my father to help provide for the family, and so he did what a great many Sicilian boys of that era did and followed in the professional footsteps of his father and grandfather, starting at age thirteen. Throughout his teenage years, my father apprenticed around different bakeries in Hoboken, Jersey City, and the surrounding area, learning both the art and the craft of pastry and cake making.

At one of those bakeries he met a young woman named Mary Tubito, who began working there as a countergirl one month before her thirteenth birthday. Buddy was taken with Mary, who had an incredible, uninhibited personality: She was a confident, outgoing, little firecracker. Like Buddy's family, Mary's had immigrated to the United States, hers from the town of Altamura in the southern Italian province of Bari.

Although Mary was just barely a teenager, Buddy liked her free-spiritedness, especially the way she'd break into pop songs spontaneously whenever it struck her fancy.

"Mom," he told my Grandma Grace. "You have to see this girl. She is something else."

He brought his mother around to the bakery to meet Mary, and Grace was also impressed with the young girl, but troubled by her son's interest. "Everything you said is true," she told him. "But, Buddy, *are you crazy?* She's too young."

"I don't care if I have to wait ten years," he told her. "I'm going to marry that girl."

Young life hadn't been easy for either of these two. Like Buddy, Mary had begun working in her teens because, in a poor immigrant family, everybody had to do his or her share. They both had an ability to take it in stride, and were eternally grateful that they had made it to the United States, which to them had made good on its social contract known the world over: Keep your nose clean, work hard, and success will follow. Like Buddy, Mary had a deep and abiding love of her adopted home of America. "If I bleed, I bleed red, white, and blue," became her motto.

Despite the difference in their ages, there was something magic between Buddy and Mary from the start. Just as he was taken with her, she responded to his big-heartedness, the way everybody did. "To know him is to love him," she remembers today. "Even at that age, I just liked him."

There were also some similarities in their background. Mary didn't come from a family of bakers, but Altamura was famous for its bread, and her father, Nicola, had also been born in America, in New York City, moved to Italy, started a family, then returned to the United States for a better life. Only *he* had made good on family obligations.

It wasn't easy for Nicolas, as he became known here in America. When he first arrived, he stayed with an aunt in Bayonne, New Jersey, until some friends from the same area of Italy helped him get a job and an apartment in Hoboken, where he found work as a longshoreman. Because he had started working as a young man, he never finished school, so couldn't read or write, not even in Italian. So that he could track his way along the bus route he took to work, he marked telephone poles and other objects with symbols etched in chalk. If a strong rain came, it would wash away his handiwork and he'd have to do it all over again. Whenever possible, however, he walked to save the fare, sending what he could to his wife and children. What he really wanted was to sock away enough dough to bring the family over to live with him. One day, his barber, who was also a leader of a local Protestant church, was cutting his hair and, noting a sadness, asked him, "What's wrong, Nicholas?"

He told the man that he hadn't yet been able to save enough money to bring his family over from Bari. The next Sunday, the man took up a collection on his behalf, raising enough funds to cover the transatlantic travel for his wife, Maddalena (who, in time, would go by the name Madeline in the States) and their five children, including my mother. It wasn't a Catholic church, but Nicolas was so overwhelmed that he began attending service there. Only in America.

Arriving in the United States, Mary loved the church her father had adopted, especially the social component, when the parishioners would gather in the basement after services and chat. Her mother resisted. "I was born a Catholic and that's how I'm going to die," she told Nicholas. He was fine with that, although he continued to attend church there until the day he died.

Once in the States, the couple had another three kids. Nicholas worked hard and the family thrived. He saved enough to buy a multifamily house and was incredibly generous to people who came over from Italy, putting them up in one of the apartments until they could get on their feet. "It was like Grand Central Station," remembers Mary.

∽

When he was in his early twenties, Buddy went to work for Carlo's Bakery on Adams Street in Hoboken. Founded in 1910, it was a small shop and catered to a niche clientele of transplanted Italians and their offspring. It sold only Italian pastries, cookies, and cakes; its only nods to American tastes were a chocolate cream pie, and a pumpkin pie it offered in the fall.

In 1963, Carlo Guastaffero decided to retire and, since his son had no interest in taking over the family business, he sold it to my dad. They didn't involve the banks; they made a deal the old-fashioned way, between themselves. My father began running the store and paying rent to Mr. Guastaffero, and in time, my father bought the building, and the Carlo's Bakery name, from him.

Buddy enlisted young Mary, then aged fifteen, right away. Not only was this young lady almost outlandishly confident, she was also a terrific student at school, and a math wiz. It was quickly clear that she was going to be doing the books at the shop. (In hindsight, my mother believes this was one of the reasons my father was so taken with her as a little girl; he always had planned to open his own place, and knew she'd be a great partner in business, as well as in life.) As Old Man Carlo helped Buddy get the lay of the land, he, too, gleaned where things were headed, and told the accountant who managed his affairs, "Anything that has to do with the books, you talk to the little girl," a line that has become legendary in my family.

One thing led to another, and as Mary and Buddy worked together and she matured, they fell in love, and were married in 1965, when she was seventeen. They made the bakery their life, assisted by Buddy's mother, Grace, who left her work in the factory to help out her son, and watched over the business like a hawk. Not only did she retain a Depression-era mentality from their days in Italy, but she also wanted to get my father's back, to make

Mama and Buddy Sr. at a nightclub, The Copacabana, celebrating their engagement.

sure that nobody was costing him money. Accordingly, she'd yell at people to not leave the water running, or to turn off the ceiling lights, which were activated by strings hanging down from the switch. (Some of the bakers used to delight in snipping the strings so that they'd be just beyond her reach.) She also had the quintessential old-world distrust of employees and was always on the lookout for thieves in the family's midst: She'd monitor the counter helpers' every move, and count every cent in the register at the end of the night, right down to the last penny. If things didn't add up, she'd launch a full-scale investigation. She also had a strict policy against anybody eating the profits; nobody was permitted to take cake home. My mother was even afraid to do it . . . and she owned the joint!

As she did at home, Grace kept a clean store; after the counter girls were done cleaning at night, she'd follow behind them with a butter knife and scrape any lingering gunk out of the corners of the room. Her standards were so high that parents of young girls sent them to work there so they could learn how to keep a good house for their future families.

Grace lived in one of my father's buildings on Garden Street. (He owned a few investment properties around town by then.) Buddy and Mary lived above the bakery and, although they had counter people to run the store, there was also a bell in the home that let them know when customers came in. If it rang enough times, they knew the store was busy, and Mary would run down and lend a hand.

It was an invigorating time for the young couple, and they were aided in their work by colleagues who would become fixtures in their lives, even though they didn't know it at the time. There was Sal Pininch, an accomplished Italian baker, and Frankie Amato, a college student who worked there as pot washer when Old Man Carlo still owned the shop. Frankie would go on to work on Wall Street, but continued to come in on weekends to help out as a finish-up guy, filling pastries and cakes. My father, displaying a gift for matchmaking that would become legendary, paired Frankie up with Nickie Clemente, who was working as a counter girl at the shop, and also introduced Sal to his future wife, Lucille.

∽

Buddy and Mary began a family in 1966, when their daughter Grace was born. The family grew quickly, with another three daughters following: Maddalena (Madeline) in 1967, Mary in 1969, and Lisa, who was born on December 31, 1974, prompting Buddy to call her his birthday present. In addition to their actual children, the bakery team was becoming like a family: There was a kitchen in the back and Mary would make dinner there, often including Danny and Sal in the meal. Just as her son had as a child, Grandma Grace had a delicate constitution—her stomach and gall bladder would often act up—so my mother made special allowances for her. For example, when she made meatballs, she made a special one that didn't have all the extra ingredients in it; to recognize it in the sauce, she made it extra-large, and the kids all knew not to touch it, because that was Grandma Grace's meatball.

The bakery was becoming known, and so was my father. He became a popular member of the community. He might

Mama and Dad holding Grace;
Madeline is on the way.

not have graduated high school, but his instincts for people and business were known to one and all. If you lived in Hoboken in those days, and, say, you needed to buy a house, or a car, you would ask Buddy Valastro to come along with you, to help you make a decision, and then to negotiate the deal. My mother attributes my dad's willingness to do this to the fact that he had grown up essentially fatherless, so he wanted to play a paternal role to as many people in the community as he could.

My mother had a similar sense of generosity. For a period of time, they took an annual trip to Acapulco with my father's best friend, Mario, and his wife, Nina, and always took along a suitcase full of clothes to hand out to underprivileged kids on the beach. One time, my mother gave away my father's shirt to a man who needed it. "Do you have the matching shorts?" the beneficiary asked. It just so happened that my father was *wearing* the shorts at the time, so my mother sent him up to their hotel room to change out of them and give them to the man, so that he could have a matching set.

From the top, Madeline, Grace, and Mary with Mama and Dad at the beach.

My mother and Grace got along great; my mother was in awe of her mother-in-law's optimism, and the fact that she still had such a life force after all she'd been through. She also understood that, while Grace could be set in her ways, everything she did was to help ensure the best for her only son, who was her entire world. One Christmas, my mother gave a box of cookies to each of her daughters' teachers. Grace, who made no exceptions to her no-taking-cake policy, said something to my father about it. Mary decided that the next year, rather than "pulling rank" and upsetting the family matriarch, she would sneak the cookies out earlier in the day and stash them in the car.

My parents hadn't planned on having any more children, but in 1976, shortly after moving into a house in Little Ferry, New Jersey, they learned that Mary was pregnant with a fifth child, and on March 3, 1977, I was born, christened Bartolo Valastro Jr.

And my sisters before I arrived, Madeline, Mary, Lisa, and Grace.

My mother strongly believed that I came along for a reason, that it was part of God's plan. At the time, she thought it was because, unless the two of them produced a son, the Valastro family name would have ended with my father.

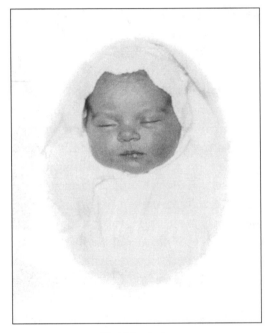

My birth photo.

2

The Prince of Pastry

FROM AS FAR BACK as I can remember, I was aware that my dad was a baker. As a little kid, I remember him leaving in the morning in his whites, and often coming home at night with flour still caked on his forearms. And coming home sometimes smelling like a street fair—all grease and powdered sugar—because he'd been making *zeppole* for an annual church fundraiser.

My favorite sign of his profession was that we had a steady supply of *tarelles* (vanilla cookies) at home that he'd bring with him from the bakery, in a glossy white box that never failed to mesmerize me.

Even though I knew that Dad was a baker, I was never sure exactly what he did at his bakery. I did know that it must have been very hard work, because he looked exhausted when he walked through the door at the end of the day. It was hard to reconcile the physical exertion he'd clearly put forth with the fragile little cookies in that gleaming white box. How hard could it be to make *those*? I wondered.

No matter how tired Dad was, it was very important to him that we all have dinner together every night. No matter how busy things were at the bakery, or what each of us had going on in our personal lives; be it homework, sports, boyfriends, or girlfriends,

Grandma Maddalena

My Grandma Maddalena (also known as Grandma Madeline) was the acknowledged greatest cook of my parents' combined families. In addition to Sunday dinner, she was the relative to whose house we would go on all the major holidays, from big religious occasions like Easter and Christmas Eve to American celebrations like Thanksgiving. She had quite a repertoire: eggplant parmigiana, baked macaroni, stuffed chicken, stuffed turkey, and roast beef, to name a few. One of my favorite Grandma Madeline food memories was when she made the stuffing for Thanksgiving every year, then sewed it up in the bird; we'd cook it in one of the big ovens at the bakery. (We also started a family tradition at the homeless shelter on 3rd Street, around the corner from her home, taking baked goods there on Thanksgiving and Christmas.)

Maddalena didn't work at Carlo's, but she had a little circle of friends—her coffee klatch—who would often congregate at Carlo's, especially in the ten years between when her husband died in 1995 and when she passed away.

I always admired my mother's relationship with her mother. Though Mama worked at the bakery, and spent a great deal of time and energy on keeping our home, she always had time for her mom, shuttling her around to do her shopping and other errands. My sisters also pitched in, driving her home after her coffee gatherings.

We were a very tight family. In fact, although it was Grandma Grace who so worshiped Saint Anthony, it was Grandma Maddalena who gave my father a gold medallion with the image of Saint Anthony engraved on it, which he put on a chain and wore around his neck his entire life.

dinnertime was sacred, the cornerstone of our daily lives. The television was turned off and everybody's focus was on the family. I think it's because he came from an incomplete family himself that it was so important to celebrate ours, and to make sure that we were a tight unit. We also followed that great Italian-American tradition of Sunday dinner, the entire clan gathering at our home, or at my maternal grandmother's, Grandma Maddalena's, a ritual that continued until many of us were grown up with our own families.

This might sound antiquated, but our house was run after a very traditional Italian fashion, and the women essentially waited on the men. From the beginning of the meal to the end, my father and I sat, and the women did all the work. Mama cooked, and my sisters served and cleared the table. Even during the meal, if I just muttered, under my breath, "Where's the salt?" one of my sisters would get up and bring me the shaker. That's just the way it was.

After dinner, my dad and I would sit and eat fruit as the girls cleared the table and cleaned the kitchen. Then, I'd go to my room, and he'd sit in his recliner, which was his favorite chair, where he'd think about things, or watch a Yankee game, often until he fell asleep. Just as I never understood what could make him so tired at work, I used to sometimes steal a look at him, almost melting into that recliner, and wonder, how many things could there be to think about in a bakery?

∽

I began to get a look at what actually went on at the bakery when I started coming around with him, when I was six years old. He'd be leaving the house on a Saturday afternoon and I'd stop him, saying, "Daddy, I want to come to work with you."

And so, he brought me to Carlo's.

I still remember my first visits as though they were yesterday. Being able to go into the back, where all those delicious foods were made, was a real treat to a young boy, and the setting was fascinating and memorable. There were two prep rooms: In the first, just beyond the retail area, there was an enormous oven that radiated sunlike heat, and a wooden bench at the end of which there was always a case of eggs. They called that end the egg-cracking station. There was an industrial Hobart mixer that dated back to the 1930s, and a smaller mixer for less taxing jobs. In the back of the back, there was a longer wooden bench that seemed to stretch on forever, where cakes were filled and decorated on the weekends, and a marble bench where cannoli were filled.

I loved the bakery from the first time I set eyes on it. Loved the equipment racked up on the wall like pool cues, or samurai swords, ready to be deployed, especially the jury-rigged implements, like the old pot tied to the end of a broomstick with wire that was used to pour filling into pies as they baked in the heat of the oven. I even loved the old, warped, wooden floors underfoot.

I'd put on an apron and stand on an inverted bucket and watch my father work. There was a beautiful rhythm to the bakery, each of the guys lost in his task. My dad would make *pasticiotti* (small, custard-filled pastries) at the other end of the egg-station bench, while across from him, Danny Dragone, a mustachioed and multitalented baker who'd come on a few years earlier as a pot washer and been trained as a baker by Dad, would be filling cakes and pastries, and behind them Sal would be loading trays in and out of that beast of an oven.

All of this gave me an idea of what could make a man so tired at the bakery; it was physical work. Dad's job wasn't just making cakes and pastries. It was also dealing with the customers and the purveyors, and pulling his weight in the kitchen. He led by example. I still remember seeing him kneel down one day, steel wool in hand, and scrubbing all around the base of the big Hobart mixer until it was spotless. No job was beneath him and, because he acted that way, the guys who worked for him did, too.

The best, of course, was watching him ply his trade. I'd watch him roll out the dough for, say, *pasta frolla*, and his touch with a rolling pin was something to behold. One moment, he'd be putting the full weight of his body behind a pin stroke, the next he'd be treating it with kid gloves. By the time he was done, whatever it was he was working on looked like it had come out of a machine, uniformly thick or thin. Perfection.

With pie dough, he was an absolute magician, his hands and the pin working in perfect harmony. He'd smash a ball of dough down, then smash it again for good measure. Then the pin came into play: He'd roll it twice, then rotate it, roll to the left, then the right. Rotate again, then roll left and right, until the dough was flattened out like a piece of Silly Putty. When he was done, he did the coolest thing: He'd roll over the dough with the pin, apply a little extra pressure, then pull the pin back and the dough would roll right up on it, like a trained animal. Then, he'd set the pin at one edge of a pie pan and unspool the dough so that it covered the pan. A few taps of the pan on the counter and the dough dropped right into place. One day, I asked Dad how he got so good. The answer was simple; he was raised in the days before sheeters (machines that eat up balls of dough and spit out flat sheets). He told me stories about those days, like how he'd have to get up on a bench and roll on his knees in order to tame a wad of *sfogliatelle* dough into something pliable.

Sometimes, after he rolled *pasta frolla*, he'd hand me a heart-shaped cookie cutter and I would press it into the dough. He'd put the hearts on a sheet pan, and I would brush them with egg wash, then we'd top them with *avelines* (nonpareil pellets) and bake them. Once they were done, then cooled, I'd pack them up in a little box and bring them home to my mom.

I didn't know at that point that I was going to become a baker. To me it was just an excuse to have a fun, Play-Doh-like experience with my dad. In fact, if I had any opinion about the baking life, it was that I would *not* be taking it up. I didn't think I had any artistic ability. I was an embarrassment at any art project in school. I couldn't paint, or even draw, anything beyond stick figures. More than that, my father didn't want me to. "No, no, no," he'd tell me in his gravely Italian-American drawl, his husky voice deepened by a smoking habit. "You are not going to do *this*. You are going to go to college." He wanted an easier life for me, I think, a life that didn't involve getting up before the sun and having to work weekends, or on holidays, which were never really normal for us. He didn't spend Christmas Eve sipping egg nog and going to midnight mass and all of that. He was working. Then, we had the Valastro family Christmas after the sun went down on the twenty-fifth; that was when we spent time together and opened our presents. Even then, there was one family member who didn't participate the way the rest of us did: My father would be laid out like a blanket on that recliner, with nothing left to give after the holiday rush.

⌘

One day, I was standing up on my bucket, observing, when Grandma Grace marched into the back, a scowl on her face.

"What's wrong, Ma?" asked my father.

"This woman out there, she's driving me crazy," said Grandma Grace. "She doesn't know what she wants."

Grace didn't suffer customers like this very well, and Dad knew it.

"Don't worry about it, Ma," he said. "I'll take care of it."

Dad walked out to the retail area, and I followed behind, watching the scene through the swinging doors. The customer, a young woman in her thirties, was pacing around nervously.

"Hi, *signora*," my father said, smiling his famous smile. "What can I do to make you happy today?"

"My husband has a birthday coming up," she said. "And I want something unique, different."

"Unique!" said my dad. "You've come to the right place. We're going to make you something that the world has never seen, don't you worry."

I watched as they continued talking, though I lost their words as the store grew louder with the gathering crowd. It didn't matter. I didn't need to hear what he was saying. The picture said it all, him making grand gestures with his hands, painting the image of her dream cake in the air, and her nodding at his every word, transfixed by the pantomime.

By the time they were done talking, she looked like the happiest woman in the world.

How did he do *that*? I remember thinking, as impressed by his handling of the customer as I was by his mastery of the dough in the kitchen.

⌘

When I was about seven years old, my family moved into a new two-story brick home on Mariani Drive in Little Ferry. It had arched windows and white columns flanking the steps that led up to the front door. My father had it custom built, and compared to the other houses in town, it was like a museum, with about six thousand square feet of majestic property situated near the end of a dead-end road, with a wooded area just behind it. There was a beautiful symbolism in that for me: All roads lead from family and all roads lead *to* family.

To Dad, that house was one of the great manifestations of how hard he worked: He loved that house, and took great pride in it, even hiring a professional landscaper, a gentle giant of a man named Steve Ortiz, to periodically freshen it up and keep it in botanical-garden-level condition.

My mother continued to work at the bakery, but she had another job: Keeping our house museum-caliber clean. Thanks to Grandma Grace's example, my father revered cleanliness, and to honor that predilection, my mother kept the house as orderly as a pastry case, and as sanitary as an operating room. She took enormous pride in that. Shoes were forbidden beyond the front door. Eating was not permitted outside the kitchen for fear that crumbs would be left behind or, worse, a carpet or some upholstery would be permanently scarred by a spilled drink. We all picked up after ourselves (okay, except for me), and then my mother would pick up after us. In the early 1990s, she hired a live-in housekeeper, but Mama did a better job. Our house was so clean that, if I spent the night at a friend's house, I wouldn't shower there; nobody's house was as clean as ours, and the bathrooms especially skeeved me out. (At home, mom kept a spray bottle of Top Job in the shower, and my sisters were expected to sanitize the basin and tiles every time they used it, and before they got out and toweled off!)

Little Ferry may be located in the Northeast, but it could have been just about anywhere in the United States. I had the typical American childhood; my friends and I would walk to school in a pack. And I had a lot of friends. I didn't think about it this way as a little boy, but I had inherited my father's open personality. As far back as I can remember, I always had friends, was always comfortable walking into a room, whether it was filled with family or total strangers. By the time I reached school age, my inner circle was mostly boys from our street: There was Bufi (Anthony Bufi), Clark (John Clark), Gary Minervini, Leo Minervini, Frank Capalupo, and Cousin Frankie.

Every morning, we'd walk to school together. I'd set out from home with Lisa, just two years older than I, and Little Frankie (the son of Frankie Amato, known to me as Uncle Frankie, who was working on Wall Street by then), and dropped him off at our house early every morning. (Uncle Frankie also had a great nickname for me: Bartolooch!) As we strolled along Mariani Drive, which led to Robby Road, then to Niehaus Avenue, other clusters of kids would flow in from their side streets until we were one gigantic pack, a blob, making its way to the schools.

I was a bit of a smart aleck, even as a little boy, and also a bit of an operator, always looking for the angle. One time, my first-grade teacher gave me a bad mark on a homework assignment.

I went up to her after class. "Do you like cookies?" I asked her.

She cut short our conversation, and next thing I knew I was getting chewed out by my mother because the teacher called her up and told her I had tried to bribe her with cookies from my father's bakery. I guess that's what I was doing, but I didn't think of it that way; I just wanted to make her happy, the way I'd seen my dad turn that nervous customer around.

When I think about my childhood, it seems to have taken place much longer ago than it actually did. Today, due to a variety of legitimate concerns, kids are with adults almost all the time. In the early to mid-1980s, when I was six, seven, eight years old, we were largely unsupervised. In the afternoon, my crew and I just hung around, playing at each other's homes or roller hockey right in the street, or playing football, soccer, or hockey at the Little Ferry Recreation Center or the local Boy's Club.

As we got a little older, I continued playing sports, like weekend-warrior football (tackle, but with no pads or helmets) in Robby Road park, up the road from our house. I was a good athlete—strong, fast, and confident—and used to get asked to play with the older kids a lot.

The thing we were most into was our bikes. We'd fly all over town, from the Burger King or Wendy's on Route 46 that served as our unofficial social clubs, to the woods behind our street, where we'd make ramps with cinder blocks and wooden planks "borrowed" from local construction sites. My bike was like my best friend, and we had all kinds of rituals: riding to nearby towns like Ridgewood and Ridgefield Park, popping wheelies, breezing through Little Ferry's backstreets and hidden crevices, pioneering shortcuts to get from point A to point B.

In the summer, Dad closed the bakery for two weeks and we piled into the family Cadillac (three in the front and four in the back) and retreated to our shore condo in Sandy Hook on the coast of New Jersey. It was a two-bedroom condo with a huge loft. Mom and Dad took one bedroom while I, as the only boy, got the other one. My four sisters shared the loft. It was a fantastic time for the whole family to be together, from the oldest sister to the little brother. We'd watch Yankee games at night, and bust each other's chops all day. Sometimes Danny would join us, prompting me to nickname him my illegitimate stepbrother, and we'd have enough people for a big whiffle ball game. (Danny was such a close family friend that when he and his wife Miriam had their daughter Daniela, my father became her godfather, a role he played for an increasing number of friends and relatives, often with my mother named godmother, as well.)

Whether out there at the shore, or back home in Little Ferry, I loved hav-

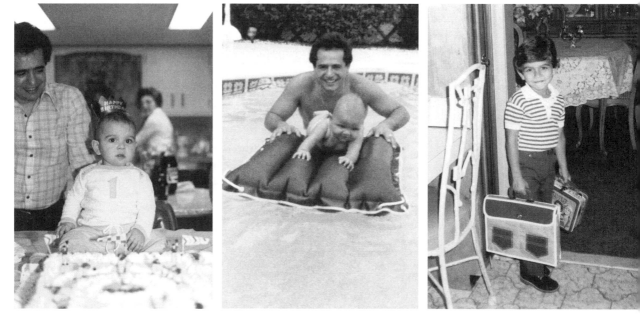

Some firsts for me: My first birthday—and my first cake!

My first "swim" with my dad before I was one.

My first day of school—and first lunch box.

A good catch!

On my communion—my own son Buddy now looks just like me in this photo.

That's me on the left with Ma, and cousin Frankie on Papa's lap.
You can see Pop's St. Anthony medallion.

ing four older sisters. We had great times together and, at that age, they all took care of me: Grace would drive me around, whether to the orthodontist or to a baseball game. Mary, who went to beauty school, used to cut my hair. Maddalena was like a second mom; she lavished so much attention and affection on me. And Lisa, just two years older, was one of my best friends, even though she was a girl.

Dad loved having that time in Sandy Hook with the entire family but, on some days, we'd divide up: My mom and sisters would opt to go to the beach with Mom's friend Jeanie, while Dad and I would go fishing with Jeanie's husband, Larry, and their son Andrew. Some of my favorite childhood moments took place out there in Larry's boat, with stillness all around. We were always so busy at the bakery, but Dad taught me the value of having a sanctuary, a place where you could get a real sense of peace.

Back in Little Ferry and Hoboken, we'd also do things that were distinctly father and son: Sometimes on Monday, his day off, he'd take me into Hoboken, to Mr. L's Barber Shop, and we'd get our haircuts, and then we'd take a walk and he'd introduce me to people. He seemed so proud, telling people, "This is my son." We'd also sneak off now and then to go bowling together. He loved spoiling me, sometimes acting more like the quintessential grandfather than father: If we went to a grocery store, I'd come out with armfuls of candy and, on Halloween night, we'd sit up late devouring all the sweets together. Good times.

Mom also spent a lot of quality time with me; Lisa and I accompanied her to church (where I was an altar boy) every Sunday, and she periodically took me on little out-of-town excursions, to the theater in New York City or the Smithsonian Institute in Washington. When we were alone, she made a point of imparting life lessons to me, like the importance of being honest and responsible. One time, a five-and-ten shop failed to charge us the right price for a Halloween costume; when I pointed it out, she marched back in and gave them the rest of their money. "I don't want anybody to steal from our business," she said. "So, I'm not going to steal from them." It was the Golden Rule brought to life. It was an awesome childhood. The only downside was that I didn't apply myself in school. It just didn't stimulate me. Math, grammar, history, and science all left me cold, especially when the teacher was a bore. I honestly believed that I could have had straight A's if I tried at all, because when I did apply myself I was a quick study. (In high school, my buddy Leo, who was a wonderful student and bit of a computer geek, and I stayed up all night cramming for a make-or-break science exam. I hadn't cracked a book all year, but processed enough information in twelve hours to sail through. "Man, if I could learn as fast as you," he said, "There's no telling how smart I'd be." That was a rare moment of inspiration for me. I'm not proud of it, but most of the time, I basically got by on B's and C's, and many of those required an assist from my sister Lisa, who acted as a volunteer tutor at home.)

One fall day in 1988, when I was eleven years old, my friends and I left our bikes at the end of my dead-end street and scampered into the depths of the woods beyond. It was cool outside, and the leaves were crisp as paper, crackling under our feet as we walked along. One of the guys got the idea that we should have an experiment and see how long we could keep a fire burning.

We made a circle out of stones, piled some leaves in the center, and then one of us lit a match and set it ablaze.

Poof! It flamed for just a few seconds, and then was gone, disappearing with a sizzle and a hiss.

We made a bigger and more diverse pile: leaves on the bottom, covered with a teepee of tree bark and branches. We set that one on fire and were thrilled with the results; after a few minutes of smoldering, it ignited into a respectable little campfire.

Our excitement, however, was soon dampened by the sound of sirens approaching. Somehow, I knew: A neighbor had called the cops. Sure enough, a few seconds later, through the trees, we saw a few black-and-whites barreling down my street.

We took off deeper into the woods. Heard the screeching of brakes and the opening and closing of car doors. One of the cops took out his megaphone and addressed us through the trees: "Come on out here and we'll work this out."

"What should we do, Buddy?" asked Bufi. "Go out, right?"

"No way," I said. "Screw that. Let's wait 'em out."

We all nodded.

"Come out," said Megaphone. "Or I'm going to take your bikes to the station."

The bikes! What were we, morons? Making a run for it but leaving our bikes right out there for everybody to see, and just a few yards from my own front door. I smacked myself on the forehead.

We came out of the woods with our hands in the air, but all the tension went out of the scene when we saw who was waiting for us: All the cops were guys we knew. Little Ferry was a small community, and they were all known to us, the parents of our friends, and baseball coaches at our school.

They didn't take us to the station. Instead, they took us home. Maybe they knew that any punishment they could dole out would pale in comparison to what our fathers would do to us. Sure enough, when Dad found out, he was incensed.

"You want to screw around in school *and* on the weekend, huh?" he said. "Well, you are not going to have this opportunity anymore. From now on, you'll spend every Saturday and Sunday working with me at the bakery."

The very next Saturday, we went to the bakery, but it wasn't like it was when I was a little kid. We weren't going to play. We were going to *work*. Where we usually talked when we drove, this drive was silent: He was the marshal and I was his prisoner. I'm lucky he let me sit in the front seat.

For all the tension in the car, I was excited, because I idolized my father and now he was really going to put me to work, to show me what he did. When we walked into the bakery, his stride didn't slow at all. He marched right past the marble bench and up a few steps to the landing where the bathroom was. He pushed open the door.

My heart sank, and he could tell from the look on my face that I was a little crushed, because I knew what was coming.

"You're going to learn what it means to work, Buddy," he told me. "You'll start here, by cleaning the bathroom."

Okay, I thought, if that's what Dad wants me to do, then that's what I'm going to do. Plus, I had my mother as a role model; when I started cleaning that bathroom, I thought of those floors at home, the ones you could eat off of. That's the image I kept in my mind while I worked, that and the picture of my own father, on his hands and knees, scrubbing the bottom of that old Hobart mixer. By the time I was done, the bathroom sparkled like never before. I looked down and saw that my fingers were bleeding from gripping the steel wool so hard. I smiled. A badge of honor.

Once I was done with the bathroom, the warden let me come out and help in the bakery. It was pretty minor stuff at first: I'd crack eggs, or bring butter and cream from the walk-in refrigerator to him or to Dominic Valenti, who had been a pot washer for my dad in the 1960s, had left for a time, and then been rehired as a full-fledged baker. (My father played matchmaker with him, too, pairing him up with my mother's sister Annette, my godmother.)

Not everybody was thrilled to have a kid hanging around the shop. Danny was like a member of the family, but when, all of a sudden I was invading his workspace, it was a different story.

"Beat it, kid," he'd grouse without looking up when I came over to see what he was doing. "Go break someone else's balls."

If the abuse ever crossed a line, my dad would stick up for me. "Hey!" he'd snap. "Watch it. That's my son. Nobody gets to pick on him but me!"

All of this, even the cold shoulder from Danny, was a good education: starting from the ground up, learning how important people's work was to them, and that no job was too small.

One of the best parts of my role was that I got to watch. I saw my father make cakes: multitiered wedding cakes and church cakes, a popular specialty cake in those days in the shape of a cathedral. I also loved watching him decorate the simple things, like birthday cakes, piping little butter cream flowers onto them.

The ultimate expression of Dad's dynamic visual style was a cake that's legendary in Hoboken: the cream puff cake, which was his signature. His masterpiece. It was born almost by accident. Dad had a good friend, his first wholesale client, Joe Orecchio, owner of the Park Casino, also the hall where our family held a lot of their big events, like communions and christenings. (He was so closely associated with his place that we called him Joe Park Casino.)

Well, one day, Joe Park Casino returned from a trip to Italy with a bottle of San Marzano liqueur under his arm. He had fallen in love with the stuff overseas and told my father, "You have to make a cake with this."

That's when Dad dreamed up his cream puff cake. The elements are French cream (Italian custard cream and whipped cream folded together and enlivened with liqueur), Italian sponge cake soaked with a liqueur, and whipped cream. This was sold as a birthday cake, so to make it into something special, he topped it with poured fondant icing (melted sugar frosting that would dry into an icing like that you might find on a doughnut) on top, and whipped cream on the sides. He then filled cream puffs with the same French cream and arranged them along the top and bottom like a border, and finished it off with chocolate shavings and whole, long-stemmed strawberries and kiwis. It was as decadent as it was irresistible, and when you saw it, you wanted to take a big bite out of it.

I also got to see Dad interact with the customers. That earlier incident I'd witnessed was no fluke. He was a real people person, able to make every customer feel as though they were the most important person in the world to him. I also saw some of his trademark generosity. If kids from the projects on Jackson Street came by, he didn't shoo them away like some merchants did; he gave them cookies.

He also had customers who hung around the shop, treating it like their home away from home, like Tony D. A good friend of my dad's, Tony D., volunteered at a church in Newark, and after visiting with us would bring our slightly stale cakes (perfectly edible, but not saleable) to the kids in a nearby orphanage.

Tony D. worked as a machinist at Maxwell House in Hoboken, along with Sal's father-in-law, Eddie, who lived two doors down from the bakery. Tony and Eddie would sometimes use their professional skills to help my father out, building, say, the wheels and board for a carriage cake. For a time, they also built the Plexiglas cages that figured prominently in a wedding cake my father made, which featured two live "doves" housed within the cake itself. (I put *doves* in quotes because we actually used white pigeons.) This is where I came in: Whenever we had an order for that cake, my father would send me around the corner to a chicken store, which I normally avoided like the plague because of the sickening stench that wafted out the door, to procure the necessary fowl.

My favorite thing to watch was the reaction of the customers when they came in to pick up their cakes. They'd throw their arms around my father and kiss him. I can still hear them: "Buddy! You are the greatest! Thank you so much!" Those cakes were the stuff of memories, the exclamation point on a birthday party or wedding celebration. It thrilled me to watch my father delight so many people, and I decided right then and there that I wanted to be able to do with cakes what he did with cakes, that I wanted to have the power to cause that reaction for people, to be the guy they turned to for their holidays and celebrations. I wanted that glory.

That was the beginning of my new life. Every Saturday and Sunday, I'd come in and be tasked with another menial chore: throw the sawdust down on the floor in the morning, clean the pots and pans, sweep the floors.

Gradually, I got to help out with some actual food preparation. Not baking, per se, but finishing work. Dad set me up at a little metal bench near the sink with a little window, perched high on the wall, through which I could see the neighboring rooftops. I quickly realized that there were lessons in every task. For example, if I was putting cherries on top of cookies with one hand, Dad would say, "Why are you doing it with one hand? God gave you two hands; do two at once." A rudimentary task became a chance to teach me the importance of working smart, of maximizing time and resources.

The first two pastries I worked with were cream puffs and éclairs. The shells were baked and frozen and I'd thaw them out, halve them, and pipe them full of Italian custard cream using a pastry bag.

Here again, there was a hidden lesson, my first introduction to one of the most important things a cake decorator can develop: the hand of the bag. I love that phrase, and how almost mythological it sounds.

"You have to have the hand of the bag," Dad said to me, as he filled a pastry bag with cream, expanding it from a two-dimensional flat triangle to a three-dimensional object full of potential.

He showed me how to pipe. There are a few crucial piping techniques, all based on pressure control: You develop the ability to squeeze and release with exactly the same pressure and for exactly the same amount of time, over and over again, and that was true whether you were piping the filling or the dough used to make the pastry itself. Today, there are machines (even at Carlo's Bake Shop) that pipe out cream puff dough, but, up through the 1980s in our shop, everybody did it by hand. My father, Sal, and Danny could all do it as well as a machine, and they could tell another guy's depth of talent by whether or not he knew how to pipe.

I didn't know it at the time, but learning how to do this relatively simple job was a great first step on the path to becoming a cake decorator, because you develop that hand of the bag: The bag becomes an extension of your hand, your arm, your entire being; it gets plugged into your central nervous system. Your brain says, "Pipe cream puffs," and it's like the signal goes right to the bag itself.

I remember my first Christmas season at Carlo's: I had to bang out one hundred pans of cream puffs and another hundred of éclairs. The cold of the cream went right through the bag and numbed my hand and, at the end of the day, when my flesh and muscle thawed out, I realized that I was sore from the repetitive movements.

I didn't care. I was really starting to love my work, and just plain adored being in the bakery. I liked feeling like one of the guys, even though I was still just a pipsqueak, and I loved the growing feeling of accomplishment.

Once my dad and the rest of the guys saw that I was serious about the work, these tasks became my responsibility on the weekends, and I'd get those pastries ready before I cleaned the bathroom, because the store was depending on me to have them in the case downstairs by the time we opened. To a kid who was underperforming in school and had a predisposition for getting into some minor mischief, this was an important milestone, being tasked with something, being counted on, was a feeling I liked. That little bit of ownership made me grow up a little.

After I'd been working there about six months, my dad let me help with some of the actual baking, starting with basics like *pasticiotti*. This was about the time that I started to recognize that I had my father's hands. He'd show me how to do something, and I'd mimic him, the steps coming surprisingly easily to me. *Pasticiotti. Tarelle. Cannoli.* I took to all of it naturally.

"Watch my hands, Buddy," he'd say. "Watch the way my hands look."

I'd look at his hands, then down at my own, which were like miniature replicas of his. In time, I became obsessed with my hands. Like many who were born into my trade, I honestly believe, and this may sound arrogant or blasphemous or conceited, but it's just the truth: I believe that my hands were touched by God.

I also developed a phobia, which I still have, that something would happen to them. As a result, I take crazy-good care of them, treating them

Meet the Sisters: Lisa

Although Lisa is two years older than I am, I've always thought of her as my little sister.

When we were kids, I kept an eye out for her, helping her out of scrapes, or loaning her money, because, even as a child, I always had some cash on hand.

Today, along with Madeline, Lisa is the sister I can always count on to go with the flow, to take things in stride, and be a peacemaker. Out of all my sisters, Lisa does not have a jealous bone in her body: She's always been the most proud of me. Today, she often helps me do the bookkeeping, because out of all the sisters, she's the most computer savvy . . . which isn't saying much!

Lisa has three beautiful children, my goddaughter Theresa, and John, who are insepa-rable from my children—and daughter Isabella, for whom my wife Lisa and I are the proud godparents.

the way some guys treat their cars: I wash them all the time, keep my nails immaculately trimmed, and if I get so much as a paper cut, I scold myself for my carelessness.

This connection with my father was very powerful. I used to have dreams about it. They were simple dreams, of me and Dad in the kitchen, working side by side, and him turning to me and saying, "Never forget your hands, Buddy. They are what make you who you are."

My sister Lisa and me.

My sister Lisa and me with my first godchild, Bartolina, at her christening.

3

Education of a Cake Boss

IN 1989, MY FATHER made a monumental announcement: he was going to move the bakery to a new location. The reason was that he wanted a few things for the bakery. As his children were growing older and approaching adulthood, he dreamed that it would provide enough jobs and make enough money so that the entire family could earn a living there. He had also become very proud of our products, of their authenticity and adherence to tradition, and he wanted the world to know the name Carlo's.

All of that added up to one thing. "We have to be where the action is," he said, "and that means Washington Street," one of Hoboken's main thoroughfares, which was beginning to flower into the *de facto* Main Street that it is today.

So, he struck a deal to purchase Schoning's City Hall Bake Shop, a large German-American bakery with which we had always had a friendly relationship because we didn't compete for the same customers: We sold Italian pastries and cakes and they offered German and American favorites. Their space was significantly larger than ours, with a grand, street-level baking area beyond the retail floor, and another area in the basement, which was mostly used for storage, but could be utilized as a production facility. Mama and Dad

poured everything into the investment, their savings as well as bank loans, and purchased the building (including apartments upstairs that they could rent out), and performed a gut-level renovation so that it would look like new when they opened for business.

Schoning's had a following in town and, while Dad wasn't going to continue making many German items, he was intrigued by continuing the store's American tradition, selling doughnuts, Danish, croissants, and American-style birthday cakes, all of which would build the enormous customer base he envisioned. He had learned how to do all of that work as an apprentice, and even had a lot of the necessary recipes in a beat-up old notebook in which he recorded his baking wisdom in pencil and, now that we were going to be on Washington Street, with its not-just-Italian clientele, it made good sense.

Dad couldn't do everything himself, so he sought out some bakers with expertise in American preparations, like Mike Vernola, better known as Old Man Mike, who was from Italy, but was one of the best American bakers around. He was a gray-haired kitchen commando with an ample belly who could work like an animal. ("Working like an animal" or "like a dog" is high praise around Carlo's.) Mike had once worked at Schoning's and, when Dad enlisted him, Mike convinced him to bring in another Schoning's alum, a bench man named John Vermil.

To honor Schoning's history and pay respect to the heritage of our new home, Dad decided to make their name part of our new name, changing it from Carlo's Bakery to Carlo's City Hall Bake Shop. My mother also devised a new logo to honor her husband: a silhouette of a baker holding a cake aloft, the name Buddy stenciled on the cake.

All this meant big changes for the family, because, overnight we went from a relatively small shop to a relatively big one. There would be no more closing up for that summer vacation in Sandy Hook, and we'd all be seeing a lot more of each other as Carlo's would become a place of employment for us. My oldest sisters began working full time in the store, running the counter downstairs. Even young Lisa, who was still in school, pitched in on afternoons and weekends. Even though we were under the same professional roof, we lived a different existence: I was in the back with the bakers, and they were out front with the customers. To this day, none of them is officially in charge, although Grace, because she's the oldest and does the scheduling, has an air of authority about her.

My father also continued his matchmaking ways in our new location: he took a liking to Mauro Castano, a framer who had helped with the construction of the new site, and Dad rang him up one day.

"I have a nice girl I want you to meet," he said.

As requested, Mauro reported to Carlo's Bake Shop and discovered that Dad was fixing him up with his own daughter, my sister Maddalena, whom we all called Madeline by then. The two met and fell in love, eventually got married, and Mauro began helping out at the shop on weekends, making deliveries.

Around the same time, Grace was getting serious with a new boyfriend, Joey Faugno, who was in the Air Force when they started dating. When he had weekend leave, he would visit us, and often bunk in my room. Like Mauro, Joey began helping out with deliveries on the weekend. Before you knew it, Grace and Joey were engaged; after he served in the first Gulf War, he came on board full time to help increase the family business, becoming one of our most trusted bakers.

As for me, my enthusiasm for my work carried with me from Adams to Washington Street. I was still working Saturday and Sunday, and when summer came, I'd become a full-timer, working six days a week.

I wanted to get better and to learn more. Shortly after we made the move to Washington Street, my father decided to teach me how to mix.

Mixing probably doesn't sound like a big deal, but it's just as important as any other part of the baking process. There's an art to mixing. Part of it has to do with mechanics. For example, we have a saying around Carlo's: "Bakers scrape." What we mean by that is that, when we're mixing, we're constantly loosening up whatever ingredients might have caked onto the side of the

Grandma Grace

At about the same time one Grace began working at Carlo's, another stopped. When we moved from Adams to Washington Street, my Grandma Grace retired, although she continued to live nearby and visit the bakery on occasion.

As I navigated my way through my teens, Grandma Grace became one of my most trusted confidantes. She just *got* me, and I could be completely honest with her about everything—my feelings and frustrations, even my budding love life. (She also had words of advice for my girlfriends. I could have a bit of a temper in those days, and if I ever became hot-headed, she would tell them, "He's got Sicilian blood. So he gets angry. But just keep your mouth closed and wait for it to pass. It'll be okay, you'll see.")

I used to love visiting Grandma Grace in Hoboken, sometimes staying over on the little sofa bed, and we'd hang out late into the evening talking, me soaking up all the wisdom she had to offer.

We all admired Grandma Grace. She was like the Energizer Bunny of the family, no matter what happened, she just kept going. Others might have taken on a Job complex when faced

with the cards life dealt her, but not Grace. Her courage and strength were always an inspiration to me, and I still call on them when I feel frustrated or disappointed. "If she could keep her chin up at all times," I tell myself, "then what do I have to be upset about?"

bowl, or sunk to the bottom. Most people, even professionals, stop their mixers to do this with an instrument, perhaps a wooden spoon or spatula in a home kitchen. The guys I learned from had such an intimacy with the machines, that they would reach right down into the depths of an 80-quart bowl while the motor was spinning the beater, and use their hands to scrape. It's like sticking your head into a lion's mouth; it takes great, intuitive knowledge to do it without getting seriously injured. (One reason we still have seventy-year-old mixers at Carlo's is that all the new models have safety cages built around them to keep you from reaching in when the motor's running. And I do not want you to ever try this at home!)

The other thing about mixing is that you need to develop an instinct for when dough has been mixed enough. Often, this amounts to a leap of faith because the consistency of the dough for some pastries, like Danish dough, is dense and moist as a wad of taffy while, for others, it's dry and flaky, and just doesn't look like it'll hold: That's when you have to use your experience to account for the magic that happens in the oven. You always have to remember that, in baking, your ingredients don't always behave in exactly the same way: Flour retains more moisture in the summer than the winter, for instance, eggs can have different ratios of yolks to whites, and so on.

A good dough to work on for developing these instincts is the one we use for making tea biscuits. The finished product is dense, but has a lot of air pockets within it, like a scone. The dough needs to be ridiculously flaky. When mixing, you need to know to stop as soon as it's mixed just enough. To the untrained eye, tea biscuit dough doesn't look like dough; it looks like something that could become dough if it were mixed for another minute or two.

This was the first thing my father taught me how to make in our new location on Washington Street, shortly after we moved here. I was thirteen, and he said to me, "You know, Buddy, I'm getting too busy to do so much stuff myself. I'm going to teach you how to mix the tea biscuits." (This was like a running joke between the two of us; early on, he almost never offered a compliment, instead toughening me up by withholding praise. This is a pretty common thing among bakers of a certain generation.)

We went into the kitchen and I gathered the ingredients: flour, shortening, sugar, golden raisins, salt, baking powder, and milk. With some recipes, such as Danish dough, you put the liquid in first; with others, like vanilla cake, it goes in last.

I'd watched the guys mix everything in the old store, so I knew that this one called for the paddle attachment, which, on an industrial mixer, is as big and weighty as an anchor. I removed one from the utility rack over the sink and snapped it into place. My father nodded his approval; I'd been paying attention.

"All right," he said. "Put in everything but the milk."

I dumped all those ingredients into the seemingly bottomless bowl.

"Now, start it."

I pushed the switch that started the machine. It hummed to life, the paddle starting to rotate slowly—*whir, whir, whir, whir*—then picking up speed, like a helicopter blade.

I watched as the ingredients came together.

"Okay," my father said, holding his hand up and watching the dough, waiting for the right moment.

"Add the milk . . . *now!*" he said, dropping his hand.

I poured the milk in, slowly, in a stream, the way I'd seen the men do it. Once it was in, I watched, excited by my first crack at mixing, witnessing the dough come together into a uniform ball.

"No, no, no!" my dad yelled. "Shut off the machine!"

I tuned off the mixer, but it was too late; the dough was ruined.

"You have to know when to stop, Buddy," he told me. To make his point, he slapped the dough down on the table. For all of his prowess with the pin, he couldn't get it to roll out, it kept springing back toward its center, like an elastic band.

"You see?"

I nodded.

"Let's try it again."

He walked away. I garbaged the dough, cleaned up the mixer, gathered up all the ingredients again, and summoned my father back.

I started to pour the ingredients in, but he put his hand up, to stop me. "Wait!"

I looked at him. He was deadly serious.

"Here's the thing," he said, imparting the next words of wisdom as earnestly as a father handing down a life lesson, the importance of knowing right from wrong, or some intel on the birds and the bees. "The dough, it's not gonna look like dough. It's gonna look superflaky, *dry*, but that's okay. You have to trust it. You have to know that that's what it's supposed to look like. Now, go."

This time my father didn't speak to me before I added the milk. He'd shown me once, no need to do it again.

Once I had the milk in there, I watched. I could feel my dad's eyes on me, but tried to shut out that pressure and just focus on what was going on in the bowl. At first, the milk collected around the other ingredients, like a moat, but then it began to be absorbed, and the mass began to come together uniformly. This is where I screwed up the first time, because the natural tendency is to want the dough to become smooth and moist, like Play-Doh.

I stopped the mixer before it got to that point, with flakes hanging off the mass like eyelashes, then turned to the umpire for a ruling.

He nodded. Good.

"Go on," he said.

I lay the dough on the table, and rolled it out. I hadn't used a rolling pin much, but I'd watched my father, Sal, and Danny, and I had a pretty good grip on how to do it. Then, I used a circle cutter to cut biscuits from the dough, which we'd put on a pan and freeze. Every morning, we'd take a dozen out of the freezer, brush them with egg wash, and bake them from the frozen state until they puffed up.

After that day, dad taught me other doughs, such as *pasta frolla*, which we use for our pies.

The next step in my education was learning real bench work. Dad's recent hire, John Vermil, was a master. Even better, although John didn't have kids of his own, he was terrific with kids and I loved being around him. A bakery is like an assembly line: One guy mixes, another guys does the bench work (tak-

Working with both hands, like Dad taught me.

ing the batter and folding in butter, or cutting and rolling shapes), then the baker bakes pans full of items when they're needed up front, or according to a regular schedule.

John spent a lot of time with me, helping me learn how to fold, cut, and shape dough, and roll out and braid Danish. He also taught me more about the proper way to use a rolling pin. This is one of those skills that really distinguishes me from other bakers today, because knowing how to use a rolling pin, and I mean *really* knowing how to use it, is fast becoming a lost art. John taught me how to use that rolling pin to make the dough do everything I wanted it to, just like I'd seen my father do. (Dad had also taught me a nifty trick that would come in handy in this and other new pursuits: how to take a fistful of flour and perfectly dust a bench by just flicking my wrist and releasing the flour

Learning bench work: the infamous dough for lobster tails.

at the right second.) By the time John was done training me, I could have gone on television and performed a whole routine in which the dough behaved like a trained animal, just as I'd seen it do for my father, hopping up on the pin, then unspooling and playing dead. Young kids learning today use a sheeter to flatten out their dough, and that's fine, but I took great pride in knowing that I didn't need more than my own two hands and a stick of wood to make whatever I felt like making.

I was starting to feel like a real baker. I had an aptitude and comfort level, and was even starting to develop my own preference for tools and equipment: I liked an old-school wood bench because doughs, especially temperamental mixes like *sfogliatelle*, were less likely to stick. The cake mavens in my midst told me that stainless steel or marble was better for working with fondant, because it was cold, and I was open to that possibility. I hadn't been allowed to touch a cake yet, although I was dying to do so. I liked having opinions like those and being able to defend them. I also loved the socializing that goes on in the back of a bakery, the manly back and forth about politics or the Yankees or the Giants, or the ballbusting that everybody, even a little kid like me, was expected to both take and dish out.

Before I knew it, I was entrusted with all kinds of bench work. It was thrilling, and I wasn't the only person who benefited. Business was flourishing on Washington Street, and my dad and his colleagues were so swamped making cakes, it was useful to them to have another set of hands in the kitchen.

❧

By 1990, it was pretty clear to me and my whole family that I was going to become a baker. The summer before my freshman year, I tried out and made the football team at Ridgefield Park, brought on to play linebacker and fullback. I was good at it, and was excited for the season to start. There was just one problem: In all my excitement, I had forgotten that the games were played on the weekends.

It pained him, but my dad put the kibosh on my athletic plans. "You're

Me and the guys
and Ma at the bakery.

not going to play for the Giants," he said, his meaning being that my future was in the kitchen, not on the ball field. I understood. It wasn't the end of the world. I ended up playing soccer instead, because the games were after school.

He might not have wanted me to live the baking life before I'd started coming around with him, but once it was decided, Dad began grooming me to one day take over the bakery. As ever, he didn't come right out and say that. Instead, he'd be a little extra hard on me. Once in a while, if I screwed up, he'd actually give me a little whack on the back of the head. (This would be frowned on today, but every boy I knew then got an occasional whack from his dad.)

His anger confused me. Dad was my confidant, my hero, and these moments of passing scorn didn't compute. Once in a while, I'd come right out and ask him, "Why are you so hard on me?"

"Because you know better," he said. "Or you should know better. You have to understand. You've got to understand. Everything here, you gotta know. And you have to be the best." (To Dad's great credit, he never let this expectation seep out of the store and into our personal life, where we remained as much best friends as we were father and son. Even if we had had a rough moment at the store the day before, he would still wake me the next morning by rubbing my back, and even let me drive the van to the shop, practicing for my driver's exam. Despite his expectations for me at the store, he knew I was still a kid, and encouraged me to go out with my friends as much as possible after work.

I think back on those conversations now, and I wonder if they had something to do with the bouts of illness Dad sometimes had. He would develop symptoms; for example, he had a recurring problem with blood clots in his legs, or just experience an unshakable bout of lethargy, and check himself into the hospital for a day or two, or sometimes a week, simply complaining that he didn't feel right. Beyond the clotting, for which he was prescribed a blood thinner, the doctors could never figure out what was wrong with him. We figured it had something to do with the way he worked himself, combined with the fact that he was a smoker and, in time, the doctor visits became a way of life, especially since, as soon as he got back to work, he was able to go right back to working like an animal.

I wonder, did he know, down deep, that something was wrong? Something that hadn't developed enough for outsiders to detect it? Something that might require me to know everything sooner rather than later?

ᥫ

When I was fifteen, I registered at Bergen County Technical School, a vocational school on River Road in Hackensack. Students spent half the day taking classes in their chosen field and the other half taking a regular academic curriculum.

I still didn't really take to the reading, writing, and arithmetic (although baking is so formula based that I had developed some math skills along the way). What can I tell you? Those classes bored me. I felt like I had found my calling, and it was in the bakery, where my father, heck, my whole family, had created a great life. What did I care what Huckleberry Finn was up to, or how to write an essay? It was a little short-sighted, but I was young. Nevertheless, I had every intention of fulfilling my father's dream of my being the first Valastro boy to finish high school.

Freshman high school photo.

I had a bit of a reputation in those days, but it was based on stereotyping. My friends and I weren't bad kids, but we'd get into some trouble every now and then. In addition to that, we were Italian-American, we dressed nicely, and my older friends had nice cars. A lot of teachers and fellow students equated that flash to the mob. Nobody ever came right out and said that, but I'd seen this profiling before, and I knew that's how some people thought of us.

Where I excelled from day one, of course, was the baking program. I was an instantaneous star pupil. This was not because of anything they were teaching me; it was because of my genes and my father's weekend lessons. That didn't matter. One of my teachers couldn't wait to show me off as the product of his teaching. If the principal or faculty wanted to watch a demo, it was me who was paraded out to show off.

I did this a few times, and let the teacher soak up the adulation of his boss and peers. Then, I told him: "I will do whatever you want, but I want special privileges." I was growing up, and was developing my father's talent for business, for negotiation.

"If I want to leave early, I'm going to leave early," I told him. "If I want to go to the cosmetology class and play with the girls, I want a pass."

Amazingly, he agreed to all of this. I had such *carte blanche* that, before long, my teacher would do anything I asked. After just a few months, I would fill out my own passes for him to sign. Where it said, *Reason* I didn't put *bathroom* or *nurse*, I wrote *to roam the halls*. And he would sign it and I'd roam the halls, free as a bird.

I also had a pretty good racket going with the instructor who ran the culinary program, sometimes called the *chef program*, where fellow students were being trained to turn out complete meals as opposed to the cakes and pastries my classmates and I were studying. One of the chef's responsibilities was to cook lunch for the faculty dining room, where the teachers paid for it. He was a good chef; I'd seen his food and knew that it was a class above the glop we were served in our student cafeteria.

"Buddy, I'd like to see your desserts in the faculty lunch room," he said.

"I will make you a deal," I said. "I'll make the desserts on the condition that I eat lunch in here every day. For free."

I look back now and realize that I probably didn't do anything to keep people from thinking I was connected. Here I was, a fifteen year old in his whites, sitting in the faculty dining room and chowing down like a king, on filet mignon and lobster, while all my schoolmates were eating in the cafeteria down the hall. I had a racket going, no doubt about it, and I'm sure others drew conclusions as to why I was receiving such preferential treatment.

Fortunately, this image was softened thanks to my father's example. I'd seen his famous generosity, like how he'd help the homeless people on Washington Street with a donation. Not only didn't he ignore these unfortunates, the way most people did, but he stopped to talk to them, making eye contact, treating them like real people. One day, I asked him why he did that.

"That could be me, Buddy," he said. "That could be me asking." (On some occasions, he'd say, "You never know.

Mom and Dad on vacation in Mexico.

That could be God testing me.") Even though he'd worked hard for everything he had, he still considered himself lucky to have bettered his situation.

As a teenager, I copied his kindness in my own strange way. If one of my friends picked on an outsider, I always stuck up for the stranger. "Hey, man," I'd say to my pal. "What are you picking on him for?" I might have had a penchant for mischief, but there wasn't a mean bone in my body. In fact, I decided that I could use that reputation I'd acquired for good, like if somebody picked on the defenseless, like calling another student *fat* or *loser*, I was even less patient, even brandishing that age-old classic, "You have a problem with him? Do you want a problem with *me*?"

Dad getting an award from the Lion's Club.

It might sound a little rough, but, I was trying to live up to Buddy, Sr.'s example.

❧

In 1992, my dad took me to visit Sicily.

He wanted me to see where he was born, and it was just the two of us, the men of the family.

I was excited about the trip: Not only were we going to see Sicily, but we were going to Altamura to visit my cousin Frederico, whom I called Freddy, a skinny kid with dark hair and dark eyes who was two years older than I was. He was a constant companion when he came from Italy to spend the summer with his Aunt Martha and Uncle Bart, my mother's first cousin, who lived next door.

Our journey began with a boat ride from the airport to my father's native island of Lipari. When we docked, three little boys, street urchins, swarmed us, asking if they could help with the luggage. They couldn't have been more than eight years old.

I instinctively clutched my suitcase handle. Hard. I wasn't going to give it up to these ragamuffins. I looked up at Dad, and saw that he had a tear in his eye.

"Let them take the bags," he said, and I let go.

"Dad," I said. "Are you okay?"

"I used to do this when I was a kid," he told me.

The kids got us out to the street and my father tipped them each one hundred American dollars.

Not recognizing the currency, one of the kids looked up at him and said, *"Che cosa è questo?"* What is this?

"Ficucia in me," said my father. Trust me. *"Portarlo alla banca."* Take it to the bank.

I knew that my father grew up penniless, but it wasn't until we were there with those boys that I really understood. Then, it all made sense to me. The way he helped out anybody he could, giving cookies to poor kids from the local projects, or handing leisure wear out on the beaches of Acapulco.

Once settled in our hotel, we rented Vespas for the week. We sputtered along the dusty ancient roads of the town until we came to a little house that looked more like a bungalow than a residence.

"This is where we used to live," he told me.

I couldn't believe my eyes. You hear how your relatives from the Old Country used to live. How they crammed into one-room houses. Until you see the confines, you can't really understand. My father was born in that house, and I swear that I couldn't picture how that was even possible.

So began our week in Sicily, and my guided tour of the history of Buddy Valastro. Dad introduced me to an old lady, Lina, who owned a fruit shop and used to give my grandmother food. He gave her a nice stack of money, a belated thank-you for all the help she'd given his family. He also took me to his grandfather's grave, in a small cemetery, with a black-and-white picture of my great-grandfather laminated right onto the headstone.

We also paid a visit to my Grandma Grace's sister, Giovana, who lived in a mental institution. Grace's father had died when she was young and, since the family couldn't support everybody, so they put Giovana in this facility, not because she was unsta-

Dad and me in the waters of Sicily.

ble, but so that she would be sheltered and fed. In time, her misery and the surroundings robbed her of her sanity, and she ended up spending her entire life there. "That's how bad things used to be," Dad said to me, as we left the hospital.

On a decidedly happier note, we visited my dad's cousins, and their children (my cousins!), and went fishing. That's when I got another potent glimpse into how different his old life was from his new. It was like he wasn't just from another country, but from another planet. We all crowded into a little canoe and went out onto the water, which was so clear that you could see thirty feet down. My dad and his cousins hopped out of the boat and plunged into the depths, farther than I would have thought possible. I saw them fiddling around in the rocks, and when they emerged, they had sea urchins in hand. They hopped into the boat and used big knives to pop the urchins open. We ate them under the midday sun.

After days of adventures like that, my father and I would sit and talk on the balcony of our hotel, with the water reflecting the moon behind us. The trip brought him back to his roots, to his humble beginnings, and he wanted me to really understand how important it was for him that we never lost sight of where we came from. He didn't just want us to be thankful for what we had, but also to always be able to relate to those who didn't have as much, especially those in our community, or in our own bakery. In a lot of food-service businesses, the anonymous men and women who wash the dishes, or clean the floors, are treated like dirt. He never wanted that to happen at Carlo's.

We also visited local bakeries. My father would pull up on his Vespa and introduce himself, ask if he could work a shift. That's not something you could do in most businesses, but in a trade as tradition based as baking, it was perfectly natural. He'd spend a day working, and swap recipes the way my friends and I swapped baseball cards. At one bakery, he picked up a vanilla-almond biscuit and taught the guys there how to make an American style cheesecake, using cream cheese, which they call there by one of the most popular brand names in the world: Philadelphia.

The pastries of Italy are region specific, just as are the rest of the foods of the country. In the places he worked, and the other bakeries we visited, you would find cannoli and pignoli cookies loaded with almond paste, and cassata cakes (Sicilian cannoli cake). I didn't work with him in those bakeries, opting to play with my newfound cousins instead, but visiting them was an invaluable opportunity, a chance to see just how authentic what we did at Carlo's was, how connected we remained to a grand old tradition.

❧

After a week and a half in Sicily, we took a boat to Naples, then rented a car and drove to Altamura, where my cousin Freddy and his family lived. They had a house in Campagna, in the countryside, and I had a look at the fabled rustic cooking of the region. One night, the family prepared an enormous feast for us; the centerpiece was *capreto* (baby goat), which Freddy's father, Mario, procured from the family farm, slaughtered, and cooked on a spit in a wood-burning oven. People came from the surrounding towns for this feast. By the time we sat down to dinner, set in a charmingly overgrown doorless farmhouse in the middle of a vineyard, there were more than thirty people assembled, toasting and laughing: There were relatives and friends of my father, many of them Italian-Americans who had migrated back to the old country after a period of time in the States, or some like us who lived in New York or New Jersey and were just visiting. There was also a staggeringly large contingent of friends my parents had made when they vacationed in Italy, but I don't know why that should have been surprising to me; Mom and Dad made friends wherever they went.

The meal was a simple and perfect banquet served on old wooden tables. There were all kinds of vegetables from the fields around us, and seafood salads, tripe, and octopus, and fresh foccacia from the wood-burning oven, that still haunts my senses.

❧

That trip was a powerful one for my dad. I'm sure it brought back all kinds of memories about his father and what he did to his family, but I'll tell you something that's true of just about any man or boy I've ever met: We want our father's approval. We *need* our father's approval. Not long after we returned, my father looked up his dad in Coney Island, and the two of us drove out there to pick him up. I remember the look he had in his eye when we were driving over the Verrazano Bridge, a sad emptiness, years of disappointment displayed there, the spires of the bridge reflected in them.

We picked up my grandfather, and the three of us drove back to Hoboken, where my father showed his father the bakery on Washington Street. It was a secret mission, orchestrated on the fly on a day when Grandma Grace wasn't around, because she still hated her ex, hated him with an unyielding passion of which only Hollywood executives and scorned Sicilian matriarchs are capable.

The two men didn't exchange many words. They didn't have to. The message was clear, even to those of us who were simply observing them:

My father, "See what I did? See what I did even without your help?"

My grandfather, "I'm proud. I have no right to even call you my son, but I'm proud."

My father brought his father to our house for dinner. At the end of the night, they left, still wordless. There was message that was clear to me, from the son to the father, "I forgive you."

About a year and a half later, when his father was on the brink of death, my father paid him one last visit and the old man came out with it and asked him for forgiveness, which my father granted him.

And when his father died, despite everything, my father wept.

•

Back at the bakery, once I mastered all those pastries, there was just one more level for me to ascend to: Cake decorating. I had succeeded at every task my father and his team had put in front of me and I had earned the right to learn about the cakes, the things I'd wanted to master since that first, punishing day on the job after the campfire incident.

After everything I've written about my dad, it might surprise you to learn that it wasn't he that first taught me cake decorating. It was Jimmy Lee, a renowned local baker who was half Chinese and half Italian, and who had started working for my Dad that year. Either of them would have been fine instructors: My father had a gift for freestyle decorating; he could come to the table with a few strawberries, a kiwi, a paring knife, and a bag full of icing, and walk away ten minutes later leaving a fanciful, smile-inducing work of art in his wake.

Jimmy was more technically oriented. He was perfection incarnate. A machine. He did everything the textbook way and, if you could do things the way he did, there'd be no room for human error. All of his cakes were iced evenly, perfectly straight, like they'd come off an assembly line. He was so good that my father would have him ice all the cakes, then they'd divvy up the decorating.

There were, however, a few final hurdles that I had to surmount before my cake education could begin. First and foremost, my father was resistant.

"You don't know how to do cakes," he told me. I'm still not sure why he felt that way, because I knew that I was ready to do cakes. I've thought about it a lot. Maybe it was that he didn't want to see his son grow up too fast. Once I learned cakes, that would be it. My education would be complete. From a baking standpoint, I'd be a man. Or maybe, I've thought, he was afraid that I'd get hooked on that great feeling that comes with decorating cakes, that I'd be unable to resist the pull of the bakery any longer, that I'd drop out of school before earning that precious diploma.

A smaller, but still significant, impediment, was that John didn't want to lose me. The store was just getting busier and busier, and he needed me on that bench, cranking out all those pastries.

None of that mattered to me. I was a man on a mission. I wanted to learn how to decorate cakes. I knew that if somebody could impart the technical knowledge to me, then I could build on that foundation with my creativity, and I'd be able to really make something of myself in this business.

I cornered Jimmy at a quiet moment one day and begged him to help me. I thought he would understand my desire, and he did. He went to my dad and spoke to him.

"I'll watch out for him," he promised. "I'll make sure he doesn't get too ahead of himself. Let's see how it goes."

Finally, my father acquiesced.

My confidence was well founded. I proved a quick study for Jimmy. First of all, I had already developed that essential hand of the bag, so when he showed me how to do something, like swags or drop lines, I could mimic him pretty well the first time, and my learning curve was steep. Good thing, too, because business was picking up even more, and there was a crazy number of orders to contend with.

The first cakes I worked on were birthday cakes, and specialty cakes for the catering halls that made up a large percentage of our clientele—huge event spaces that hosted two or three weddings every Saturday and Sunday. A major fixture of weddings in those days was the Venetian Hour, a reception buffet from which the guests would feast on pastries and cake. The Venetian Hour included a set combination of items from the bakery. There were assorted pastries, such as tiramisu, a fruit log, a chocolate volcano mousse (a layer cake shaped like a volcano), a cream puff log, and strawberry cheesecake, California cheesecake (topped with a variety of glazed fresh fruit), and the cream puff cake. Those were the first cakes I learned to make.

Cakes were one of the few areas in which I struggled, not with everything, but with specific aspects of decorating that really kicked my butt, like leaning how to ice with buttercream. I kept in my mind a piece of advice my father once mentioned to me in passing: "The thing with cake decorating is there's nothing you can't fix." And so, if I messed up, say, the swags, I'd just patiently scrape them off with one of the cardboard squares we used to smooth icing and start over. I really applied myself to getting better, patiently riding out these frustrating storms until I could get the bag and the spatula to execute my brain's every command, the same way the rolling pin did.

On some weekends, at the end of the decorating day, I'd go out on deliveries with Danny.

One of our biggest stops was Macaluso's, a catering hall owned by Joe Macaluso, a notorious grump and one of our most impossible-to-please customers. He had an itchy trigger finger; if he were disappointed, he would just let fly with a tantrum, but, at the end of the day, he was a fair businessman, he always paid his bills, and, although his family no longer owns Macaluso's, it remains a valued client today.

A few months after we took on their account, Danny and I were making the Macaluso delivery and one of the strawberry cheesecakes got damaged, nothing too catastrophic, but a little smushed on one side.

"What the hell is this shit," said Macaluso, who had a Sicilian accent and a hot temper.

I was only fifteen years old, but I whispered to Danny, who was twice my age, "Get out of here."

He gave me a skeptical look, but shrugged and headed back to the van.

Macaluso was lobster red by now, and spit was spraying from his jowls as he laid into me.

"This looks like my ass," he said.

I put my hands up. "Whoa, whoa, whoa," I said.

He stared down his nose at me. "Excuse me? You're a fifteen-year-old punk. Who do you think—"

"I'm Buddy's son," I said.

It was like having a magic spell. He was speechless.

"Mr. Macaluso," I said. "Yelling and screaming isn't going to resolve anything. Just tell me what you need."

"Let's start with this cake here," he said.

"No problem," I said. I looked at the cake. "You have any chocolate in the back?"

"Of course."

"Okay, have somebody bring me some. And a knife."

Macaluso sent for the items and I took the knife and shaved chocolate all over the cake, masking the imperfection. I remembered my father's line about how you can fix anything in decorating.

Macaluso watched, and nodded. He could tell I knew my way around a cake.

A couple of the beautiful wedding cakes we used to turn out before fondant became the rage.

"Okay?" I asked.

"Yeah," he said.

"Is there anything else?"

"Well, last week I ordered three mousse cakes and only got one."

"No problem," I said. "Soon as I get back to the shop, I'm going to make sure those aren't on your bill. And I'm going to take this strawberry cheese-cake off, as well."

I paused, then added, "Don't worry about it. I will take care of it." That was the first time I ever said those words to anybody. I don't know how I turned the magic on, but that's what it was: magic. Macaluso was appeased. He knew that I meant what I said and that his concerns would be addressed. From that moment forward, whenever he called the bakery, he'd mutter to whoever answered the phone, "I only wanna talk to Buddy, Jr."

The first time it happened, Danny reflexively shot back, "What the hell do you want to talk to him for?"

"Don't be jealous, Danny," I said, feeling my stock in the bakery rise a little.

I had a growing list of responsibilities at work, but one of my top concerns became making Joe Macaluso a happy man. One of the cakes that was part of the Venetian Hour at Macaluso's was the Buddy Delight cake, a chocolate cake with whipped cream, bananas, and strawberries inside and gigantic chocolate shavings on top. It was a great cake that really showed off my Dad's stylistic gifts because it put a big smile on your face when you saw it, and an even bigger one when you tasted it.

I wanted to have a cake of my own, and one day, when Macaluso told me he wanted a cake with cannoli incorporated, I saw my chance.

I set up at one of the old wood benches in the bakery. I had a ten-inch Italian sponge cake and a rough idea of what I wanted to do. I started work-ing . . . and . . . I drifted away.

It was the first time I went into what I call *the zone*, when my brain stops working, and my hands take over. It's a state of euphoria, a happy place where the rest of the world melts away and I am unaware of my surroundings. My four sisters could be arguing two feet away and I wouldn't even know they were there.

On a good day, I can stay in the zone for hours. That first time, I think, I was there for about ninety minutes. When I emerged, I was spent, both physically and emotionally. When I looked down and saw what I had made, I was consumed with a sense of pride at what I had created: a vanilla cake, soaked with a little Galliano liqueur, filled with cannoli cream and with little cream roll wafers sticking out of it like curlers. Then I'd dressed it up with chocolate shavings and drizzled chocolate over it.

There was only one thing to call this: The Buddy *Junior* Delight Cake.

Macaluso loved it, and our relationship developed into one that I treasured, founded on mutual respect. In time, I forgot all about his reputation for grumpiness. He treated me like an equal when I came by, even feeding me in the middle of my delivery day.

The whole Macaluso experience was a real turning point for me. It's fun to be a wise guy, to hang out with your friends, but there's just nothing like the feeling of being recognized for a job well done.

∞

My mother was proud of the way I turned the Macaluso account around, and so was my father. Not only because I was developing as a baker and a businessman, but also because Old Man Macaluso was a difficult customer, and I was able to take that problem off Dad's desk. I can relate to this now better than ever: If anybody can keep things off my desk, they are my friend.

The thing about Macaluso was that he was never difficult with me. I understood him. It's a gift, as sure as having my Dad's hands is a gift. I get people. Macaluso just needed somebody who understood what he was all about and knew how to make it happen for him and, just as important, how to talk to him. As time went by, I even customized his Venetian Hour, creating more original desserts to satisfy his personal passion for hazelnuts and cannoli cream. It wasn't long before I actually considered him a good friend.

One day, my Dad's friend, Tony D., was in the bakery and he said to my father: "Man, look at your son. He is going to be great." Sometimes he'd tease him: "Your son is going to be better than you one day."

Once in a while, the praise would go to my head. I'd bring a freshly designed strawberry cheesecake over to my father, lay it down on the table, and look at him with a self-satisfied smile.

"Look what I did!" I'd say.

He'd look it up and down, then damn it with faint praise. "Not bad."

"Not bad? What are you talking about not bad? It's *great*."

My cockiness was not appreciated. "Ahhh," he'd say, waving his hand dismissively. "What I've forgotten about cheesecakes, you still gotta learn." I knew he was proud, that this was just his way to keep it from going to my head, to keep it clear who the boss was, even though it was him who pushed me to get that good in the first place. Fortunately, my mother was there as a counterbalance, offering me all the positive reinforcement a growing boy needed. She'd come through the kitchen on occasion, see one of my cakes, and beam. "You did that yourself," she'd exclaim. "Look at what my son did! I'm so proud!"

I kept at it, kept working on my skills, fanatically, obsessively. Sometimes, if one of the other guys began prepping a cake at the same time I did, I'd turn it into a race. There were no words. It was just like when two runners find themselves alongside each other on the track and suddenly they're trying to see who can go faster. I'd trim the top, then the sides, and have the first layer of icing down before the other guy even had the bag in his hand. That's how fast I was getting. And the quality of my work? Forget about it! I was piping like a pro—swags, drop lines, filigrees, borders—my repertoire was complete.

Finally, even Dad couldn't hold back his praise. One day, when I was sixteen, he paid me the ultimate compliment by asking me to ice the wedding cakes for him because I did them better, same as he used to do with Jimmy. And then, I reached my personal promised land: wedding cakes, where my talent really flourished.

Finally, that glory I'd witnessed on that first Saturday at the bakery, all those years ago, was mine.

There was another reason I was glad that my baking graduation day had arrived: Dad was in his fifties, and I wanted to be able to take some of the pressure off his shoulders, to help him enjoy life a little more, and maybe get enough rest so that he'd be able to stop checking into the hospital.

One of my first wedding cakes.

✂⌒

When I was sixteen, I returned to Ridgefield Park Junior Senior High School, which had a vocational program as well; I'd take academic classes in the morning, then hop on a bus to Teterboro High School for my afternoon baking classes.

Once again, the teacher made me for a wise guy; on the very first day, he pulled me aside and said, "Listen, don't disrupt the class, don't bother nobody, don't whatever, and I will give you a C."

I probably shouldn't have, but I took that deal. I look back now and I'm not proud that they thought I was a mobster but, at the time, the illusion of being connected came with a raft of fringe benefits. Plus, I knew I was going to be a baker, and a C would get me through school. From a bottom-line point of view, it made sense. It was a solid business decision.

✂⌒

The thirtieth-anniversary celebration of my dad's ownership of Carlo's—the whole crew.

In 1993, we had a big party to celebrate the thirtieth anniversary of the family taking over Carlo's. At the celebration, my father made a toast, acknowledging my sisters and brothers-in-law. He thanked his mother, and my mother. He thanked so many people that I thought he was going to forget me!

Then, he told our assembled family and friends that he was glad, relieved, that he had me to carry on the family tradition. That he was just waiting for me to grow up and take over the shop. It was a rare show of emotion for Dad, who had tears in his eyes by the time he was finished, calling me up and giving me a big hug and a kiss for everyone to see.

☙

As 1994 began, and my seventeenth birthday approached, I was so obsessed with baking that I would come to the shop after school, pulled there by an almost magnetic force. Baking was the thing that gave my life meaning, that kept me out of trouble and gave me a sense of accomplishment, a sense of self. I knew that it was a force for good in my life. No exaggeration: It was my salvation.

I was getting to know the business on a real fundamental level, and applying my brain in a way I rarely did at school. For example, I began to notice some inefficiencies in the system: When we would decorate cakes, we'd pick them up off the rack, put them on a turntable to ice them, let them set for a few minutes, then set them on the bench and apply icing flowers to them. I was doing four racks, with ten to twenty cakes per rack, every Friday, Saturday, and Sunday. I had never seen an assembly line, but it occurred to me that if we had an assembly line, that would make things more efficient.

I devised a system where we'd line up six turntables, each with a cake on it, and I would ice them all, then turn around and put the flowers on them. I never put the bag down. I was like lightning, working like a dog, there was no thought involved, just the rote repetition of a task. It got to the point that we'd have three gallons of heavy cream at the ready because I'd go through a pot of cream by the time the next one had been whipped.

Just as I'd been obsessed with mastering different techniques, now I was consumed with discovering new efficiencies. No more picking up a knife six different times to ice six different cakes: Get all those cakes down on turntables, pick up the knife once, and do it right.

I had a rite of passage awaiting me outside the bakery as well: My seventeenth birthday was approaching. I was going to get my driver's license and my dad had promised me a car. We had visited a bunch of dealers in the area and I had settled on a white 1994 Mitsubishi 3000 sports car.

The bakery was doing well, but my father always had an appetite for more. Once in a while, we'd take a cake to a local television news show, like channel 7 (the local ABC affiliate in Manhattan) or channel 4 (the NBC affiliate). One time, Chauncey Howell, a local features reporter, focused on my dad in a piece on Saint Joseph's zeppole. Dad didn't talk much in the pieces, because he was fundamentally a shy man, and I didn't talk, either, but you could sometimes see me in the background, making pastries and cakes.

Besides our local television exposure, Dad always wanted to be in the bridal magazines. We'd pass a newsstand, or a bride would bring a magazine into the shop to show us what she wanted her cake to look like, and my father would turn to me and say, "Can you imagine what it would do for our business if we could get into one of these magazines?"

"Don't worry, Dad," I said. "One day, we will."

I believed it, too. Because my father and I had the same iron will: Whatever we set our minds to, we accomplished. With me fully installed in the bakery and feeling like a completely trained workhorse, it felt like the beginning of a special time for the family and for Carlo's.

However, the truth was that the golden age was coming to an end.

4

Calling Saint Anthony

ON MARCH 3, 1994, I turned seventeen and my mother took me to take my driver's test so I could get my license.

You might think that my dad would have accompanied me to such an important milestone and, normally, you'd be right. However, my father was in the hospital for one of his periodic mystery stays. This one, in New York City's Columbia Presbyterian Hospital, was longer than most. It had lasted a few weeks, but even so none of us thought too much of it. We visited him, joining him for meals in his room, or strolling the halls with him in his gown, pushing his IV stand alongside. Then we'd come back to Hoboken and run the bakery with Mama. It was nothing out of the ordinary for us.

As for my driving exam, as usual, when the subject intrigued me, I was a star pupil: I passed the test with flying colors and strutted out of the DMV office coolly holding my license, still warm from the lamination machine, aloft for my mother to see. She beamed with pride; her little boy was growing up.

I had wanted a license for the longest time and had fantasized about my first day as a state-recognized driver, imagining myself making the rounds, picking up my crew, and taking to the local highways, really opening up the engine as we rocketed off to some adventure. Instead, I had a family obligation to attend to: I opened the passenger door for mom, then got behind the wheel and drove her into the city to see Dad and tell him the good news.

We arrived at the hospital room the way we always did, as though we were greeting him at the end of a work day.

"Check it out, Dad," I said, pulling my wallet out to flash him the license.

He just nodded, barely reacting to news he normally would have high-fived me over. My mother kissed him on the check, but his return kiss was perfunctory.

We both picked up on these cues right away. This wasn't the man we knew, the one who was able to put a good face on just about anything and always make you feel that everything was going to be all right.

"You two better have a seat," he said.

It was a tone of voice we'd never heard. Mama and I looked at each other, instantly fearful. I dragged two enormous armchairs over to the side of the bed and we sat down, leaned forward.

"Buddy, you're scaring me. What is it?" my mother said.

He took a deep breath, bit his lip, and looked me in the eye, then Mama. "I have cancer," he said.

My mom gasped, a sharp intake of breath that I'll never forget. She sounded as though she'd just had the wind knocked out of her.

I reacted the way a kid reacts, looking to my hero for comfort: "Maybe it's a mistake," I said.

My father shook his head. "No, Buddy. No mistake. It's cancer. Lung cancer."

He looked off to the side, as though he were staring right into the abyss. I had never seen my father look scared before, but that's how he looked that morning. And I'll never forget the look on my mother's face, pure desperation that pleaded, "What are we going to do?"

We didn't say much. What was there to say after *cancer*? The bottom had just fallen out of our world. Before you knew it, the three of us were hugging each other at the edge of his bed and my parents began crying and looking into each other's eyes.

I'm not ashamed to say that I bawled my eyes out, too. My father was my hero, my rock, the man who had the same hands as I did, and who showed me what to do with them. He was the guy who took me fishing and bowling and taught me what it meant to be a man, to run a business, and to care for your family. He was also patriarch to a large and growing clan that depended on his leadership and vision for survival.

I was a full-fledged baker, but I was supposed to finish high school, to be the first Valastro man to earn that distinction, then I was supposed to go to college. Once I regained my composure, my problem-solving brain—yet another thing that I'd inherited from him—kicked into gear. I knew what had to be done. "Dad," I said, "I am going to drop out of school. I am going to work full time."

That very afternoon, my mother drove me to Ridgefield Park school and signed me out.

My father tried valiantly to get back on his feet. A few days after he told us he had cancer, he checked out and came home. I'd seen him work endless hours and put forth a superhuman effort all the time at the bakery, but the depths of his constitution and spirit weren't completely clear to me until I saw him will himself out of that hospital. It was pretty clear to all of us that he should stay in the hospital, but he insisted. He wanted to be with the family, and he marched himself out of that hospital like the proud man he was; and my mom drove him back to Little Ferry.

Once he was back at the house, without all the attention and services of a hospital, it was hard for him. He couldn't get comfortable in that recliner, so he passed his days lying on the couch. He was getting chemotherapy, which nauseated him and heightened his sensitivity to smells. When I came home from the bakery, he couldn't stand the scent of me: That sweet, sometimes greasy aroma we all barely noticed anymore made him even more sick to his stomach.

"I can't stand the smell of you," he'd say, "but I don't want you to go upstairs." I'd sit down on the floor at his feet, and with him stroking my hair, he'd say, "Just stay with me, Buddy. Stay with me . . ." and he'd nod off.

Within a few days, reluctantly, he went back in the hospital, but he still kept tabs on what was going on at home. Amazingly, mindful of my recent birthday, he dispatched my mother to take me to buy that car he and I had picked out before he got sick. With everything on his mind, he still found the energy to be upset that he wasn't able to make the deal. After all the cars and houses he'd negotiated on behalf of others, his wife and son had to go out into the jungle and fend for themselves. It would have been funny if it weren't so unfair.

Ever the good soldier, my mother did as my father asked, and took me to the Ramsey Mitsubishi dealership on Route 17 in Ramsey. That car that had beckoned to me weeks earlier didn't seem nearly so exciting any more, not with everything else going on.

The sticker price was thirty-six thousand dollars, and my mother was so despondent she would have gladly paid it just to get out of there and get back to the bakery, or the hospital.

I felt a sense of responsibility well up in me. This was no time to let my mother take care of me. It was time for me to take care of her, and the family. It was a time to act like a patriarch, even if the real Boss were still alive and kicking.

"You know what," I said to the dealer, flashing him the same smile I'd seen my dad flash so many times. "Thirty-six seems a little high. How about we give you thirty-two for it?"

The dealer smiled that pained grin that salesmen display when they know they're in for a fight.

"Thirty-two?" he said incredulously, feigning a chuckle. "That's more than ten percent off the sticker."

I just smiled and shrugged. It was like that time with Mr. Macaluso. I was just barely seventeen, but that same confidence that had come over me at the catering hall had sprung up once again.

"Tell you what," he said, "How about thirty-five?"

I shook my head from side to side. Looked at that car, that car that I wanted so badly, as though it were a lemon I wouldn't be caught dead in.

"I really think it's worth thirty-two," I said. "I'm just being honest with you."

I turned to my mother and winked. She looked away, stifling a laugh. It was a sorely needed moment of comic relief.

"C'mon," the dealer said. "Work with me here."

"Okay," I said. "I'll give you thirty-two thousand *one hundred* dollars."

My mother looked at me like I was nuts. She couldn't believe my nerve.

I don't know how or why, but I knew what I was doing. That talent I'd seen my father display so many times, for peaceful negotiation, had come to me, just as his baking prowess had come to me.

I wore that poor guy down, and when our standoff was done, we paid thirty-two-five for the car.

My mother used the occasion to teach me a lesson about the value of money, and made me pay for half out of my bakery earnings. (Years later, she revealed that she had actually stuck the sixteen grand in a bank account, and gave it to me when she thought I'd treat it responsibly.)

Back at the bakery, everybody knew my father was sick, but nobody knew how bad it was. Carlo's was, and remains, a family operation. We didn't post a notice, or circulate a memo. The family knew what was going on; the other employees knew what they overheard, or what somebody chose to tell them. The truth was that we were all doing the best we could to get by, taking it one day at a time. Nobody knew what was going to happen and though we all knew the worst might be on its way, we prayed for a better outcome. (Ironically, I later learned from my mother that Dad himself, having seen a dear friend of his, Sonny, waste away fighting cancer for two years, was praying that, if there were suffering ahead, he'd rather God spare him, and take him home to heaven.)

For his part, my father spent a lot of time visiting with priests. There were four priests with whom our family maintained a strong bond: Father Gene, who was our priest in Little Ferry; Father Pagnotta of Saint Joseph's Church in Jersey City, a dear family friend for whose church Dad baked carnival zeppole every year; Father Guenther, who had been our priest in Little Ferry but had moved away; and Father Michael of Saint Francis church in Hoboken, for whom my father baked Saint Anthony's bread every year.

I'm told that, talking about me, Dad said to Father Gene: "I wish I could have shown him a few more things." He wasn't talking about life, I don't think. He had already shown me, by example, enough to set me on my way. He was talking about the bakery, which would fall to me to run after he was gone.

One night, my father and Father Pagnotta were talking,

The St. Anthony's bread Dad made every year.

and my father, in his typically selfless fashion, told the pastor how bad he felt that he was leaving my mother with all the responsibility of the business and the family, especially because he knew that he never could have built it all without her by his side. She was his partner, in every sense of the word.

One day, after visiting Dad in the hospital, my mother and I were driving home, and she turned to me and said, "You know, Buddy, you should try to spend as much time with your father as you can right now."

I took her words to heart, but on the very next day, March 20, we were all working at the bakery when I heard a scream from the office. It was my sister, Grace.

"Something's wrong with Daddy," she said, running into the back of the shop in tears. "We have to go to the hospital."

We all scrambled into one of our cars and went to the hospital. My father had had a stroke, brought on by the Coumadin adjustment he had had to make when he went on chemo. By the time we got there, he was essentially brain dead. The doctors wanted to try a procedure to relieve the swelling in his brain. Mama authorized it, and we all sat for what seemed like an eternity in the waiting room, joined by Father Pagnotta. The operation was successful, but our relief was short-lived because, within hours, the other side of his brain swelled.

That was it. He didn't make it through the night. He died, at the incredibly unfair age of fifty-four.

Before we left his side, I carefully removed the necklace bearing the St. Anthony's medallion from around his neck, kissed the medallion, and put it around my own. We had never discussed it, but I knew that he'd want me to have it, and that maybe, in some way, even need it, before too long.

&cs;

My father's wake lasted three days, and for three days there was a line of people to see him. I wanted to be strong, as he would have been, and so I stood by that coffin all day, every day, greeting all the mourners. By the time the day was done, my cheeks would be sore from all the kisses applied by friends and family.

Everybody tried to say something, but nothing helped. In time, I became grateful for those who just came right out and said the inescapable truth: "There are no words."

❧

The day before my father's funeral, our front doorbell rang. My mother and I answered and found Steve Ortiz, our landscaper, standing there with his hat in his hand, his head bowed, gently sobbing.

In his Spanish-accented English, he spoke: "I'm so sorry about the Boss, Mary," he said.

"Thank you, Steve."

"Listen," he said. "I'm going to plant flowers in all the beds for tomorrow."

My mother had no idea what he was talking about. "Absolutely not!" she snapped.

He put a hand up, gently, respectfully.

"Mary," he said. "I'm going to make the house look beautiful."

"Thanks, Steve, but I'm not interested," she said. "I'm too sad."

He pressed: "Mary, I want to do it for the Boss. I want the house to look the way he liked it. I'll rip every flower out the day after, but I want the house to look perfect when he passes by for the last time." He was referring to the funeral procession that would be driving by our street the next day.

She nodded her consent, and went back inside.

Through our living room window, I watched Steve work that day. It was still winter, and the ground was cold and hard. He spent hours out there, softening up the earth with a hairdryer and chipping away at it with his tools until it gave way. He planted fresh flowers in the cold ground, then patted down the soil all around them, working patch by patch, into the evening, until the house looked like it had time-warped into spring.

Dad's funeral was so well attended that you might have mistaken it for a town hall meeting. Everybody was there, from old friends to loyal customers, relatives and neighbors going back to the time he first set foot on American soil. It was an incredibly sad occasion, but the somber mood was lifted by the stories everyone told, recounting what a great boss he'd been or how he helped them find and buy their house, or, in the case of my sisters and me, stories of vacations on Sandy Hook and nightly dinners.

All four priests eulogized my father. One of them, Father Michael, addressed my grandmother from the altar.

"Remember, Grace, when you almost lost him fifty-three years ago," he said. "Saint Anthony and God gave him to you for another fifty-three years, so you have to be grateful." It was wonderful perspective, and a reminder to be thankful for what we have every day. I wouldn't have my father any more, but I had one of the all-time great dads for seventeen wonderful years, and enough wonderful memories and lessons to last a lifetime.

After the funeral, we all got into our cars, headlights on, and formed a procession that wound its way through Little Ferry to our house on Mariani Drive, so Dad could see his dream house one more time. I was glad that Steve had come by the day prior to work his magic. I knew that Dad appreciated it, too.

At the cemetery, on Ridge Road in North Arlington, we carried Dad's casket into a mausoleum. On the way out, I pressed my face against the cold granite and wept. Even through my grief, I never really felt like he was gone, that he was in that casket. I felt like, in some way, he was with me still, an angel on my shoulder, still watching out for his son.

As I turned and walked away, I squeezed that Saint Anthony medallion between my fingers. This might sound like an exaggeration, but I kid you not: I have never taken it off since that day at the hospital.

And I never will.

Customers and Friends 'Buddy', THE MAN who made life sweeter for thousands, has passed on. His memory will live on forever. It is our greatest LOSS

The Valastro Family

The announcement of Dad's passing in the window of Carlo's.

5

Big Shoes

WE BURIED MY FATHER on a Friday, and on Saturday, we all went to the bakery and worked. We were wrecked, emotionally and physically depleted, but we poured every ounce of ourselves into keeping the business going, even though we were aware that people around Hoboken were whispering that without Buddy, Sr. at the helm, there was no way Carlo's would make it. It was tough: We were baking, or selling, cookies and pastries—happy foods—with tears welling up in our eyes. When a family or couple came in to pick up a cake, it was surreal. The idea that something positive was happening beyond our doors seemed downright impossible.

My mother, too, came to work that day, but she didn't get anything done. She sat in her office at the back of the downstairs bakery, behind a closed door, and sobbed the day away. The only person who I think took it as hard as my mother was Grandma Grace. I honestly can't imagine what it must be like to lose your child. It crushed her, and made her question her faith.

"I'm mad at God," she'd tell us in those days, shaking her head at this latest injustice that had been heaped on her meager shoulders. "I'm mad at Jesus."

Who could blame her?

Lobster tails—the unassuming pastry that would present my biggest challenge.

77

I was mad, too. Mad at the universe for taking my father away. My anger came out sporadically. I'd hold it together for days on end, then crack, go out and party too hard, showing up for work at ten o'clock the next morning, which in a bakery is like showing up after lunch. When it happened, I'd get the silent treatment from my brother-in-law Joey, or if it happened on a weekend, from Uncle Frankie, whose quiet wrath was severe. He would make like I didn't exist, or shoot me a dirty look, until finally, one Sunday morning, we had it out.

"You're a disgrace," he said to me.

"What do you know about what I'm going through!" I yelled. "I lost my father! My best friend!"

"Hey!" Uncle Frankie said. "Your father was like a brother to me. I miss him, too. But he would have wanted you to do the right thing!"

He was right. I was the son of the Boss. It was like Dad always said, I had to be a little better than everybody else. I wasn't entitled to any slack, no matter how much I felt I needed it.

Still, I was a mess, and so was my mother. We saw more of each other than anybody else did, because we were the only two people still living in that big house in Little Ferry. We both put on the best face we could at the bakery but, at home, I'd sit in the living room, passing my nights in front of the television, my father's old recliner a constant reminder of our loss, while I'd hear her faintly weeping in her room. It was almost funny: I was in such sad shape myself, and yet I was worried that *she* was going to crumble. Our isolation and grief made us closer than we'd ever been. Before long, I was telling her that I hoped she'd meet somebody else; it was the only way I thought she'd ever fully recover. It went against every old-world bone in my body. Back in Italy, if the husband died, the widow wore black and toughed it out for the rest of her life, but I really found myself wishing only the best for her. She was too young not to have romance in her life.

My mother became housebound in her personal grief, but after a month or two I was doing just the opposite. I'd always been a social animal, but I was really going overboard, for a number of reasons: First of all, despite all the responsibility that had been heaped on my shoulders, I was still a seventeen-year-old kid: I had tons of energy, raging hormones, and a lot on my mind, not to mention a relatively new driver's license and set of wheels. How better to honor all that than by going out? Motoring around the local highways in my new car, I'd turn up the stereo, cranking the hard rock and club music I favored in those days to earsplitting levels, pushing all the thoughts right out of my head. I'd screech up to one of my favorite clubs, and once I was inside the sensory overload was just what the doctor ordered: more blaring music, flashing lights, beautiful people. I'd just take it all in and forget about my troubles, if only for a few hours. Going out was like a morphine drip for the pain; every time I lit out into the New Jersey night, I got some temporary relief.

Even after my grief began to lift, I continued to go out, because I had actually started to enjoy myself. It came at a cost, however, and I was spending money with utter abandon. I'd always had a taste for nice things, but was really going overboard: I spent loads on clothes, lavished a series of girlfriends with gifts, and tipped doormen and bartenders as though I were a millionaire.

My mother might have been grief stricken, but she was present enough to notice all of this, especially the big spending. She thought I was being foolish with my money, and it didn't sit well with her, not after how hard she and my father had worked for everything they had, and when she saw how hard I worked myself.

One day, I picked up my pay in her office, and immediately noticed that there wasn't enough money in the envelope.

"Mama," I said. "There's a mistake. The envelope is light."

"You're not getting all your pay," she told me flatly. "You need to learn how to respect money. You're just going to go blow it. I put some of it in the bank for you."

"Give me my money!" I bellowed, in spite of being in the bakery's hallowed halls. "I work hard!"

"No."

I was furious, even though deep down I knew the truth was that I would have spent all that money. Every last cent. I relented, and with her socking it away for me, by the time I was twenty-one, there was enough money in that bank account to buy a house.

I was leading a double life. At night I was a carefree kid, but by day I was a stress case. On top of the actual work, and there was plenty of it, because the bakery just kept getting more and more popular, there was a power struggle underway. Our bakery has always run spontaneously, an improvisation fueled by flour and family. This worked because there was my dad, the original Cake Boss, and my mom, who ran the books, and they established order. With my father gone, there was a void, and it was as big and as threatening as a black hole. We weren't a corporation. We didn't have manuals and guidebooks. There was no emergency contingency plan in the safe, no chain of command. The closest we had to an heir to the throne was me, the only son of the fallen king.

Everybody knew, or had heard around the nook just beyond the retail area, or on lunch breaks, that it was my father's intent for me to step into his shoes and take over the business, but *eventually*, not when I was barely old enough to drive and still too young to vote. I wasn't up to the task yet. I was just a soldier. I didn't know anything about leadership. I had never managed anything in my life, not even myself. There's no point beating around the bush: I was afraid and underqualified. People needed me to fill a void, and I choked. I didn't step up.

We were lucky, though. We had a good team, so, even though nobody was taking the reins, the work was getting done. Dominic and Joey were especially helpful, managing the production team with their easy style. The flip side was that everybody thought he were the one who had the stuff to run the show, which led to daily dustups and arguments.

Every time something like that happened, I'd cringe. Because *I* was supposed to figure this all out. I was the one who was supposed to take over the back of the house and make the bakery run smoothly. It was up to me to make order out of chaos, harmony out of infighting. I knew it in my bones, but despite the fact that I was surrounded by people who loved me, it was the first time in my life that I felt afraid to act and the fear embarrassed me. Every time I walked through the bakery, I could sense everybody's eyes on me, feel them wondering when I was going to rip off my shirt and turn into Superman and save the day. The look in my sisters' eyes was especially haunting. After them taking such good, loving care of me all my life. I wanted so badly to be able to take care of them, by doing what was expected of me at Carlo's, but I just couldn't muster the courage.

Every week, the stress would come to a head on Friday night. The decorating room then was where my office is now, looking out on Washington Street. I had a bench set up parallel to the old windows that look out on the scene, and on Friday night, after doing my part to run the shop, I would do my decorating work for the weekend. I'd have twelve cakes lined up on the table, and I'd go to work.

It was tough, but it was something I knew how to do and offered me a sense of accomplishment. And so, I'd get into the zone, and let my instincts take over, making borders and drop lines while I processed what was going on. I'd get as lost as I could in the work, until hours later, I'd look down and see that the garbage can of buttercream (we buy rubberized cans and use them to store various creams and flours; they are just the right size) I'd started the night with was empty, and that the pastry bags that had been so crisp and new a few hours earlier were twisted beyond recognition. Stretching my back, I'd look out the windows and see my friends out in the street, on their way from one bar to another, their work for the week done, their lives in order for the moment. That's when the pain would settle in. My right arm would be swollen and throbbing, and I would trudge down the hall, put the cakes in the refrigerator, lock up the bakery, get in my car, and drive home, feeling years older than my actual age.

Sometimes, after nights like that, I'd be driving, and my thoughts weren't thoughts at all, just wave after wave of despair, consuming me. The truth is that sometimes I thought about running my car right off the side of the road, right off Route 3.

Of course, I never did. Too many people were counting on me, even if they couldn't count on me yet.

Once I got home, I'd just sit there, in my father's old recliner, understanding for the first time what it was that he had on his mind all those times I'd watched him there when I was a little kid, finally comprehending how much there could be to operating a bakery.

❧

Amazingly, things got better. Time worked its magic and week by week, we all got back on our feet.

There was still a leadership void, but the bakery was cranking out what it needed to, as each of us pulled our own weight.

From a production standpoint, the only problem was the *sfogliatelle* dough used to make lobster tails. My dad was the master at pulling that dough, but we were struggling with it. Sal had helped my father do it, so he was able to do a passable job, but it just wasn't the same. He didn't have the same finesse that my father did, or the time to do it himself.

It was a problem, because our lobster tails were a real signature item at Carlo's. For a bakery that prided itself on staying true to tradition and doing things the old-fashioned way, the lobster tails were one of the jewels in the crown. I can't tell you how many customers would take one bite of them and positively swoon with delight at the airiness of the pastry, the richness of the filling, the decadence of each and every bite. Elderly Italians, relocated here from the old country, would rhapsodize in Italian about how feathery

Mama, in the middle, and her girls: Lisa, Maddy, Grace, and Mary.

they were, how all the other lobster tails they'd ever eaten in America were hard as rocks, with layers so thick they could cut your gums.

Probably no one ever realized that almost every lobster tail that had ever come out of our kitchen had been rolled and pulled by my father's own hands. Every so often, he'd set aside a good chunk of a day and pull ninety to one-hundred-twenty pounds of dough. After refrigerating it overnight, the rest of us would cut the salami into discs, open them up, fill them with cream puff dough (which provided crucial support, keeping those fragile layers from collapsing), bake them, and freeze them until they were ready to be thawed, piped full of cream, and dusted with powdered sugar.

Mama and me: Through the rough patch.

I finally decided to take matters into my own hands and take a crack at that *sfogliatelle* dough. I made up a huge batch in one of the mixers, ran it through the sheeter to flatten it out, then went to work on it with a rolling pin until it was about sixteen feet long and three feet wide. Periodically, I'd stop to get under the dough, which seemed as big as a tent by then, sticking my fingers up against the surface from below and massaging it out wider, thinner, stretching and pulling it until it was just about see-through. Because that's how thin *sfogliatelle* dough needs to be to achieve that light-as-air effect in the final product.

I couldn't do it. No matter how hard I tried, I'd either rip huge holes in the dough, or fail to pull it evenly, so the roll would be bunched up on one end, or in the center, or too loose. I kept at it, though, trying batch after batch, until I was huffing and puffing and glistening with sweat, my T-shirt soaked through. I felt like a surgeon must feel when he's trying valiantly to save a patient, only to realize that his powers aren't going to be enough that day.

"Damn it!" I yelled.

Everybody looked up from their work, but when they saw how upset I was, they turned away.

"I'm going home," I said.

More frustrated than I'd ever been in my life, I went back to the house, into my room, pulled the covers over my head, and fell into a deep, deep sleep.

Out of the darkness, came a white, the white of heaven, or a bakery, or both.

It was the most vivid dream I'd ever had. I was standing in the basement of Carlo's Bake Shop, awash in white: the walls, the table, the flour that's always hanging in the air. Suddenly, my father was standing there. We always look like ghosts, we bakers, because we're in cook's whites and aprons, dusted with flour. That's how we looked in my dream. I couldn't tell which of us was alive and which was visiting from the hereafter.

I threw my arms around him.

"Dad! Wow! I haven't seen you in so long. I miss you."

He gently removed my arms and fixed me with a serious look.

"Listen," he said. "I am not here to dick around with you. I am here to show you how to pull *sfogliatelle* one more time."

I nodded, shifted gears.

We moved to the table, wordlessly, the way you sometimes do in dreams, and we stood next to each other.

"Now, watch what I do," he said.

We started working, with me mimicking his every move, just as I'd done with so many preparations. Even in my dream, it occurred to me that this was one of the things he'd told Father Gene he wished he'd had time to teach me. But here he was, showing me anyway. As he massaged the dough, I massaged the dough, watching how his fingers did their magic. As he pulled, I pulled. As he stretched, I stretched. We were in perfect sync. And, somewhere along the way, something changed, and instead of him standing there, there were two of me, two Buddy Juniors, working in harmony. And then those two Buddys came together and I was looking down at my hands, my father's hands, one and the same. I was alone in the bakery, a perfect roll of dough stretched out before me.

I woke with a shock. I'm not going to lie to you: I was spooked. I walked around in a daze that morning, unsure of what to feel, looking at my hands. They felt different, as if they'd been touched by God for a second time.

On my drive to the bakery that day, I held the wheel with one hand, and with the other I squeezed the Saint Anthony medallion that hung over my chest. It's like I told you earlier, that medallion isn't just for show. I believe in Saint Anthony, and I believed with all my heart that my father visited me that night, that he had come straight back from heaven to teach me a crucial lesson.

By the time I got to work, I felt a sense of peace, which in turn led to a sense of excitement. I pushed the doors of the shop open and called out to Sal and Dominic, "C'mon guys, we're going to do this today."

They looked up from their work.

"Do what?" they said in unison.

"The *sfogliatelle*!"

I marched through the bakery possessed by a positive energy I hadn't felt since before I learned my father was sick. Bakers had to jump out of my way to avoid getting mowed down. All I wanted to do was get in that kitchen and have it out with the *sfogliatelle* dough, show it once and for all who was boss.

When I got to the bins that hold the flour, Sal and Dominic were nowhere to be found. I'd left them in my dust, way back in the corridor.

I started shoveling flour into the mixer. Then gallons of water. Some salt. I turned it on and let it come together into a thick wad of *sfogliatelle* dough. It takes a good fifteen minutes for that to happen, and it seemed like the longest fifteen minutes of my life. I couldn't wait to get going on that dough and paced around the mixer the entire time. People were stealing glances at me, then at each other. I could read their thoughts on their faces: "Buddy's finally lost it."

Finally, the dough was ready. I sent it back and forth through the sheeter, narrowing the settings on each pass, until the rollers inside were almost touching. Then I met the thin sheet that came out on the other side, and went to work on it with a confidence that had eluded me on previous attempts. For the first time ever, I got into the zone with the *sfogliatelle* dough. The rest of the bakery fell away and I was having an out-of-body experience. At first, I felt disconnected from my fingers, just watching them do their thing, watching them dance under that dough, coaxing it out until it was almost as transparent as a pane of glass, then I felt disconnected from the entire room, as though I were watching myself from above, as I knew my father surely was, the two of us united once again.

Meet the Sisters: Grace

True to her name, Grace is the sister who most reminds me of our Grandma Grace; she has that slightly suspicious Sicilian gene that sometimes tells her that everybody is out to get her or her family. Those instincts sometimes serve her well; when our father died, Grace really rose to the occasion and helped keep the retail counter running smoothly, and she has managed the schedule there for the last twenty years. She's incredibly honest and devoted to Carlo's Bake Shop.

Grace is also the only member of my generation of Valastros to graduate college—Ramapo College in New Jersey—earning high honors on the dean's list, before returning to work with the rest of us at Carlo's. Grace has always been a hard worker, and tends to take all aspects of the business personally, like if there's a small amount of money missing from the register after an insanely busy Saturday, which more likely than not was the result of an honest mistake by one of the kids who works for us. I sometimes have to tell her to let these things go.

They say that opposites attract, but Grace and Joey actually have a lot in common: both are industrious and devoted to the business and the family. They have two beautiful children, Robert and Bartolina, who was my first godchild and was named after—who else?—my father.

When it was all over, I came back to myself and, couldn't believe how depleted I was. I paced around the table like a marathoner who had just crossed the finish line, sucking in as much oxygen as I could, unable to stop moving, fearful that maybe I'd cramp up.

I looked down at the table, at the perfectly pulled roll of dough there.

That's right, I thought. *That's right, you pain in the butt. Now, you know who the boss is! Now, you know who the boss is!*

I looked up and realized that the entire bakery had come to a halt. Nobody was doing anything.

Normally, the dough is refrigerated overnight, but I didn't want to wait for the results. We cut it right then, then pushed it out into little cones, stuffed them with the cream puff dough, and baked them. I waited around for the verdict, but I didn't need to. I knew they'd come out right. And, sure enough, when they emerged from the oven, they looked light enough to float away.

The room burst into applause. I had my mojo back, and so did Carlo's Bake Shop.

Things were looking up.

6

Making My Mark

MAKING THOSE LOBSTER TAILS was a turning point in my life, and in the life of Carlo's Bake Shop. A young prince can ascend to the throne, but he doesn't truly have the respect of the knights he commands until he's shown his mettle in battle.

Well, the day I made those lobster tails, power was conferred upon me. It was the day the prince demonstrated that he was the king's true and rightful heir, not just because of genealogy, but because he had the same *abilities* as his father. Word spread through the bakery that day—Buddy did it! He made the *sfogliatelle*!—and by the end of the day, when I passed through the kitchen, or walked along the cases in the retail area, I could feel the sea change that had taken place. People were looking at me differently, even my sisters.

I felt different, too. Much of it had to do with finally cracking the code of those lobster tails, but it had just as much to do with that dream. When Dad came to me that night, he didn't just want to teach me how to make lobster tails. He knew that somebody needed to step in. Somebody needed to take the rudder of Carlo's Bake Shop and steer the ship to calmer waters. He was telling me that it was okay, that I didn't need to feel guilty for taking his place, that I didn't need to be afraid that I wasn't ready. He was telling me that somebody had to jump in, and that it was me.

I had proved something to myself: I was capable of stepping into those big shoes. I had the goods. Maybe I wasn't yet the man my father had been, maybe I never would be, but at least I could become the baker he had been, and I decided there and then that that's what I'd do. I don't know why I'd forgotten it for so long, but that was the day I remembered, finally, that whatever I put my mind to I can accomplish.

Next thing you knew, I was the boss of the bakery, overseeing the production schedule, deciding who would make which specialty and wedding cakes, and managing all the little crises that come up on a day-to-day basis. Unburdened by doubts, I took right to it, effortlessly mingling my father's management style with my own personality. The disorder that had consumed Carlo's Bake Shop after Dad had died was beginning to lift.

I had become the boss of the bakery, although, make no mistake, Mama continued to run the *business*. ("You're the Cake Boss, but I'm the Boss Boss," she liked to remind me every once in a while, and she was right; she was still the one who cut the checks.) Nevertheless, with my swelling confidence came a sense of ownership, a sense of responsibility, and I began to notice things that I wanted to change. Not out of ego, but just because I saw that they could be improved. I was seeing with new eyes, and it would have been downright irresponsible not to use my perspective and ability to their fullest to help Carlo's Bake Shop be the best bakery it could be.

The first area I addressed was creating greater efficiencies in the system. It seemed so very minor at the time, but one of the most important lessons my father had taught me when I was a little kid was using both my hands to apply those cherries to the top of pastries. That really resonated with me; it's what had led me to line up all those turntables at once for cake decorating.

And so, the first big change I instituted, ironically, was to the lobster tails. The more I made them, the more I realized they could be produced more efficiently. Normally, the guy who stretched and rolled the dough would apply the shortening himself. It occurred to me that we could move much more quickly if a second man put the shortening on. And so, I recruited Danny, and as I pulled and rolled, he would stay one step ahead of me, rubbing shortening onto the dough, greasing it up and keeping it pliable, which freed me up to move even faster. This was when I discovered that I had an alter ego, who I like to call the Hulk, who I can call on when things need to happen faster than humanly possible. Don't ask me how, or why I'm able to call out this being; all I can tell you is that when I need him, he is there, in all his green glory.

Before you knew it, I was banging out those salami in record time, going through five hundred to six hundred pounds of dough at a time. To hurry me along, I'd crank up Metallica on the boom box, which also made Danny go faster . . . because he couldn't stand that noise. It got to be like a game. The Hulk was so fast, that Sal would get the next piece of dough ready to go, passing it back and forth through the sheeter, and I would try to finish pulling the current one before he was done sheeting the next one.

As the weeks and months passed by, I started to notice things about some of our actual products that I thought could be improved. Like the buttercream. The elders in our shop made buttercream the old-fashioned way, whipping it to increase the volume as many times over as possible and get the most bang for their buck, which many feel is just good business. Fair enough. But I'd always secretly felt, even though I didn't admit it, even to myself, that that airiness made it hard to decorate with our buttercream, because the air pockets kept you from being able to get into a flow with it, to pipe and smooth it with any consistency.

Now that the buck stopped with me, I decided to see if I could improve our buttercream. I became a detective, calling shortening companies. I wanted to understand the *science* of buttercream, which meant understanding the science of shortening. After talking to a few sources, I realized that buttercream needs to be mixed at seventy to eighty degrees, so that it would be light and fluffy and easier to manipulate. I also learned that my instincts about the effects of too much oxygen were correct; it's crucial to not allow all that air into the mix. I began mixing buttercream with a paddle instead of a whip, and completely submerged it from the get-go so as not to swirl in any additional air.

Then, I got into my lab, the kitchen, and spent days trying different formulas and techniques, starting at lower and higher temperatures and whipping for different lengths of time. When I was done, I had a buttercream that looked like shaving cream, a cake decorator's dream.

I had great respect for the old ways of doing things, but moments like these taught me the value of questioning tradition. Of course, not everybody agreed. You have to remember, Carlo's Bake Shop is an old-school joint. There are days when you can walk into the kitchen in the morning, hear the oldies on the radio, see the vintage Hobart mixers in the corner, and hear the guys' sentences punctuated with the occasional Italian word or phrase, and you'd have no way of knowing if you were in 2010 or 1958 (except for the giant flat-screen television on one wall, or the desktop computer parked in the corner).

Put another way, this was not exactly an ideal breeding ground for systematic change, which was soon demonstrated to me by the pure venom that greeted my next little project: making over our vanilla cake, one of the basic cakes that we use in everything from birthday cakes to wedding cakes to cupcakes. As I opened my mind up to the possibility that not everything in the bakery was perfect, I had noticed that our vanilla cake was inconsistent, that it could sometimes be a little dry. I wasn't the only one: Lisa asked me one day why it wasn't always as moist as it should be. I knew what it was. The recipe was a little temperamental; if you didn't make it exactly the same way every time, it didn't come out right.

I began tasting sample after sample of the cake on a daily basis, and came to realize that I didn't really care for the grain, either: If you cut it down the middle and looked at a cross section, the grain was too airy, and if you popped it in your mouth, the texture was sometimes too gritty.

I want to be clear about this: I never saw this as a flaw with my old man. It's like I said earlier, mixing is an art unto itself, and I'm sure that any of the elders in the place, if they devoted their full attention to making the cake batter, would have been able to nail it every time. However, that wasn't the case anymore. We had younger and more inexperienced mixers on the line, and that was the source of the problem.

So I set a goal for myself: Create a vanilla cake recipe that was stupid-proof, which is Buddyspeak for foolproof. It was yet another thing I got from my father. If I asked certain questions when I was a kid, Dad would say to me, "Let me do all the thinking." Finally, now that I was in the captain's seat, I understood what he meant. You don't want your workers to ask questions; you want them, in the best sense of the word, to become human machines, executing the same steps over and over with the same results. The problem was that there was room for error in our vanilla cake recipe. Even with some experience and the best of intentions, a baker could end up with a sub-par specimen simply because they mixed it for a few seconds too long, under-mixed it, or over- or undercooked it.

Now, it was my turn to do the thinking, and I wanted to devise a recipe that anybody could follow successfully, which meant something that could survive any of those pitfalls.

I imagined a supermoist cake in my mouth, and found myself thinking of a pudding cake. I decided to add some Italian custard cream—the closest thing we have to pudding in the shop—to the batter, but it came out too mushy. I knew the problem was that the fats in the recipe weren't getting along, it was like trying to give a transfusion to somebody with an incompatible blood type. I set about investigating different shortenings I might be able to use, asking my suppliers for some candidates. They were only too happy to share: Nutex, Wesson Super Quick Blend, Fluid Flex, and a few that I can't remember. I bought up samples, and began experimenting, trying different combinations and amounts of various shortenings and the custard cream.

I have to stress again that this was no small thing. It was almost like questioning one's religion to start screwing around with a cake recipe at a place with roots as deep as Carlo's. My hesitancy was alleviated only by the fact that this particular recipe wasn't Dad's; it had been developed by one of the bakers. I shook off whatever discomfort I felt, and plowed forward. As I tried to solve this problem, it was all I could think about. Going to the supermarket became an almost painful exercise for me because, inevitably, I'd find myself in the baked goods aisle, staring longingly at the perfect slices of cake on the boxes for Duncan Hines and Entenmann's products, obsessing over the uniform grain of the sponge. *Why can't I do that?* I wondered.

The answer came as I was looking through Dad's old recipe book one night and came across his formula for an American vanilla cake that used Nutex, one of the shortenings I'd been experimenting with. I made that recipe the basis of my new recipe, tweaking it to get the grain just right, then began adding the custard cream to the batter. This caused the cake to not rise properly, so I then had to tweak the amount of baking powder.

By the time all was said and done, I'd been at it about every other day for a month, usually working at night when I had time for side projects, and when nobody else was around to ask me what I was up to. It was a long slog: Three small batches would come out wrong, then one would come out right, but when I scaled up the recipe to do a larger batch—a normal-sized Carlo's batch—it wouldn't hold together, or it would be too moist, like bread pudding. I was a mad scientist, scribbling notes, making two or three batches at once, and being driven to the brink of insanity; sometimes, I'd be so frustrated that I'd take it out on the cakes, squishing them through my fingers, or throwing them violently into the garbage.

Finally, I nailed it. Made a cake that came out just right: moist, firm, and delicious. The only remaining step was to solve why the cakes, while perfect in texture and flavor, were crowning, puffing up a little at the top.

My mind raced back to those Entenmann's products in the supermarket. They always came out the same, I thought. You never see an Entenmann's cake that doesn't look just right. Why? It occurred to me that the factories that crank out those products always make the cakes the same way every time. There are no humans involved; it's all machines. Then it hit me that I'd never been taught much about the *science* of baking; I knew how to take certain ingredients, mix them a certain way, and bake them at a certain temperature to end up with this or that cake or pastry. However, I knew nothing about the why of it. *Why* did things get mixed in a certain order? *Why* did some items get baked at three-hundred-fifty degrees and others at three-hundred seventy-five?

I'd never been to one of those big factories, but I started to visualize what went on there. Same ingredients we use, more or less, I figured. Basically, the same techniques. What was different? Then it hit me: *temperature control.* They must obsessively control the temperature of *everything*, not just the ovens but the raw ingredients that go into the ovens. Ditto the way things are mixed. I bet that every time an industrial-sized vat of batter is produced at Entenmann's, it's whipped for exactly the same number of minutes.

I started playing with all of those factors, recording the mixing times and temperatures, both of the batter and of the oven, and, of course, the cooking times. Ultimately, I realized that the batter itself should be at seventy degrees before it goes into the oven, and baked at 350°F. Do *that*, and it would come out flat as a top hat.

The next day, I went into the downstairs kitchen, where the cakes are baked, and brought samples of the new cake to the crew.

"Guys," I said. "Taste this."

They did, and they all nodded their approval, which is the baker's equivalent of moaning with delight.

I produced the recipe from my pocket. "From now on," I said, "This is our vanilla cake recipe."

The pronouncement was greeted with dead silence. Crickets. Eyebrows were raised. Tongues were swallowed. Everybody knew what was coming: The new recipe set up a conflict as fraught with tension and possible bloodshed as a heavyweight fight. In this corner, me, Buddy Valastro, Jr., heir to the Cake Boss throne. In the opposite corner, Old Man Mike, proud practitioner of the ancient art of baking, and creator of the Carlo's Bake Shop vanilla cake recipe that had been in use for almost a decade.

While everybody else, regardless of their personal feelings on the matter, fell into line, I knew it was going to be a battle with Mike, and he did not disappoint. At first, it was a quiet protest. He just kept on using his recipe, leaving me to discover that the batches he baked weren't up to snuff.

I'd go up to him, trying to be polite. "Mike," I said. "This is what I want you to do."

"What do you want from me?" he'd say, barely stopping in his stride as he unloaded a tray of cakes from the oven.

It was hard to get mad at Mike because not only was he a hard worker, an animal, but he also was much older than I was.

Finally, I decided to appeal to his sense of pride, and threatened to take some of his precious work away from him.

"Mike, if you don't do it the way I want you to, you're not going to do it at all."

Finally, he relented and tried it my way. I made of point of tasting the first batch. It was delicious, if I did say so myself.

"C'mon, Mike," I said, trying to lighten things up. "Have a taste."

He did, but offered nothing.

"Isn't it moist?"

He thought for a second, then said: "Oh, sure. It's moist. Of course, it's moist. There's custard inside." His message was unmistakable: Don't think you're a better baker than I am, because you're cheating.

I took his point in stride, because his coming on board was the tipping point after which other changes became easier to sell through to the troops.

And other changes did come: I changed the chocolate cake recipe, incorporating that same shortening I'd brought to the vanilla cake. Cookie recipes that were made with shortening only would henceforth be made with half shortening and half butter, for a more luxurious texture. Similarly, the *pasta frolla*, which had always been lard based, would now be butter based because lard was an acquired taste, and truth be told, we had always used it simply because it was cheaper. (Although lard does have its place: it remains the best, most authentic fat to use in cannoli and St. Joseph's zeppole.)

I also started to take a hard look at all our raw ingredients which, for all of our attention to quality, had never been that closely examined. Again, this traces back to the age of the bakery. Back when my father learned his craft, there was no artisanal movement in this country. To bakers like my dad, one brand was as good as the next. So, when he needed cocoa, he'd tell his supplier, "Give me a bag of cocoa." He didn't say which brand, or variety, or specify a butterfat or cocoa content.

I inherited my role at an exciting time in American cookery. For just about any ingredient you can think of, there are oodles of options, from premium brands made by large corporate producers to small-batch products turned out by farmers and artisans. You can specify the amount of butterfat you want in your cocoa or chocolate, which was also not a concern in the old days.

I decided to take advantage of these enlightened times we live in and upgrade our inventory. I started using Callebaut cocoa in our cakes and their chocolate in our chocolate-chip cookies and chocolate dip. I also began using European margarine instead of American because it was less greasy.

This time, it was my own mother who took exception, because, in order to use more expensive ingredients, we'd have to charge more money for the pastries and cakes. It was yet another sign of the gap between the old and new generation. If you think about it, so much of the food my ancestors, and even my parents when they were children, were raised on was created by the poor out of necessity. Take *bruschetta*, for example, which is stale bread, grilled, and topped with chopped overripe tomatoes. That dish was engineered for the sole purpose of utilizing food that was past its prime, stuff we'd throw away here in the United States. But, go to a fancy restaurant these days, and you'll see modernized *bruschetta* made with freshly baked bread, organic tomatoes at the height of freshness, maybe even flecked with fresh herbs and microgreens.

That's what I was trying to do with our product. Not mess with the integrity or the tradition, but just make everything a little better by using what was available to us, in the 1990s, here in America. I also believed that if we followed this path, customers would happily pay the extra price, and even greater success would follow.

I always secretly believed that my mother was upset with all these changes for another reason, and that Old Man Mike was, too: Carlo's represented a little bit of the world they'd all left behind right here in America. Although all my relatives are proud to be American, they are very proud of their Italian heritage, which was kept alive in every pastry and cake that we made in the bakery.

I was raised in an environment in which we ate dinner together every night as a family and the entire extended family congregated every Sunday night. But, today, as each of the siblings has his or her own family, with both parents working and lots going on in our lives, that's just not possible any more. That's upsetting to my mother and her generation. I think that when I started to mess around with formulas that had been honored for decades, it felt like I was Americanizing the one thing about us that shouldn't be Americanized, that I was cutting loose the last of the untampered-with rituals.

I understood, but I also felt that making these changes was essential to Carlo's resonating with the next generation of customers, that, in order to keep the bakery viable as a source of income for the growing family, it was crucial that we keep up with the demands of the modern food lover. When you looked up and down our pastry cases, nothing looked any different than it always had, but a lot of it just tasted better and, for the most part, we were able to achieve that with no extra work or skill, but just turning to better ingredients.

I stuck to my guns, and it wasn't long before the plan was validated. Sure, some customers took note of the higher prices on some items, but we trained our counter people to explain the reason and, before you knew it, everybody had adjusted.

Even so, the more things change, the more they stay the same. Despite my attempt to adapt some classic recipes for the modern customer, a lot of things are still done the old-fashioned way at Carlo's Bake Shop. For example, we adhere to an age-old method of tracking an order from the time it gets taken from the customer to the moment the final cake is picked up or delivered: the slip.

When a cake is ordered at Carlo's, an order form is filled out, which we call "the slip." The original stays with the counter team and the carbon goes to the bakery. That slip stays with the order from the time it's placed to the time the cake is baked, decorated, refrigerated, and delivered. This system has cost us our fair share of disasters because, unlike computerized systems, where orders are traced electronically, those little pieces of paper tend to float away, or get coffee spilled on them, or get set down next to the wrong cake. It makes for some heart-pumping situations, but we always manage to get it all straightened out by the end of the day.

We also still use a lot of equipment that was made before my father was born and has been with us since our old location on Adams Street. There's the ancient Hobart whipped-cream machine that has a pedal on the side that activates a compressor and pipes air into the cream. They'll have to kill me before I surrender that beauty. Ditto the seasoned black pans that we bake our cookies on, which used to belong to Old Man Carlo as well. God only knows how many millions of cookies have been baked on those relics. And, of course, there's our trusty old Hobart mixer still cranking along after more than seven decades, and our Rondo sheeter, which Dad bought in the 1960s.

Some things have changed. We have an industrial-sized dishwasher now. We used to wash everything by hand, a chore that was useful for motivating apprentices like me when I was young because being the dishwasher used to

Meet the Sisters: Mary

Of all the family characters who appear on *Cake Boss*, I probably get asked the most questions about my sister, Mary. Scarcely an episode goes by in which she doesn't get into a fight with me, or another sister, or a customer. People ask me, "Is Mary really like that?"

The answer is *yes*. And *no*.

Mary, who's seven years older than I am, definitely has a big mouth, but she also has a big heart. Sometimes, I think maybe she just has a hearing condition: tone deafness. She doesn't think she's doing anything wrong, which seems incredible, because when I see her going off on an employee or, worse, a customer, it still makes me cringe, same as it did when I was a teenager.

When she's in sweet mode, Mary and I get along just great. As much of a terror as she can be on an off day, when she's on, she's the very best at managing the counter, an absolute master at multitasking, making sure the cash in the drawer adds up, that all the cookies and pastries are constantly replenished, that the specialty-cake customers are getting what they need, and that everybody is happy.

Mary is the one sister whose husband doesn't work in the store: Her husband Joe, who we jokingly refer to as Handy Joe for his lack of handyman skills, is a pharmaceutical broker, specializing in oncologic drugs. He has a great personality, best described as happy-go-lucky. Mary and Joe have twins, Lucia and Joseph (my godson), who are age-wise right between our kids Sofia and Buddy, and the cousins are inseparable, the way my sisters and I were growing up.

leave me with bloody fingers. ("Better not screw up today," I used to think. "Don't want to end up doing that later on.")

Most important, we still make a lot of things from scratch that many other bakeries order from food-service companies, such as cannoli shells and, of course, lobster tail shells; that's something that will never change because, if it did, we wouldn't be Carlo's anymore.

7

Polishing the Diamond

BY 1996, CARLO'S BAKE SHOP was in full stride and bursting at the seams. All three floors were humming like a well-oiled machine, and we were doing a brisk business, often with a line that snaked just outside the door and onto the sidewalk. Of course, behind the scenes, things continued to be imperfect, our working life punctuated by drama. But, you know something? That's just the way it is. We're all family at Carlo's—at some point, even nonrelations began calling my mother Mama—and, at some point, I realized that we liked it this way. Sure, I want my production line to be regimented, but who wants to come to work in a place where everybody has to act exactly the same and every day is just a repeat of the day before? Not me! Our little foibles made us unique, gave us an energy like no other bakery, and I honestly believed that that liveliness showed up in the food we baked.

There were things that changed at Carlo's over the next few years, setting us up nicely for the coming new millennium.

One of the most significant evolutions involved my brother-in-law Mauro. We had a hilarious little bit that we did every weekend, although to us it wasn't a joke. Mauro always felt great urgency to get his deliveries made, which is a good thing. But in order to move things along, he'd often loom over me as I was decorating the next cake he was waiting for.

"Buddy!" he'd plead. "I need this cake! Please! It's gotta get done! You're killing me!"

I'd keep my absolute focus on the cake, not even responding, until finally I'd snap: "You need the cake? Then *you* can help decorate the cake. C'mon, put the cream up! C'mon, fill a bag for me!"

That's how Mauro learned to become a cake decorator. Before too long, he wouldn't be helping me finish a cake, he'd be in such a hurry that he'd have started working on the next one all by himself. It could have made me angry, but the truth was that he was a natural. And, the more he did, the better he got. He also enjoyed the challenge, and began coming around and helping out whenever he had free time on his hands, often staying late into the evening to help me with wedding cakes so he could learn.

He got so good, and enjoyed it so much, that in 1996, I hired him and he came to work for us full time. I trained him personally, and not only is Mauro a skilled decorator, but he quickly evolved into my right-hand man, because he has terrific people skills, able to manage and watch over the entire decorating room when I'm not around. (The only area in which his people skills fail him is that he has an almost metabolic inability to remember people's names, which is why we've nicknamed him "Chef Mario," tagging him with the wrong name himself.)

Mauro came along at just the right time, because another change was about to take place that would begin to pull me out of the back of the house more often. It had to do with how cake orders are taken at Carlo's, and it happened in fits and starts, beginning at around the same time.

Historically, if you wanted to order a cake at Carlo's Bake Shop, you'd come in and flip through a book of designs, perusing your options. Then you'd select your cake, frostings, and any special flourishes you wanted. Fundamentally speaking, a birthday cake was a birthday cake and a wedding cake was a wedding cake. Flavors and colors would vary, but there wasn't much personalization.

However, as the store did a brisker and brisker business, my sisters and the young women who worked for them would sometimes be too busy to step out from behind the counter and take a cake order. And so, once in a while, one of them would intercom me, asking if I could come out and help take care of a customer. I was happy to make the time, just as my father did back in the day, and it turned out to be a real treat. I'd done everything you could do in the back of the bakery, but I'd never been a counter guy, and I loved getting out of the back and among the people. I loved hearing about a couple's wedding, or the sweet sixteen party that parents were planning for their daughter, or the baseball-themed party another family was throwing for their five-year-old son.

I'm a good listener, and I developed an ability to home in on the key words in their conversation. From a ten-minute monologue, I'd latch onto "simple," or "classic," or "extravagant," and I'd know the essence of what they desired. And, because I express myself through my baking and designs, as soon I began throwing out ideas for what I thought they'd like their cake to taste and look like, it was as though I had psychic abilities, because my success rate was close to one hundred percent; I'd pitch a concept and their eyes would light up and they'd say, "That's it!"

Before long, I realized that the same social gene that had allowed me to make so many friends in my life, and to handle clients like Joe Macaluso, made me a natural at dealing with our retail customers, even the more high-maintenance ones, who would come in with an attitude and leave kissing me on both cheeks.

I can't put words to why. I just key into people. I shake their hands, and look into their eyes, and listen to their words, and I just *get* them. It's just like the gift of my hands, or the hand of the bag, something I was born with.

✦

Mauro wasn't the only one to take an unconventional route to the Carlo's creative team. During these years, a number of employees transitioned from less specialized jobs into decorating, at precisely the time when we needed as many hands on deck as possible. A good example is the story of an Ecuadorian pot washer named Alex.

Alex was a hard worker from day one, a head-down, no-nonsense, service-with-a-smile employee, which instantly endeared him to me. There was also something about him, something I couldn't put my finger on, that told me that there was more to him than met the eye.

In time, I came to realize what that "something" was—Alex wanted to learn to do what I did. He'd hang around the bakery late into the evening, finding excuses to pass by the decorating room upstairs, where I'd be working into the wee hours.

"What's up, Alex?" I'd ask him.

"Nothing," he'd say shyly, before retreating to some other part of the bakery.

Finally, one night, I couldn't take it anymore. "Alex!" I said. "What are you doing here?"

"Well," he said. "I want to learn how to do it. To make the cakes like you guys do."

I thought about it for a moment, and decided, "Why not?" If he had the motivation and desire, who was I to deny him the opportunity? But I wasn't going to just let him start decorating right away; he'd have to earn that privilege, same as we all had. So I let him begin by putting up the whipped cream. After he did this, I showed him how to fill a bag, and before you knew it, we had a little dance going, me piping until the bag in my hands was empty, and him handing me the next one. I'm sure it wasn't especially gratifying work, but Alex did it with perfect attention. I could tell that he wasn't just waiting to hand me the bag, he was watching my hands up close, watching them do their thing on the cake.

I explained to him what I was doing, the different techniques I'd employ for different effects, the drop lines and swags and all the different borders, and the various bag techniques used to realize them.

Once all the cakes were done, we cleaned up together, rolled the cake-bearing racks into the refrigerator, and closed up the shop. We shook hands and I knew that this was going to be the beginning of something.

After that night, Alex started staying every night, which I respected, because he'd been at work since six o'clock in the morning. My official decorators punched out at six in the evening, but there were always more cakes to make. So, he and I would stay up there working until ten o'clock some times. As a reward, I'd teach him everything I could.

It was fun. I would showboat for him, really strut my stuff. For example, if

I was icing birthday cakes, with seven or eight of them lined up on turntables, and he brought me a three-gallon tub of whipped cream, I'd try to go through it before he could get the next batch whipped up. To do this, I called out the Hulk yet again, and with him unleashed, I'd be piping the cream out with a bag, then smoothing it with a spatula, so fast that I was a blur, and Alex would be frantically eyeing the mixing bowl, trying to *will* the cream to whip up faster.

It became an assumed thing that Alex would stay after work to help me, and once he'd mastered all the tasks of being my wingman, I started to let him help with the decorating.

"Here," I said, handing him the bag, one evening. "Try a drop line."

He took the bag in hand, and piped drop lines, over and over, running them around the edge of the cake like theater curtains. For a first-timer, it was impressive and I knew right then and there that he had the hand of the bag. I talked to him about it, the same way my father had talked to me, the two of us carrying on a conversation that had happened countless times, in English and Italian, here in America and back home in Sicily, going back to the previous century.

After a few months teaching Alex the nuts and bolts of decorating, I decided graduation day had arrived, that he knew how to put all the pieces together. It was time for him to do a cake on his own.

And so, one night, as he was bringing over the second batch of whipped cream, I stepped aside and gestured toward the turntable in front of me, a vanilla cake sitting there, naked in the overhead lights.

"Okay, Alex," I said. "Let's see what you've got."

"Yeah?"

"What?" I asked. "You don't want to?"

He jumped into action, putting into effect all the little things he'd been learning over the past six months. He piped the cream out onto the cake, then took a spatula and smoothed the top, then held it perpendicular to the sides, spinning the turntable to rotate the cake against it. For a first-time effort, the result was spectacular.

That was all I needed to see. I promptly promoted Alex to the decorating team, where he did everything from birthday cakes to wedding cakes, executing each of them with real flair, and in time developing his own signature flourishes and areas of specialization; he was especially adept at fashioning flowers, which he picked up more quickly than most people do.

What can I say? The guy simply blew me away. I was reminded of the way Tony D. used to talk to my dad about me: "One day, this kid is going to be better than you!" That's how I felt about Alex. He was going to be at least as good as me. That didn't threaten me in the least; if there's one thing Carlo's can always use, it's a great decorator.

&

As the years ticked by, business just kept booming at Carlo's, and we had the right team in the bakery, and upstairs in the decorating room, to keep up and maintain our high standards. Eventually, desperate for more space for our growing team, we built a new, expanded decorating room on our roof, and converted the old decorating room into my office. In these hectic times, Mauro proved to be invaluable, taking charge of that construction job as I ran the bakery with Joey, who similarly kept on top of all the baking production downstairs.

Around this same time, my Saturdays became more and more consumed with cake orders.

Beyond the human value of these interactions, I also loved doing business with the customers, which sometimes can be like a great, big game. For the most part, transactions were straightforward: I'd name a fair price, the customer would agree, we'd shake, and I'd pop the slip in the back.

There were exceptions, though, lots of them, and once again, my instincts served me well. For example, I could tell a penny-pincher coming a mile away and knew to jack the price up a few hundred bucks so he could feel good when he thought that he had negotiated me down. On the other end of the spectrum were the couples who became my favorites, the ones who came in bedecked in custom jewelry, expensive watches, and designer glasses. You can literally see couples like this coming from a mile away because they sparkle in the sunlight. Inevitably, when I sat down with them, they all said the same thing, "We want your most expensive cake." To which my reply was always, "You got it!"

As much as I prided myself on being a savvy businessman and world-class negotiator, there were those poignant occasions when I could sense that a couple was on the verge of ordering a cake beyond their means. If I picked up on the fact that somebody couldn't afford a real showstopper, I'd try to subtly talk them out of it. I heard a couple once whispering about the expense of sugar flowers, an expensive flourish that I had to purchase at that time because I didn't yet know how to make them. The bride had had a picture of this cake in her head since she was a little girl and they were about to describe to me a cake that would cost thousands of dollars. And yet, somewhere in their discussion, I overheard that they were throwing their wedding at the local VFW (Veterans of Foreign Wars) hall. I waited for the right moment, then told them, "You know, I can make this cake look just as pretty with real flowers and your guests will never know the difference." They exhaled in unison and took my suggestion.

Another time, a couple told me that they were trying to scrape together enough dough to buy a house, but it was clear that they were struggling. Nevertheless, they were about to buy a $3,000 cake. I talked them out of it, selling them on a less expensive but perfectly lovely one instead.

There were times when these conversations left me feeling like a cross between a bartender and a marriage counselor or psychologist, which helped me understand the role of a bakery in people's lives: Whether it's a little treat to get them through the day, a weekend indulgence for their kids, or ordering a cake for a big occasion, our products were a source of joy for people. More than ever before, I developed an appreciation for what an awesome responsibility we had, and how we needed to treat our customers right. It's the same reason that if, a wedding gets called off, despite our strict no-refund policy, we always return the deposit. If I kept the money from a canceled wedding, I wouldn't be able to look at myself in the mirror.

Before I knew it, I was pretty much spending my entire Saturdays taking cake orders, which offered a window into a side of our business that, strangely, I had had very little contact with on a daily basis: our customers, the people who actually ate the food that we baked and designed. It provided crucial insights. The more people I met, the firmer my grasp became on what the public was looking for. This gave me new ideas, and directly inspired the most daring decision I made as boss of Carlo's Bake Shop. I realized that couples were gravitating toward wedding cakes decorated with rolled fondant (a pliable sugar icing made with glycerine and gelatin), which were being depicted in more and more bridal magazines. They brides especially were drawn to the clean, polished look of cakes covered with perfect, smooth, satiny fondant as opposed to buttercream, which could be beautiful, but would never have the same elegance. Properly rolled-out fondant on a wedding cake could be as lovely as the bride herself. Not only that, it allowed for the design touches to have more impact, enabling the designer to mold and sculpt three-dimensional effects like drapes, bows, flowers, and cutouts.

Even though I hadn't done much work with fondant, as soon as a customer voiced a concept to me, I'd be able to visualize exactly what the finished cake would look like. I'd close my eyes, and go into a zonelike place. I couldn't draw it on paper, but I could describe it to them in such a way that they put their trust in me and placed their order.

The first fondant cakes I made took forever to produce, but I had a feeling, an instinct, that this was going to be the wave of the future, so, even though it wasn't time-effective from a cost standpoint, I was happy to spend extra hours mastering this new form. Bakers, including my father, had been almost afraid of fondant, because they thought it was hard to work with, and time consuming. All of that was true, but I knew that if I could devise systems and efficient techniques it would pay off. Not only that, but for us, as craftspeople, it was a whole new medium with endless possibilities for self-expression, which was irresistible.

Additionally, fondant was inherently special, which people were willing to pay top dollar for, so I saw it as a chance to dramatically alter our business model. Up to that point, most of our wedding cakes were produced for big catering halls, so, while we did a substantial volume and were proud of our work, we were, relatively speaking, paid peanuts for acting as a cake factory.

I also knew that most people who worked with fondant were decorators, not bakers. Under their beautiful designs were cakes that didn't taste as good as ours. If I could marry world-class fondant artistry with our old-world recipes, I knew we'd be able to corner the market on this emerging niche category.

As I began down this road, I had a secret weapon: I'd always had a theory about fondant, which many people found too thick, chewy, and sweet.

I believed that was true because everybody rolled their fondant too thick. When I began experimenting with it, I used all of my rolling-pin prowess to roll the fondant paper thin. Where most decorators applied a very thin layer of buttercream under the fondant to help it adhere to the cake, I went thicker with the cream, for a more traditional taste. As a result, the inherent flavor of the cake itself was preserved, and I was on my way.

As the months and years wore on, if a customer didn't suggest fondant, I would, and, in time, my team and I became experts at working with it and I became a master at selling it. I cut loose a lot of the catering halls, instead deciding to focus on this designer business moving forward and, within a few years, we had flipped our model. Where maybe one or two of our wedding cakes a week out of fifty were made with fondant up until the mid 1990s, we gradually developed the business until, eventually, forty-eight out of fifty were made with fondant and two were made with buttercream.

Some of our beautiful fondant cakes in our window at Carlo's.

Our dedication to these customized, boutique-style wedding cakes, in turn, led to the formalization of what has become a trademark Carlo's offering: the consultation.

The whole idea behind the consultation was to treat the discussion and creation of a cake as seriously as you might treat a visit to a doctor or a lawyer. You had something big going on in your life, and you needed time with an expert to sort it out and make a decision. The big difference, of course, was that the something big that brought people to our door was decidedly more positive than most things that send them to an attorney or a medic.

I began looking for ways to beef up the consultation. For example, we started making actual appointments with customers, inviting them to call and book some time. That way, when they came to the shop, they would walk past the increasingly long line, identify themselves to one of the counter people, and tell them Buddy was expecting them, which made them feel special.

For the consultation itself, I created a sampling plate of different cake types so that the client could actually taste the options. Although we still have a book of standard designs, it began to gather dust because now people could sample the most popular choices—vanilla, chocolate, vanilla chiffon, chocolate chiffon, red velvet—and make their selection based on more than a name and a photograph—no different from bringing home a paint chip or fabric swatch from a design store before making a home-décor decision. (I have to admit that the sampling plate was partially selfish; I knew that if clients tasted our product, they'd be sold, and also knew that by narrowing the selection, I was limiting the number of different cakes we had to crank out on a regular basis.)

Once they had selected their cake type, I'd jump in with my suggestions as to how to customize the cake.

Before you knew it, the consultation grew into something special, a boutique-like experience for our customers, who I noticed were beginning to come from farther and farther away to order their own custom-designed Carlo's cake. The best part was that once they'd indulged themselves in this new ritual, and enjoyed the cake we produced for them, they came back to us for all their cakes needs in the future.

The only downside to the consultation was that by offering extreme customization, we sometimes invited confrontation. There were occasions when even my social skills were pushed to the limit, if not the breaking point. Most of the time, I knew I could make a customer happy, but every once in a while, I could just smell that it wasn't going to turn out that way. For example, I would get a request for something that I knew would look or taste nasty, like the bride who requested a bright purple cake to match her bridesmaids' dresses, or the occasional description of hues that were going to be so mismatched I wondered if the bride were color blind.

My response plan was pretty straightforward: "Listen," I'd say. "I have to be honest. I will tell you right now that this is not going to look good. Personally, it will kill me to make this and sell it to you. But, if it's what you really want, then you're the customer and I'll do it for you." After hearing that from a baker, nine out of ten brides would take my advice and ask me for another recommendation. If they didn't, I'd go on the record: "Okay, I'll make this, but remember what I said." Translation: Don't ask for your money back when you think the cake looks like something that just swooped down from outer space to ruin your wedding day.

I generally felt that if I said those things, I was covered. If, however, I saw trouble on the horizon, getting that sinking feeling that when they saw their finished cake I'd have an irate and inconsolable customer on my hands, I'd do an end run by jacking up the price ("No problem, that'll be $10,000, payable *now*, in *cash*, and no refunds, for any reason.") or feigning unavailability ("Oh, you know what, I misread my schedule. Can't possibly work this in. So sorry. Nice to meet you."). These tactics usually succeeded in driving the sure-to-be-dissatisfied customer off to some other baker's shop. (Sorry, guys.)

There was only one time that none of the above seemed adequate to the occasion, the day that a bride came in and requested all kinds of crazy combinations of fillings and frostings: hazelnut, champagne, apricot, and on and on. I had never put those flavors together in the same cake, but I didn't have to in order to know that it was a train wreck in the making.

"I don't care," she said testily. "I am the bride and I want what I want."

If you saw the *Bridezilla* episode of *Cake Boss*, you know I will try to make the best of any situation, but this particular bride was a piece of work. My spider sense was tingling something fierce, and I just knew that it was going to end in pain, and I felt it deserved nothing less than a shock and awe response.

"Listen," I said. "I don't think I can make you happy. We're just not connecting in the right way. I don't want you to be disappointed. I want you to enjoy your wedding day. Go to somebody else."

That might seem like a bad business decision, but I knew that relationship was going to end in pain, and if this customer was going to have anything bad to say about Carlo's Bake Shop, I'd rather she said that she didn't like me than that she didn't like the cake we made for her.

❧

Small changes were also afoot behind the pastry case. Having noticed that national coffee-bar chains like Starbucks had popularized different flavored biscotti, and that we were beginning to get requests for fancy biscotti ourselves, I decided to put on my thinking cap. We already made a version of classic biscotti at Carlo's, *quaresimali* (page 162), but I wanted to see how creative we could get. Since nuts are a defining ingredient in biscotti, I decided that I'd base my new line of biscotti on changing the nut choice, using almonds, hazelnuts, and pistachios.

I had a bit of a head start in my research and development on this project, because as the baker-in-chief at Carlo's, I was constantly sent samples of products by purveyors, and one that most intrigued me was nut flour, which is toasted nuts pulverized to the point that they resemble, and can be used as, flour. I started playing around with Dad's biscotti formula, replacing a quantity of regular flour with nut flour, to really drive the flavor home. So, if a biscotti would have, say, pieces of hazelnut in it, I'd use hazelnut flour in the dough; same for almonds and pistachios. These ingredients were expensive, leading to another classic disagreement between me and Mama, but I was vindicated as soon as we began selling these biscotti because the customers went nuts for them.

Biscotti in the United States can be big and heavy as paperweights, but I made our new designer biscotti a little smaller. Traditionally, they are meant to be eaten with espresso but I wanted these to be more like American cookies, something even kids might enjoy. By the time we were done, we had devised eight different cookies, and some of them were downright fun: Like the pistachio variety, turned green by the nut flour (we sell a ton on Saint Patrick's Day), or the ones we make with chocolate chips. These would have been unheard of in Italy, but here in Hoboken continue to be popular years after we introduced them, a new tradition of our very own.

⌘

The other big development that grew out of our consultations was that more and more people were beginning to ask for cakes that didn't look like cakes; in other words, *theme cakes*. Occasionally, in a consultation, something unprecedented would come up. Because they felt an instant bond with me, a cus-

One of the early theme cakes. Joey is in the middle, Mauro on the left.

tomer would say, "Hey, instead of making a cake with a picture of a football on it, you wouldn't be able to make a cake in the *shape* of a football, would you?" Sometimes the requests would be more outlandish, like, "Would you be able to make a cake that looks like our fraternity house?"

These concepts never failed to intrigue me, because they represented a chance to challenge myself and to grow as a baker and decorator. By this time, I had done so many fondant cakes that I knew anything was possible with fondant. Even when the customer didn't have the budget for what he or she wanted and what the cake really should cost, I'd do the job on the cheap, back then, just for the experience of learning how to make, say, a beach-themed cake, or a stack of cakes designed to resemble a set of luxury luggage for a bridal shower, for which I made the leather out of fondant.

Initially, these requests were few and far between, but at around this time I had an epiphany: When it comes to cakes, adults want the same thing that

End of an Era

Things were moving so fast and furiously at Carlo's that it was especially jarring when something sorrowful would hit, but that's what happened in October 1999, when Grandma Grace passed away.

We had some time to say good-bye. Her delicate system, the one that had required her to watch her diet, finally gave way and she found herself in the hospital. Somehow we all knew the end was near.

My mother spent some especially meaningful time with Grace in her last days.

"I know that I'm dying," Grace told her, "but I want you to know that I'm going to die loving you." She thanked my mother, thanked her for being "more than a daughter" (let alone a daughter-in-law) to her, and for being a great wife to her son and mother to her grandchildren, and for taking care of her after my father was gone.

Grace made one last request of my mother: She wanted to be buried with that Franciscan robe in the coffin with her, and my mother promised her that she would and, when the time came, she did.

Then, always mindful of the value of a dollar, Grace said, "Now. I want to tell you how much money there is left." It was a reference to her personal savings. There wasn't a lot of money in her bank account, but she wanted to be sure my mother got her share. Just as she'd always watched out for my dad, she left this world getting my mother's back.

Grandma Grace with Buddy Sr.

kids do. Just like a kid wants a cake with his favorite superhero or her favorite princess, adults love cakes that are individualized, customized, that express who they are and what they love to do.

The true potential of theme cakes, both as a creative challenge and as a game-changing signature offering, wasn't really driven home for me until a family asked me to create the first grand-scale theme cake I ever produced. Their son was being bar-mitzvahed, and the party was to have a Las Vegas theme. For the cake, they wanted to replicate a section of the famous Las Vegas strip. I took the job and my team and I created a Vegas scene with three hotels and casinos, as well as the street outside, with cars driving along and Elvis impersonators walking on the sidewalk. It was produced for a kid's party, but it occurred to me that it would delight any adult I knew as well.

Theme cakes became one of the new signature items we offered at Carlo's Bake Shop, inviting customers to sit down with yours truly and create their dream cake. The majority of our cake business continued to be wedding cakes for several years, but these theme cakes were always a highlight of our week, and something we wished we could do more.

In order to contend with my increasingly busy days, I developed a daily ritual: the morning walkthrough, my attempt to get a grasp on everything that I needed to know about and also head off any potential crises as best I could in our rapidly growing business.

The walkthrough is always the same. I arrive at the bakery between six and eight o'clock and fix myself a coffee with milk and one sugar. Then, I walk around like General McArthur, surveying the equipment and the troops, making sure that we're ready for battle.

There's no area of the shop that I don't inspect in the morning: I scrutinize the retail counter to be sure all the pastries, cupcakes, biscotti, and other items are fully loaded. If they're not, I have to ferret out the source of the problem: Did my guys screw up and not make enough, or did my sisters forget to tell them that they need more?

I also make sure that everybody is getting along. If any of my sisters are going at it, I do what I can to break it up. Early. Before it snowballs out of control.

In the bakery, I'm on the lookout for all the little things I've learned to anticipate: are all the cakes ready for the day's deliveries, and, if not, what needs to happen to get them over the finish line? Is there a reservoir of our most popular pastries in the freezer, and do we have all the butter, flour, and sugar required to get through the long day ahead?

There are times when I feel like my father on these walkthroughs. One day, I saw one of the counter girls transferring cookies from a pan to a platter with one hand. *One hand!* I was reminded of the day Dad taught me to apply those cherries with both hands.

"You're a lucky young woman," I thought to myself. "Back in the day, you got smacked in the head for using one hand." Well, okay, it was only me that got smacked, but I don't smack anybody. Just another adjustment to these modern times.

8

Brides and Grooms and Sweet Little Things

THE TIME RIGHT AFTER the holidays is always special for the Carlo's Bake Shop family, because, although the bakery was operating on a regular schedule, it felt like a half vacation after the sheer, twenty-four-hour, nonstop, pressurized insanity of the holidays. In 2000, January was all the more enjoyable because cousin Freddy had come from Altamura to spend the holidays with his cousins, so we were hanging out, just like old times.

One cold, sunny Sunday afternoon, Freddy called me up.

"Buddy, I'm eating at Gloria and Mauro's tonight, then we're all going to go out to a club. It's me and Lisa. Can you get us in?"

It was the kind of request I lived for. I loved knowing everybody around town, and it would be my pleasure to serve as the concierge for my cousin and his pals. Plus, since Monday was my day off anyway, Sunday was always my big night on the town, when I'd meet up with my core crew: Dino, Paul, Jeff, and Cousin Vinny. These guys were

117

my best friends, and we were treated like high rollers all over the area, the result of years of paying off doormen, bartenders, bouncers, and anybody else that stood between us and a good time. Freddy and I agreed that we would all meet at my house and the bunch of us would go to Joey's, a club in Clifton.

After work, I took my customary disco nap from seven to ten thirty, showered, and got into my nightclub regalia: a sharp pair of slacks and a fitted shirt. I tucked my Saint Anthony medallion into my shirt, squirted a dab of hair gel into my hands, worked it in, checked myself in the mirror, and I was ready to go, just as my crew pulled up in the driveway, and Freddy and his friends were walking over from next door.

It was a dreamy scene: snow on the ground, lawns still decorated for Christmas with everything from manger scenes to Santa and his reindeer, and flashing holiday lights on every house in sight. Paradise.

When Freddy had told me that Lisa was coming along, I thought he meant my cousin Lisa from next door, but the Lisa in his group was Lisa Belgiovine, whom I'd known since we were little kids, because she used to hang out with my cousin Lisa. I never really paid much attention to her. She was three years younger than I, so I always thought of her as a little girl. Not that night. She was all grown up, and dressed in black pants and a silvery black tube top. She looked *great*.

Wow, I thought, though I tried to play it cool.

My friends had the same impression. As they would do whenever we saw a pretty girl, they started whispering to each other, each one boasting that they were going to hit on her.

"Guys," I said. "You can all forget about it. I'm going to win."

"Ohhhhh," they said in unison, affecting mock intimidation.

I laughed along, but the truth was that I was annoyed. That kind of talk never really bothered me—most young guys talk that way about women, whether they admit it in mixed company or not—but I was instantly interested in Lisa. I wanted to spend some time with her, as soon as possible.

As we hung out in front of my house, my wish was granted, as Lisa gravitated to me. I looked over at my buds and winked. In your face, fellas.

We formed a motorcade and headed out to Joey's. When we got there, there was the typical nightmare club scene: red velvet ropes hanging like drop lines from gleaming silver stanchions. Following behind me, my gang marched right up to the bouncer. I didn't even have to say "Open, sesame." He just gave me a big smile and a high-five shake, and cast the rope aside.

Inside, the scene was anything but glamorous. The dirty little secret was that my friends hated that Sunday was my big night out, and with good reason.

"Guys," said Cousin Vinny, "I forget. Who is it that has Mondays off again?"

Jeff was ready with the regular punch line, "Bakers, strippers, and beauticians."

That was the truth. And the characters before us bore it out, the women wearing too few clothes, or too much makeup, and the men—the bakers— with their bellies hanging over their belts.

Lisa and I found one another and parked ourselves on a sofa, talking. It was easy for us to talk, the way it's always easy to talk to somebody you're meant to be with. She caught me up on her life: She still lived with her parents in East Hanover. Was working for an orthodontist. We talked for hours, having a pretty deep conversation, despite the surroundings. We discussed what we wanted out of life, and it was pretty similar: We both wanted to meet the right person, settle down, raise a family.

If we weren't talking, we were dancing.

And that's how it went, all night long.

"You know," I said to her at one point. "I like you. Let's not play any games with each other."

She knew what I meant. None of that waiting three days between calling, or mentioning other people to inspire jealousy. We vowed not to pull any of that, not to screw it up.

At the end of the night, as we all said goodbye in the street outside my house, Lisa gave me a kiss—a sweet little peck—and pressed a piece of paper into my hand.

"Here's my number," she said, making good on the no-games pact. "You *better* call me."

I kept up my end of the bargain, too. Later that same day, I rang her up and invited her to lunch, as it was her day off, as well, and we made plans to meet at my house. When she got there I was still upstairs getting dressed and she was in the kitchen, sitting at the table talking to my mother. I came downstairs and, before either of them saw me, I just stood outside the room watching them. The two of them seemed totally natural there, visiting, like Lisa had been part of the family all along.

I was starting to feel some good vibrations, thinking she could maybe be the one. And, the truth was, I was ready for the one to come along. Much as I loved partying with my crew, who were like brothers to me, the baking life is no world for a playboy; I may have only been twenty-two, but the life I'd been leading was burning me out: getting up at five in the morning, working all day, napping, then going out until three or four, then reviving with just an hour or two of shut-eye. It was no way to be. Beyond the perpetual exhaustion, I had a sense of emptiness. I wanted to be with somebody who mattered. My friends gave me a hard time when I started opting to be with Lisa instead of them, but I know they all secretly wanted the same thing for themselves and, deep down, they were really happy for me.

Next thing you knew, Lisa and I were inseparable. She'd come around the bakery after work and we'd grab dinner. We hung out on our days off. Besides being a cut above as a person, Lisa was able to relate to me in ways previous girlfriends hadn't. Her father owns a pizzeria, so she had grown up witnessing the long hours and sacrifice it takes to operate a food-service business, and never gave me any grief for working the hours I had to in order to honor my responsibilities.

We also came from similar families: She had a big, crazy (in a good way) family just like I did, and I fit right in with them. I got along especially well with her mother Gloria and father Mauro, not to mention her sister Daniela, who fast became like a fifth sister to me, and her kid brother Maurizio, who I considered the little brother I never had. I could not have asked for a kinder, more generous group of potential in-laws.

Scarcely a month after we began dating, I saw the ultimate sign that she was the one. Just two days before Valentine's Day, Lisa had some minor surgery and was home recovering. Valentine's Day is one of the busiest days of the year for Carlo's, with customers crammed into the shop all day long. I worked like a beast that Valentine's Day, so that I could get out of the bakery as early as pos-

My beautiful bride-to-be, Lisa, and me at our engagement dinner.

sible, get into my Corvette (I had upgraded from the Mitsubishi somewhere along the way), scramble around town to procure flowers and chocolates, then pick up Lisa and take her to dinner. When I got to her house, however, I discovered that despite the pain she was in, she had gone shopping and prepared a candlelit lobster dinner. I couldn't believe the thoughtfulness and the selflessness. I didn't need to know anymore: She was a keeper. *The* keeper.

That June, I picked out a ring, which I kept hidden in a suit pocket in my bedroom, waiting for just the right moment. Before I proposed, there was a necessary middle step: When shooting pool with her father, Mauro, one night, I asked him for his blessing. He granted it.

I had planned to pop the question in front of the whole family, to make a big deal out of it, but I just couldn't wait. One night in early July, when we were hanging out at my house, I went into the closet, got the ring, and proposed. As ever, making good on our no-games policy, she said, "Yes," without missing a beat.

A New Tradition

Lisa and I weren't officially family yet, but it felt like we were, in part because of a tradition we started that fall. One day, when visiting Lisa's house, I saw her mother, Gloria, in the kitchen, lost behind bushels of tomatoes and pots of simmering sauce. She was in the midst of her annual tradition of making sauce from the last of the season's tomatoes, a popular ritual among many Italian-American families, especially in New Jersey, where we have the best tomatoes in the United States. (We aren't called the Garden State for nothing.)

"Ma," I said, "Why don't you let us do this at the bakery for you? It'll be so much easier. We have tons of room and equipment, and people to help and to clean up."

She took me up on the offer and when word spread around Carlo's, I was delighted to discover that all my sisters wanted to get in on the act. The prospect of having jars of homemade sauce on tap was irresistible. (We all love long-simmered Sunday sauce, with its variety of meats, but to have sauce ready to go on a weeknight . . . what could be better?) We bought ten bushels of tomatoes, a special machine that seeded the sauce, and, for one day, turned the bakery into a sauce factory: Working in a steam kettle (it functioned like a double boiler, preventing the tomatoes from scorching), we sautéed olive oil, then added onions, then the tomatoes, fresh basil, and a little sugar and salt. We let that simmer for a while, then ran it through the machine to get the seeds and skin out, then simmered it for a few more hours. At the end of the day, Gloria had her sauce, and so did all my sisters, and the coming together of the two families was a terrific bonding experience.

By the time we were done, I knew we'd embarked on an annual tradition. (Sure enough, we now haul in about a hundred bushels of tomatoes for this enterprise and, as the family has grown, most of the kids have gotten in on the act.)

I have to admit that I couldn't help from bringing my restless experimentation and taste for innovation to the process: Usually when you seal sauce or preserves in a jar, you have to first sterilize the jar in boiling water in order to create the hermetic seal that keeps the foods fresh. We discovered that, if you put the sauce in the jars while the sauce itself is still boiling, it creates the proper seal. The lawyers advise me to tell you not to try this at home, but it works for us!

We had a long engagement, setting the date for October 14, 2001.

I was happier than I'd ever been, except for one thing. My dad never got to meet Lisa, and she never got to meet him. "He would have loved you," I told her. "I would have loved to have met him," she said.

Over the next year, energized by romance and encouraged every step of the way by Lisa, I went on a tear at work, improving in any area that I could. For example, I enlisted Betty Van Nordstrom, who's one of the world's finest sugar-flower crafters, to spend three days with me, imparting her wisdom. I still remember when I called her, and was greeted by her sweet, elderly voice. She invited me to come to her home for the tutorial, so I drove up to Pough-keepsie, New York, even though I was a bit skeptical.

"What is this woman really going to teach me?" I wondered.

My doubts were put to rest the moment we began working. We were a bit of an odd couple, but had an instant rapport, and her ability to create lifelike flowers from gum paste was astonishing. She taught me both the craft of flower-making as well as such practical things as the best brands of paste and manufacturers of implements, and where to find them.

The only disconnect was that she was more meticulous than we can afford to be, actually taking a nail file and sanding the edge of every petal to make them perfectly smooth. When I got back to my bakery, I spent a day making flowers the way she taught me, and it took a whole day to make ten of them. That wouldn't work in our business, because we can't charge what those people-hours are worth. So, I began playing around with what she taught me, devising a way to make the sugar flowers on a greater scale. Where she worked with a quarter pound of gum paste at a time, I worked with twenty pounds; where she rolled by hand, I used the sheeter. I'd put flowers together, then take them apart, looking for ways to divvy up the work into an assembly line. In time, I came up with a system where six of us could line up along a bench and make five hundred flowers in a day.

Though I had no choice but to find a time-efficient way to do it, making sugar flowers is one of the few things I could do more slowly, because they really take me into the zone. I find incredible peace when I make sugar flow-ers, a godlike sensation that I'm mimicking nature herself.

Red Velvet Comes to Carlo's

One of the quirks of Carlo's Italian-American roots was that we never offered a red velvet cake (a Southern staple made with both vanilla and cocoa and colored and flavored with food coloring and, sometimes, beet juice), not even after moving to Washington Street and hiring bakers with an expertise in American cakes and pastries. I first got interested in it because I saw great potential for it as an addition to our wedding-cake arsenal. Traditionally iced with white frosting, red velvet's contrasting colors are eye popping. In my mind's eye, I saw red velvet covered with white fondant and knew that the contrast would be stunning.

I embarked on a mission no less obsessive and time consuming than reinventing our vanilla cake. I began by Googling a ton of red velvet recipes and cross-checking them against my vanilla-cake recipe. I got in the lab and began experimenting, just like old times, removing some ingredients from the vanilla recipe and adding varying amounts of cocoa, buttermilk, and vinegar. Truth be told, one of the secrets it took me a while to unlock was that you really need to use a lot of food coloring. Bakers are conditioned to ignore the flavor of food coloring, because when we use it in icing, its flavor doesn't register. However, when you use enough of it in a recipe like that for red velvet cake, it contributes a subtle sweetness that helps pull the other flavors together.

Flowers were just one part of the repertoire we developed. Our rolled-fondant wedding cakes were becoming known far and wide, and our theme-cake business was picking up as well. Additionally, I saw ways to work fondant into our everyday inventory, designing signature cakes such as the Bow and Dots (a fondant-covered cake with a big, loopy fondant bow and polka dots) and the Groovy Girl (a psychedelic cake with daisy-shaped patterns, all achieved with fondant). We make those cakes daily and display them in the case along with the pastries and cookies, a moderately priced, spontaneous way for our customers to avail themselves of the wonders of fondant. No special order required; come in and pick one up.

One day late in 2000, a young woman named Joanna Saltz came into the bakery asking for me. She told me that she worked for *Modern Bride* magazine and was planning a story on winter cakes. We displayed fondant cakes in the window and, not surprisingly, it was these that had drawn her in.

"It's just a little, little story," she said, almost apologetically. "Would you be interested in making a cake for the magazine?"

Inside, I was doing cartwheels. There were fireworks going off in my head. My father's wish, his eternal wish, had been for the bakery to get into one of those bridal magazines, just *once*.

"I'd be delighted," I told her.

They set up a photo shoot at the magazine offices, and I showed up the way I always show up to events like that, with boxes of cookies and pastries for the editors and the crew. Everybody seemed surprised by that, but I was just following my old man's example. It was just the way he treated people. Everybody has something they can contribute and his gift was pastry, so if there's a photo shoot, and I'm going to be there, the crew is going to be well fed.

As for the cake itself, they had asked for a winter cake and I created a gingerbread cake with candy cane stripes and holly.

Again, they seemed surprised. Surprised that I knew how to follow direction, I guess, and that I was able to connect with their vision.

When the magazine came out, I bought ten copies. I cut the page out and carried it with me everywhere and showed it to everybody who knew my dad.

"Can you imagine if he saw this," I'd exclaim.

Before too long, Joanna's editor, Linda Hearst, began coming to the bakery on a regular basis. She would stock up for the holidays at Carlo's, and became a real fan of the bakery. I think it all began with those treats I brought to the shoot, which is a real credit to my old man.

Before long, Linda asked me to do more cakes for the magazine. Every time they asked for one, I knocked it out of the park, whether they wanted something pink or blue, or four tiers tall, or an oceanic design, or *whatever*.

I became their go-to guy. They knew that if they had a shoot scheduled, whether it was next month or tomorrow, that they could throw up the bat signal and I'd be there with the goods.

In time, they confided to me that some designers had a case of amnesia: They forgot who the boss was. I was never confused on this point: The customer's the boss. And so, sometimes, I made a cake that wasn't the sort of thing I would come up with on my own, or for my own wedding, but they got what they wanted. And, in return, they'd sometimes give me a theme and let me run with it and do my own thing; it was a two-way street, what corporate types would call a win-win situation.

From 2001 to 2006, I was in just about every issue of *Modern Bride* magazine, and I've been in other publications as well, from *Brides* to *For the Bride*, more than two hundred individual issues in all, which helped our burgeoning fondant-based cake business continue to skyrocket.

ℂ

Love was in the air for the family. Shortly before Lisa and I got married, Little Frankie and his girlfriend Maria tied the knot. His father, my Uncle Frankie, had had a lot of brothers, but he had picked my father to be his best man. Little Frankie didn't have any brothers, so I was the closest thing he had to a big brother, and was picked me to be his best man. And, just as Little Frankie was my parents' godson, Lisa and I would go on to be godparents to his daughter Nicoletta.

In the wake of the September 11 terrorist attacks, Lisa and I canceled our planned honeymoon to Hawaii, but went ahead with our wedding plans on October 14, 2001, which was one of the happiest days of my life. For the cake, I designed a checkerboard with chocolate mousse, chocolate ganache, and fresh raspberries, covered with white fondant and positively strewn with sugar flowers in four different colors. I spent two and a half weeks on those flowers, making every one of them myself. Carlo's also did all the pastries for the Venetian Hour, and I personally came into the shop on the morning of our wedding day to whip the zabaglione by hand.

We had a huge Italian wedding at the Rockleigh Country Club in Rockleigh, New Jersey. When I first saw Lisa in her wedding dress walking down the aisle, my heart skipped a beat and tears welled up in my eyes. She was my soulmate and I couldn't wait to make her my wife.

Four-hundred-and-fifty people were there to watch us tie the knot, and it was an awesome night of toasts and dancing. One of the highlights of the day for me was a private one: Uncle Frankie, who had been one of my harshest critics during those painful months after my father died, had his son give me a letter expressing the kinds of thoughts that men, especially men of that generation, don't always share with one another. In the letter, he told me how proud he was of me and of the man that I'd become, and how proud my father would be of me. It meant a lot. And it confirmed what I was feeling as well: That falling in love with Lisa, committing to her, to the family that we'd create, was a final step over the finish line of growing up for me.

From watching my father, I knew that the old line about there being a wonderful woman behind every great man was an understatement. Without Lisa in my life, I never would have become the man I am today. Nor would I want to be. I loved her with all my heart and vowed that we would be together forever, no matter what.

Following in my father's footsteps, I owned two pieces of investment property at this time, and Lisa and I ended up moving into one of them, in East Hanover. It was my wife's hometown, and also had good schools, which was important to us, because we hoped to need them before too long.

↭

Our first child, our beautiful daughter Sofia, was born on April 23, 2003.

The day she was born was probably the happiest day of my life. I'll never forget the first time I saw her. It made me remember my father, and how he used to look at me. She was the newborn, but it was me who cried like a baby that day.

It was a powerful time for remembering my

The happiest day of my life, marrying my soulmate.

father. I thought of the continuum of life, of family. Sofia has the same cleft chin that I do, which made it easy to pick her out in the nursery. For the first time ever, I knew what he must have felt when he looked at me, that feeling of love that wells up in you when you look at your own child.

I missed my father more than I ever had, and it became something that I'd feel over and over in the coming years. Whenever there was a big moment in my life, an accomplishment or a milestone, I wished I'd had him there to share it with me.

✑

Strange as it may seem, that monumental event in my personal life led to one of our biggest sellers at Carlo's Bake Shop.

That year, I began to take note of a burgeoning trend in the baking business: cupcakes were hotter than ever. Across the Hudson River in Manhattan,

We leave the real center of the world, Hoboken, New Jersey, to visit Times Square in New York.

in shops like Magnolia Cafe and Cupcake Cafe, designer cupcakes had been an out-of-control fad for years with customers lined up around the block just to purchase a traditional vanilla or chocolate cupcake with colored frosting.

In the early 2000s, the trend grew. All of a sudden, cupcake towers became an alternative to wedding cakes. I wanted to take advantage of the trend, especially because our cupcakes were made with the vanilla cake recipe I'd tweaked back in the mid-1990s, meaning they were a world-class product. As it was, we sold four to five hundred cupcakes a week, but I knew there must be some way we could at least double that number.

The opportunity nagged at me. I was disappointed in myself as a businessman, but what could I do? The inspiration just wasn't there.

Mother's Day that year was extra special for me, because my Lisa had become a mom. As the holiday approached, I decided I wanted to do something special for it, something flower-themed. Our yard was full of flowers by that point in the spring, and it occurred to me that a flower is about the same size and shape as a cupcake top. And that's when I created our first signature cupcake, the flower cupcake.

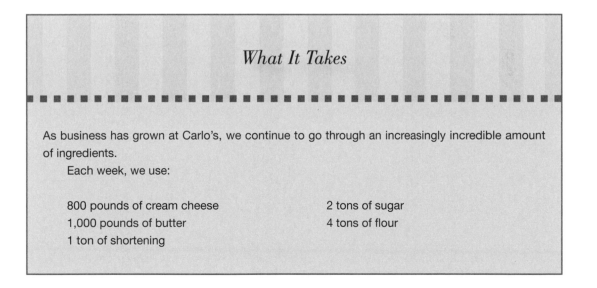

What It Takes

As business has grown at Carlo's, we continue to go through an increasingly incredible amount of ingredients.

Each week, we use:

800 pounds of cream cheese   2 tons of sugar
1,000 pounds of butter   4 tons of flour
1 ton of shortening

The Baking Life

Even before television made me the Cake Boss to a national audience, being the Cake Boss at Carlo's demanded more than any devoted father can give to his profession. I'm not special in this regard: Every baker faces the same dilemma. To do your job right and provide for your family means that you sometimes can't be around for life's little moments. Just as my father had to work every Christmas, I sometimes can't be at my kids' baseball games or other special occasions. (One of the great reasons Lisa and I make such a good team is that she's always understood this; her father often had to be at work at his pizzeria during milestones in her life.)

Carlo's also provides us things we can do as a family: I love taking the kids around the bakery, showing them little tricks of the trade the way my father did for me. Taking them in the decorating room is an especially rich source of memories. The one who's taken to it the most is Buddy, Jr., who I call my Cake Boss in Training. "Watch my hands, son," I tell him. "Watch my hands."

I try to break free of the bakery when I have to. One year, every kid in my daughter Sofia's class had to bring in a gingerbread house. When the teacher asked her who she wanted to make it, she said, "My dad." It wasn't just because I was a baker; it was because we have a great relationship. Somehow, despite the fact that it was in the midst of the holiday crush, our busiest season, I found the time, and when she marched that house into her classroom, telling everybody that her dad made it, it was one of the great moments in my life.

I'm blessed: My father wanted to be a great father because his dad had let him down. I want to be a great father to live up to my dad's example. When I come through, I feel like I'm honoring him as well as my own kids.

In hindsight, it was an obvious thing to devise, because piping is my strong suit, and piping is how we designed our cupcakes to look like a variety of flowers: roses, daisies, sunflowers, and puffy fantasy flowers. The idea is to craft them quickly: The cupcake set on a turntable, a green frosting band applied with a pastry bag, and a series of petals and leaves applied working from the center outward. Because it was Mother's Day, I made them in a variety of bright, springlike colors. I made a pan of them—forty-eight cupcakes in all—and put them in the retail case.

Not fifteen minutes later, one of the counter girls buzzed my intercom to tell me they were sold out.

I couldn't believe it. I grabbed another bunch of naked cupcakes called out my old friend, the Hulk, and made up another pan. And that's the way it went all day, with the counter team selling them as fast as I could make them.

The only problem was that the cupcakes were all crowned which means they were high and I had to trim them. It wasn't the waste that bothered me, because we could always use that scrap to make crumbs. No, it was the *time* that got on my nerves, the time it took to trim them.

I applied the science that I'd learned when I reworked our vanilla cake recipe to these smaller cupcakes, and began baking them at a lower temperature, 375°F instead of 400°F. That did the trick; the cupcakes were flat as could be.

It wasn't long before we applied all the tricks we'd been incorporating over the years into our cupcake production. It sounds like a joke: How many Carlo's Bake Shop employees does it take to decorate a cupcake? The answer is four: one to rotate the turntable and take the cupcakes on and off, one to pipe the green border, one to pipe the petals, and one to pipe the center.

Once we had that assembly line mastered, we began making cupcakes in huge quantities, lining up sixteen turntables along a bench, eight on each side, with the pipers going around in a circle like a choo-choo train.

The very next year, on September 29, 2004, our first son was born and we named him—what else?—Bartolo Valastro.

Right from the start, people said that Buddy (of course, we gave him the

Meet the Sisters: Madeline

She may not be the oldest, but of all my sisters, Maddalena, better known as Madeline, has always been the most like a second mother to me. About ten years older than I am, she has been, or seemed, to be an adult presence all my life. Madeline is what some people call an old soul: She's got a wonderful peacefulness about her, a knack for avoiding confrontation, even when it's happening right in front of her, and she wants others to get along, too. At the bakery, where things can be chaotic and sometimes confrontational, she's a calming influence, doing her job and interacting wonderfully with the customers.

Madeline and I get along so well that, when she and Mauro were building a new house around 2007, the two of them and their three children—Mary, Dominique, and Buddy—stayed with us for year and a half in our home. In most families that would have been a recipe for disaster, but we all got on great, especially my wife, Lisa, and Madeline, who are like sisters, and Dominique, one of my goddaughters, who was like a second mom to my kids, same as Madeline had been with me. Nothing cracked me up more during that year-and-a-half than walking downstairs to our finished basement and catching Mauro in his tighty whities. We really bonded over that time, even more than ever.

nickname as well) was like my father reborn; he had the same eyes, the same gentle but confident expression.

I was ecstatic to have a son, somebody to share all that guy stuff with as he grew older. The amazing thing was that I started to notice that we had similar tendencies, even as a baby he seemed obsessed with his hands. He has the same body type as me, and the same posture. He was a hard worker even from a young age, finishing anything he started, from an art project to a sand castle, just like his old man.

Before long, I started to think of Buddy as my clone, my mini-me, and I wondered if he'd grow up to be like me, though, even when he was a little kid, I knew that I wanted him to go his own way, whatever that might reveal itself to be.

The family in 3-D glasses.

Our third child, Marco, came into this world on February 26, 2007. He's Lisa's clone, with blond hair and blue eyes. Sometimes I'd look him in the eye and say, "Where did you come from?" He'd just smile.

Marco, too, had some of the tough Sicilian in his blood. We call him the Baby Who Fights Back because he doesn't take any nonsense from his older brother. He seems to be in a hurry to grow up. Of our three kids, he was the first to walk and talk, the first out of diapers.

I've been proud of him at every step of the way, but sometimes I want to tell him to slow down. Before I know it, they'll all be grown. Was it already fifteen years ago that I was seventeen? I feel like I blinked and the last fifteen years were suddenly behind me. I blink again, and those boyhood days at my father's side seem almost so close I can touch them, even though they are three decades in the past, lost to time's endless forward march. How do you explain to kids to enjoy their youth while they have it? How do you tell them that life is like those little cupcakes right out of the oven—best enjoyed when fresh and full of promise.

9

Ready for Our Close-up

SO, HOW DID I GET from this great adventure of a life, with all of its ups and downs, to the television screens of America on my TLC show *Cake Boss*?

That journey took about five years, and required its own learning curve, determination, and that little something all of us need to really succeed: a touch of good luck.

My television odyssey began in 2004, when I was asked to participate in an episode of the series, *Food Network Challenge*, which featured a different type of cooking contest every week. The producers were putting together an episode called "Holiday Cake-Off." It was yet another benefit of all the press coverage we'd been enjoying; the producers had seen us in multiple bridal magazines, and asked if we wanted to be included.

I'd never been on stage or screen. Didn't have a garage band in high school. Didn't sing or dance. The truth was that I had never had much interest in it, probably because I expressed myself through my baking. At the same time, however, I wasn't afraid of being on a stage, or even on television. I wasn't afflicted with anything resembling stage fright; my feeling was that, even though we wouldn't be in the same room, I'd get along with whoever was watching me on television the same way I'd always gotten along with just about everyone I'd ever met.

Plus the prize—a cool $10,000—was pretty appealing.

I said "yes," and next thing I knew I drove down to Sea Island, Georgia, to a production facility where the special was shot, accompanied by Mauro. (I opted not to fly so I could bring along my beloved sheeter.) The studio stage set blew me away, big as an airplane hangar and jam-packed with equipment: lights hanging from steel beams overhead, cameras around the perimeter of the set, and soundboards and control rooms at the outskirts of the space. It looked just like the sets I'd seen in movies about making movies. Although we were in Georgia, I felt like we were in Hollywood.

I was pitted against five other well-known bakers for this challenge. Whenever the host asked me a question, I was ready with a snappy answer, and everything I said seemed to delight the producers, who loved my accent and the way I bantered with Mauro. I think they thought it was an act, but it wasn't; all those years of shooting the breeze around the benches in the back of Carlo's, or with my buds in the parks and woods of Little Ferry proved to be perfect training for being an on-camera personality.

Even though I was comfortable on stage, I was a rookie, and I made a big-time rookie mistake by not paying enough attention to the fine print in the contestant briefing materials. The producers had been drawn to me because of our wedding cakes, so I produced a wedding cake with a holiday theme—a ten-tiered monster, each tier topped, naturally, with rolled fondant, and decorated with little fondant gift boxes and sugar poinsettias resting on the individual tiers.

It was spectacular, but there was just one problem: The challenge had nothing to do with wedding cakes; all they wanted was a holiday cake. Period.

Not surprisingly, I lost. Badly. The only silver lining for me was that Chris Russom, the guy who won, really had the goods. He made a jack-in-the-box cake that looked like an honest-to-goodness jack-in-the-box with a giant Santa's head popping out. He deserved it. I *hate* to lose, but I was happy for him.

I was asked back to subsequent episodes of the show, and quickly became more and more comfortable on camera. But I did have some frustrations. Some of the episodes were what I think of as "gimmick shows," like the second one I did, where we were each paired up with another baker, which is the most unnatural thing in the world if it's somebody you've never worked with before. Ditto the third one, taped in 2006 in Tulsa, Oklahoma, called "Wedding Cake Surprise," in which we were introduced to a bride and groom the night before the contest and, by the next day, had to create a theme cake based on our conversation.

Though I hadn't won a challenge, all of this exposure began to change my life. I've always had a lot of friends in Hoboken, but all of a sudden, it seemed like everybody in town knew me. I'd walk down the street to grab some lunch and people would stop and say hello, or honk their car horns. Sometimes, they'd ask to have their picture taken with me. It was a little crazy, but I took it in stride.

Things rocketed to a new level, when the *Today Show* asked me to participate in their "America's Wedding" series. In it, a young couple volunteers to be married on the show, and in the weeks leading up to the nuptials, the audience votes on everything: the dress, the food, and the cake. I designed the winning cake decoration, which I titled "Majestic Dreams," draped with fondant to look like fabric, decorated with old-school piping, and topped with a bouquet of sugar roses. Then the hard part came, figuring out how to actually make it. It was like the old days when I took on a challenge just to improve my skills as a baker and decorator. It took me two days to figure it out, but the exposure was incredible, and we now sell that cake as part of our repertoire, only now that we know how to make it, it's a more time-effective undertaking that takes a few hours instead of a few days!

Later that year, two of the *Food Network Challenge* camera guys, Tony Cacciavillani and Greg Verspohl, approached me with a potentially life-changing proposition, "Hey, Buddy, you're awesome on camera," Tony said. "You have a great personality. You should have your own show."

I thought about it for about two seconds, and I realized he was right. Not just about my on-camera presence, but that my day-to-day life would make for a great television show: the cakes, the clients, my sisters, the bakers, and the story of Carlo's Bake Shop. There was more comedy, drama, and cooking going on under the roof of our store than there is on most television shows I could think of. Plus the cakes themselves, especially the wedding and theme cakes, were spectacular.

This was also the time of *The Sopranos* and, although Tony didn't say this,

Welcome to the Family

I think of shooting *Cake Boss* as like panning for gold. In order to get enough material for a half-hour episode, the production team shoots hour upon hour of footage, which is then edited down to what you see on television. To get to the good stuff for one half-hour, they sometimes have to shoot as many as ninety hours as they wait for us to figure out how to make a cake or get lucky and capture a mishap on camera. As a result, a camera crew is present at Carlo's more often than not; in fact, there are so many extra people there during production, at least ten every day, that it takes us from crowded to overcrowded. During filming, we add a shift to the bakery production schedule, spreading out the day so there are fewer bodies under the roof at any given time.

While filming our second season, it occurred to me that the crew has become an extension of the Valastro family, just like all those employees who called my mother Mama. Carlo's Bake Shop is like a giant sponge; spend enough time there and you will be absorbed. As I write this book, we're working on our third season, and many of the same camera people, crew, and production team are back with us: Rafael Sienkiewicz and Arnold Finklestein (the sound guys), Steven Schlueter and Gary Azzi-naro (the camera guys), Richard Kathlean (our production manager), and Nick Budadin and Sarah Steinfeld (our on-site producers), among many others. I do whatever "the talent" can to make sure we have the same team back season after season. I love them all and feel like they're my good luck charms. It's just another way in which the show has enriched my life. I truly enjoy having all these people around all the time, especially the way the crew salivates when they hang out in the kitchen. Sometimes, I'll stop everything and feed them because I can't watch those faces of anticipation for another second.

As anybody who watches *Cake Boss* knows, things can get pretty tense in a place as busy and crowded as Carlo's Bake Shop. To let off some of the steam, we love playing pranks on each other, like dumping a bag of flour from the roof onto an unsuspecting delivery guy, like Stretch, and I love that we've captured those moments on the show. (Believe me, even though I'm the Boss, off camera, I've been the victim of those pranks as well: In my case, a bucket of water was dumped on me from the roof.) Though we of course don't show it on television, when they became honorary members of the family, the crew became subject to our in-house high jinx. Just as I get a kick out of tormenting Stretch, I take a sadistic delight in picking on my producer, Nick. I was even going to pay him the ultimate backhanded compliment one day when we planned to dump flour and water on him from the roof. We were doing one of my interviews for the show from an off-site location, when one of my staff members called my cell phone and told me to hurry back. It was all a ruse, though, and when Nick came back to the shop looking for me, we had the back door locked, trapping him out there like Sonny Corleone at the toll booth. The only problem was that Little Frankie, perched on the rooftop with the flour and water, wasn't listening to his walkie talkie and missed the call to drop his arsenal. I'll get Nick one of these days. Hopefully, we'll have many years together on the show.

I knew that part of the allure of that show was the public's fascination with Italian-American culture. I thought that my family—my hardworking, honest, on the up-and-up family—would be a welcome counterbalance to the other type of *famiglia* being portrayed on television.

By the time I came home that day, I could picture the show. I stormed through the front door of our house, and Lisa was standing there in the kitchen and I said, "Baby, I am going to do a television show!"

"What are you talking about?"

I told her about my conversation with Tony and Greg and what I thought the show was going to be and by the time I was done, she was fully on board. Lisa's always supported me in everything I've wanted to do. In a world where there are doubters everywhere, her optimism and belief helped me believe in my own dreams, whether it was taking Carlo's to the next level, or this latest goal of making the television show a reality.

I became obsessed with the idea and, when I showed up in Denver for the fourth *Food Network Challenge*, I marched right up to the producer, Art Edwards of High Noon Productions, which was the production company for *Challenge* and other Food Network shows, and said, "Let's do a show."

"What are you talking about?" he said.

"I want to do a show."

I briefly told him about the idea that had been taking shape in my head—a series that was about my family and its heritage, both personal and professional, with all the highs and lows and of course the cakes that made us famous.

"I like it, Buddy," he said. "But Food Network is already doing something with Ace. They're not going to do another cake show."

Oh, no! "Duff" Goldman, better known as Ace of Cakes, had already inked a deal, beating me to the punch. Not that anybody would have been that interested in me after my appearance on that particular challenge, the "Disney Villain Challenge." I created a caked-out version of Scar from *Lion King*, but when the time came to present . . . its head fell off! It was all my fault. I had messed up the support, which is something I *never* do. I also didn't win challenge number five, the "Extreme Holiday Cake-Off," coming in a tantalizingly close second.

When I finally saw *Ace of Cakes*, I realized that there was a big difference between what he does and what I do. Duff's primarily a cake maker/decorator, where I am a pure-bred animal baker. My family's bakery has been in business for a century and all of that history has been funneled into me and my fingers. I am one of the last of the all-around bakers capable of doing *anything* in the bakery: Italian pastry, American pastry, French pastry. And when it comes to dough, I can fold it, I can roll it, I can mix it, and I can stretch it out. I knew that if I had a chance to really show off all my ability, that the show would shine, and that, if we could weave my family in, then all the better.

A few months later, I got called back for yet another *Challenge*, the "Battle of the Brides" in Denver. I was glad, because I wanted to go back. Wanted another crack at the title. I had never set "television cooking champion" as a personal goal of mine, but I can't stand failing at anything, and I wanted to turn the situation around, to master this new Everest in my path. Why? The same reason most people climb Everest. Because it's there.

I headed to Denver full of enthusiasm and energy. When the cameras started rolling, there was a big surprise sprung on us: We each were paired with an actual bride and had to work with her to create a cake based on her design. It wasn't comfortable for me. Not because of anything my bride partner was doing, but because I needed to be free to do my own thing and couldn't do it with somebody chained to me. I used all the wisdom earned in years of consultations at Carlo's to make my bride accept my vision—a cake buried under hundreds of sugar flowers. But while I was pleased with my rapport with her, I grew even more annoyed at the constant need to create a new gimmick for every competition, and at the things they did to up the ante. This all seemed so unnecessary to me. Why wasn't it enough to just watch great bakers do what they do best, I wondered? Now *that* would be a cool show.

I kept my annoyance in check and gave it my best shot. I also was beginning to get the idea that the producers liked me, because they spent a lot of time interviewing me. And I seemed to have a gift for the one-liner. "I'm the baker and you're the bride," was one that I let fly before the baking commenced.

My perseverance and positive energy finally paid off: I won that challenge. (A big, mounted blowup of the check hangs like a poster in my office to this day.) Afterwards, Tony, Greg, and I went to dinner at a Longhorn Steakhouse with Danny and Mauro, who were along for the show. By then, I had the concept firmly in mind. *My* show would focus on a few specialty and wedding cakes every week, interspersed with slice of life from the bakery, from the pranks we play on each other to blow off steam, to the drama that often ensues when cakes are delivered to their destination, to the family dynamics—the good, the bad, and the ugly—that define the joint.

"We've got to do this," said Tony. "We really believe in it."

We hatched a plan for the most down-and-dirty low-budget sizzle (demo) reel of all time. Tony and Greg would come to New Jersey, sleep in my house, and shoot some footage at the bakery, which would then be edited.

The next time I was in Denver, I mentioned the show to Art Edwards again. "You're good, Buddy," he told me. "But Ace is doing great. Food Network not going to do another cake show."

"It's not a cake show," I insisted. "It's a *bakery* show."

I was a little more aggressive this time. I convinced Art to have a meeting with me and we holed up in his office for two hours, kicking around ideas for the show, developing it right then and there into something for which we both had great passion. Our vision was so similar that I knew that if the show ever came to be, I'd move heaven and earth to make sure that Art and his High Noon colleagues were brought on board to produce the show.

Driving Me Crazy

■ ■

By far, the hardest cake I ever made up to the end of season two was the NASCAR cake, produced for an hour-long special.

Working on that cake was a mind-boggling experience. In addition to the pure size—the same as that of an actual car—just determining how to start was a project in itself. It took an entire day just to build the frame.

It was also a crash course in management, as NASCAR arranged for the Johnson & Wales College of Culinary Arts students to help us out, so my pit crew had fifty-six people on it. I had never honchoed that many people so even something as simple as ordering them to knead dough or fondant became an important decision. And because of the sheer volume of cake required, we used brand-name bag mixes (which we *never* do at Carlo's), and had to have half of it baked on site and half at Johnson & Wales.

Down the homestretch, it was one surprise, one crisis, after another: The icing (also donated, and out of a can) developed a skin as soon as it met the air, so the fondant wouldn't stick; we had to steam it just to get it to take to the cake car. And, because it was so heavy, a part of the front end broke off and had to be reinforced with cereal treats.

I'll tell you a secret: My producers love nothing more than to see me at my wit's end. That drama makes for great television, they tell me. Well, guys, I hope you enjoyed yourselves while we were making this episode, because that cake took years off my life.

"This is going to be great," he said. "Have Tony and Greg make that sizzle reel and send it to me."

The plan was for Tony and Greg to shoot at my bakery for two or three days, but when I called Tony to set it up, he hit me with a big surprise.

"Buddy," he told me. "I'm going through a divorce. There's no way I can make it."

I was sorry to hear that, but I felt opportunity in the air. "C'mon. This is the time."

"Sorry, Buddy."

Here's where the story gets a little crazy: The very day I was planning to leave for Denver to do a seventh *Challenge,* I appeared on *Good Morning America,* presenting a cake for Britney Spears's birthday that imitated the color scheme of her new CD.

When I got back to Carlo's, I received a call from a man I'd never met, Andy Strauser, director of Talent Development and Casting at Discovery Communications, who own TLC and a bunch of other cable networks.

"Buddy Valastro?"

"Yes?"

"I came across one of your *Challenges* because another competitor we're considering for a new baking show sent us a tape and you were on it. We ended up being drawn to *you.*"

He asked me about myself and I gave him the *Reader's Digest* version, focusing on all those elements that I thought would make for a show.

He was interested and wanted to see some footage of all the things I was talking about.

"Listen," I told him. "I have to run. I'm leaving town this afternoon."

"Okay," he said. "But I need you to do something before you go. *It's very important.* Take a video camera and go through the bakery and introduce me to all the people and things you're talking about. Then, overnight it to me in Los Angeles. Can you do that for me?"

I looked at my watch. I was supposed to leave for the airport in two hours.

"No problem," I said.

I hung up and speed-dialed my pal Rick Edrich, who does production work for a New York–based company called Spot Creative.

"Hey, Buddy."

"Rick, I need you," I said. "I need you here *yesterday* to do me a huge favor." I told him the situation and next thing I knew, he was pulling up outside the bakery, running in with his equipment with all the urgency of a paramedic.

With him following me, we walked through the entire shop. I spoke right to the camera, introducing all the bakers and decorators—Mauro, Joey,

Little Frankie—and all my sisters, and, of course, Mama. Nobody knew what I was up to, which was a good thing because everybody was being themselves.

We sent the video off to Andy Strauser in Los Angeles and then I took off for Denver.

Then, the most amazing thing happened: The day before the *Challenge*, Strauser called to tell me that we had already been green-lit. They wanted to shoot a pilot! Without so much as a meeting or an audition, I was going to have my own show.

"We want to send a contract to your agent," he said, and I was laughing inside because I didn't have an agent.

That was the worst *Challenge* I ever did. My head just wasn't in it. I didn't beat myself up over it, because a new chapter was on the horizon. In fact, the new chapter was so close at hand, that while I was in Denver taping that *Challenge*, I had a meeting with Art Edwards and Jim Berger, CEO of High Noon, to tell them the news about TLC and let them know that I was going to be sure they were on board as my production team.

Back in New Jersey, I moved like lightning to secure an agent and make it official between TLC and me. Although my contract simply referred to the show as "Untitled Cake Show," there was a name being kicked around: *Cake Boss*. I wasn't crazy about it. Thought it maybe sounded a little arrogant. But, within a few days, I was positive it was the only possible title. It just worked.

∽

At a big family dinner one night, I told everyone about the new show, and they were understandably excited about it.

Before we began shooting, we had a meeting at the bakery with Nancy Daniels, Howard Lee, and Jon Sechrist, the core production team for *Cake Boss*. I was nervous, because I had never hung out with TV executives, who have a reputation just slightly nicer than great white sharks. To my surprise, these guys were nothing like that. They were down-to-earth, inspiring, creative, and excited about *Cake Boss*. By the time we were done, I already thought of them more like family than as colleagues.

Next thing I knew, we were in production. There were cameras everywhere, we were all miked up, and even though I had my own office, there was a trailer parked outside for me to hang out in and get my makeup done. There was also a production assistant assigned to follow me around, updating the director on my whereabouts, but instead of referring to me as Buddy, he called me "the talent," as in "The talent is in wardrobe." "The talent is in makeup." "I'm bringing the talent to the set."

In all, we shot about 120 hours of footage for the pilot, and I didn't know what to make of any of it. Jim Berger, who was fast becoming a good friend, was ecstatic.

"Dude, it's going to be awesome," he told me.

After we wrapped up shooting the pilot, Jim, Art, and their team packed up and left, edited it, and sent it off to Discovery.

Next thing I knew, the network had gone gaga for the pilot and ordered another twelve episodes for the first season. A week later, even though I still hadn't seen the pilot, we were filming again.

There was a big event scheduled in New York about that time, the Upfronts, where the networks announce their lineups for the next season (often showing clips to the audience of media and advertisers). The night before, I went out to dinner with David Zaslav, president and CEO of Discovery Communications, TLC's president and general manager Eileen O'Neill, and Joe Abruzzese, president of Advertising Sales for Discovery. David, Eileen, and I hit it off right away. I also formed an immediate and special bond with Joe. He is older than I am, but we have a lot in common. He is from New Jersey and had lost his father at a young age. He was a legendary figure in the business, and watching him work the room at dinner, and the next day at the Upfronts reminded me of my dad. Before too long, I had taken to calling him Uncle Joe.

I still hadn't seen the pilot, but at the Upfronts, a number of strangers approached me, telling me that I was going to be the next big thing. I have to admit, I was beginning to get excited.

❦

And so it began. Our debut episode opened with the bakery in all its chaotic glory—the team and me upstairs baking away, and me praying (aloud, for the benefit of the camera) that my sisters give me the room to breathe. As if on cue, Mary intercoms me asking where some pastries are for the case. Just another day in the life, only it was all captured on film.

One of the great triumphs about the show for me was that I got to introduce America to my father in the very first episode, with snapshots of him, and the two of us side by side, and him with my sisters, intercut with my interview.

"What you have to understand," I said to the camera. "Is that my father was a god." If you watch that episode closely, you can see that I started to get a little choked up in those first few seconds, because I knew that I was realizing his dream. Carlo's Bake Shop was already generating income for his entire family, and now it was about to become, as he'd always wished, and I had promised, a household name.

Then the episode kicks into high gear, when I get a call from Maria McBride of *Brides* magazine, seeking a cake for the inside back cover of her magazine. I hang up and turn to my crew, describing the six-tiered monster we'd have to create in addition to all the work already laid out before us.

The show also had its little melodramas, as when we happened to run out of sugar, causing a dustup between Joey and Little Frankie.

That very first episode also featured our own special effect. It might not have been *Avatar*-level, but I happen to love it: As I imagine what the cake I'm designing is going to look like, the viewers get to see it brought to life with computer generated images that depict the visions I get in my head. For that cake for *Brides* magazine, they got to see the six layers come together, depicted in white, then the double-zero piping appeared as if being written on with an invisible pen, then the red flowers I had in mind, which were then replaced with white anemones that Maria McBride preferred. That's right, I was *overruled* in my very first episode.

The episode also gave viewers the first look at one of our famous theme cakes: a man fishing on a boat in an ocean made from piping gel. It turned out that the cake was actually meant for *me*, for my own surprise birthday celebration. We didn't touch on it in the show, but that, too, brought back wonderful memories of those summer days on Sandy Hook, fishing with my dad. I still go fishing today, often by myself. It's one of the few times I turn

The Computer versus the Crayon

Thank God, Art Edwards came up with the device of showing my thought process via computer-generated images, because although I have a perfect picture of what I want to design in my head, I've never been able to draw it well. I'm glad viewers have been spared images of my actual drawings, which I make with crayon or marker in hand as I try to communicate what's in my brain. If we depended on those drawings to sell our theme cakes, we'd have gone out of business years ago.

off my always ringing cell phone and take time for me and me alone. It's important to run the bakery and give it all the time and attention it demands, and the same goes for my family, but it's also important for me to take time to recharge, so that I can be at my best when I am parenting or working. That little guy depicted on the cake might have looked lonely out there by himself, but for me it was a depiction of pure life-giving bliss.

All of these little revelations helped me realize that *Cake Boss* was more than just a side project. The show quickly became a way for me to relive moments from my own life, and to share them with the public. More than that, it was a chance for me to work out things about my life and my feelings about what I've been through. Psychotherapy might be a big industry across the Hudson in Manhattan, but it's not all that popular in my circle. To have a chance to reflect on all of it—my personal history, my relationship with my sisters and brothers-in-law, my mom, and; of course, my late father—was a real gift. In the midst of the most public thing I'd ever done, I was having a deeply personal and private experience.

Many of the personal elements of the show, of course, exist on the margins. Most of each episode is dominated by what actually goes on at Carlo's, especially those theme cakes, but even these provided fodder for a personal expression of family history. Our second episode featured a fire-truck cake and a fashionista cake, but it also focused on a tribute cake to my dad, on the fifteenth anniversary of his passing. Every year, beginning the year after he died, we host a commemorative dinner to mark his passing. For the one we held in 2009, in his honor, I made a cream puff cake, bringing back his signature creation. The San Marzano liqueur used in the cake has since been discontinued, so the episode has become especially poignant to me. (We now make the cake with a custom blended liqueur, which approximates the flavor of San Marzano.)

Then, there was the time a young couple asked me to re-create that signature dove wedding cake from the 1980s, and I got a chance to breathe new life into that memory along with Sal and Danny, who still work with us today. On another early episode, I demonstrated the technique for making *sfogliatelle* dough, which took me right back to those days when I came of age after my dad's passing, including my final, transformative mastering of that dough, which, in some ways, was the biggest turning point in my life. Sometimes the show captures family history in the making, as in the first episode of Season Three, when Mama—after almost forty years—retired, leaving the bakery in the hands of the next generation.

I've also loved being able to show off my wife and kids on the show, and sharing some of the traditions of the family, like that annual tomato-sauce ritual in the Carlo's kitchen.

Sometimes, the connection to my life is indirect. When the world-famous Grucci family, creator of sensational and historic fireworks displays, asked me to create a cake for their centennial, I instantly thought of how New Yorkers and New Jerseyites, myself included, have the same experience of fireworks, watching them over the rivers between our shores. When they asked me to include the Brooklyn Bridge, because their late father once did a huge show celebrating its centennial, we worked in all three landmasses. We then found a way to work fireworks into the cake presentation. Best of all was the little figurine of Mr. Grucci sitting on the shore, detonator switch in hand. I'd never met the man, but their close-knit family reminded me of my own, and their patriarch reminded me of my father.

Woulda Made a Great Episode!

One of the great things about having a television show is that it provides an instant silver lining to the kind of disasters that would normally ruin our day. If a cake can't fit into the truck, or takes a spill down the stairs, or gets dropped ten feet from its destination, we might have to scramble to find a solution, but at least we can say to ourselves, "It'll be a good story for the show."

That's why sometimes I find myself wishing the production crew were here all the time to capture some of the monumental mishaps.

The most ironic story occurred the day after our last week of shooting season two. We wrapped on a Saturday and, when we walked in Sunday morning, discovered that one of the walk-in refrigerators had been left open overnight and that five wedding cakes were down, one of which was a five-thousand-dollar cake for four-hundred people. We had to get all hands on deck immediately and re-create all five cakes from scratch.

Those moments used to leave us screaming all sort of unprintable things at ourselves, but now we have an instant joke that lightens the moment as we triage the emergency: "This woulda made a great episode!"

Cake Boss hasn't only been a way of looking backward. It's also been a tremendous source of inspiration and growth in moving forward. One of the keys to remaining a vital and creative baker is keeping things fresh and challenging day after day, and the show has brought some of the greatest challenges of my career to the door of Carlo's, whether it was making a cake representing an apple orchard, or the Bronx Zoo. Some cakes let us put our creativity to work in service of our community, like the one designed to commemorate the opening of a new movie theater in Hoboken, or the time that we fashioned a cake featuring two forty-eight-inch tanks, so that live fish could be included, for an aquarium in Camden, New Jersey.

When viewers see me struggle on the show, it's not an act. Any new cake requires the team and me to push ourselves, to learn new ways of applying what we know. When we were tasked with creating a Leaning Tower of Pisa cake, the breakthrough was incorporating a wedge to support the tower; a cake that was actually crooked would have fallen, for sure. Then, there was the time that a group of hackers asked us to produce a robot cake that actually moved. I jumped at the opportunity. What a challenge! We had a rough time devising a mechanism powerful enough to make the hefty cake roll. Mauro's carpentry instincts came in handy as he realized we needed to put two sets of motorized wheels under the frame. Problem solved!

It's not always the construction of the cakes that challenge me; sometimes, it's little things that prove deceptively difficult. For the "Extreme Mammals" exhibition at the Museum of Natural History, we created an Indricotherium. Replicating the texture of the animal's skin was brutal; to mimic the brittle texture, we used a mixture of modeling chocolate and fondant. In the end, it came out better than I ever expected. The episode also featured one of our trademark dramatic deliveries, which are just as tense in real life as they are on the show. Even when cakes aren't that big, they can weigh a lot; for years, I've had bruises on my arms from picking up cakes.

As the show has become more popular, we've gotten a chance to meet and interact with some iconic people, and even some nonpeople. One of my favorite episodes of the first two seasons was when the producers of *Sesame Street* asked us to create a cake for its fortieth anniversary. I grew up watching that show, and the opportunity to visit the set as part of our due diligence was like something out of a dream. It was truly awesome to meet Big Bird, Elmo, and of course, every baker's favorite character, Cookie Monster. We did the show proud, re-creating an entire street scene, and my team of elves, especially Sunshine, outdid themselves with their figurines of the characters. The cake was a huge hit and, when we delivered it, I brought Cookie Monster the biggest chocolate chip cookie we'd ever made at the bakery, which Joey fashioned in a twenty-inch-round cake form.

ⅎ

Cake Boss has been many things to me. It's been a chance for me to make Carlo's as well-known as my father always wanted it to be. It's helped ensure that

Inspired by a favorite of the American South, Red Velvet Cake (page 226) is a relatively new but very popular addition to the Carlo's Bake Shop repertoire.

Lobster Tails
(page 175).

Opposite: *Freshly filled (from lower left corner) Cannoli (page 182), Cream Puffs (page 179), and Lobster Tails (page 175) Pipe them with cream just before serving to preserve the character of the pastry.*

A match made in heaven:
Espresso and Classic Biscotti (page 162)

Bet you can't eat just one of some of our most popular cookies: Tarelles (page 160), Chocolate-Chip Cookies (page 167), Pignoli Cookies (page 169), Classic Biscotti (page 162)

*Far out: The Groovy Girl Cake
is a tribute to what you can do
with fondant and a little imagination.*

Flower power: Created for Mother's Day, our beautiful floral cupcakes are now available all year long.

The Italian pick-me-up, Tiramisu (page 189).

For a fruit tart, it doesn't get much easier than this Crostata (page 192), filled with jam beneath a traditional lattice top.

The cake of a lifetime: The wedding cake I made to honor my beautiful bride, Lisa.

Nothing takes me into The Zone like making sugar flowers; they require intense concentration, and the finished product is the ultimate decorator's illusion.

Two classic styles: Filigree piping, which I think of as "drawing on the cake" . . .

. . . and a more formal cake with drop lines, crest emblems, and lattice work.

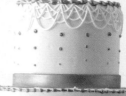

Born to be wild: Our 110th Anniversary cake for the Bronx Zoo reflected the natural habitats in which its animals live.

the shop will provide a living for our ever-growing family. And it's a fun addition to our lives, something that adds excitement and drama on a daily basis.

The show has also provided a constant source of professional challenges for me and the other bakers and decorators. Since the mid-1990s, we'd done a handful of theme cakes any given week, but once the show started airing, it became an even bigger part of our business, and the requests only get bigger and more outlandish with each season. That drama you see on the show is sincere; often, I have no idea how we're going to pull off what someone has asked us to do. All I know is that we'll find a way.

Thanks to the show, the bakery is also more crowded than it's ever been and we've had to go with the flow to keep up. Counting the basement, we have three floors of space and every inch of it is taken. Shelving runs all the way up to the ceiling on some walls, holding boxes of icing, buckets of fondant, and so on. Above every refrigerator you'll find cake boxes and other miscellany piled up to the heavens as well. There are walk-in refrigerators on every floor; open one and you'll find a speed rack in your face, because every freezer in the joint is jam-packed with everything you can imagine: lobster tail shells, cookies, cakes, tea biscuits, pie, and *pasticiotti* shells. In 2009, I started planning a factory, and when the architect and kitchen designer came to see our existing setup, their jaws dropped in disbelief. "I can't believe how much you are able to produce in such a small space," the designer said. "This should be utter chaos, but you've managed to control it." It was one of the truest things anybody has ever said about me.

When that factory is completed, it'll be a 30,000 square foot facility where we'll produce as many of our signature desserts as possible, not just cakes, but cookies and pastries. I'll be honest: Things move fast at Carlo's, and in my life, and that's how I like it, but I'm taking my sweet, sweet time with the factory, because I'm in uncharted territory and I want to get it just right. I'm excited about the factory, because it'll let America taste what my family and I can do.

My favorite thing about the show is that it introduced the world to my father. Even after all these years, he remains my inspiration, my North Star, and just as I sometimes feel that I'm baking with his hands, I often have the comforting feeling that I'm watching the bakery's evolution through his eyes.

My Secret Weapon

■ ■

Cake Boss viewers think they know my family and, to some extent, they do, but our family is actually much, much bigger than we could ever squeeze into the confines of a television screen: a sprawling network of parents and children, in-laws and cousins, aunts and uncles, nieces and nephews, cousins and godchildren, scattered all over the towns of New Jersey and across the country. Not all of them work at Carlo's, of course, but they're all connected to it in some way.

Given the size of the family, it's amazing how well we all get along. Sure, there are some squabbles, but it never gets in the way of what's important. We are always there for each other: helping out with each other's kids after school and on the weekends, shuttling each other around from the shop to our homes, and in those sad but inevitable moments when tragedy strikes, doing whatever it takes to get through a tough time.

I think of our tight-knit family as my secret weapon. Without them, the bakery would never be able to run as well as it does and I never would have been able to become the Cake Boss. Even if I hadn't become that, I'd still be eternally grateful for the richness all of these people have added to my life.

When I see my whole family together, at a birthday or anniversary celebration, filling one of our homes almost to the breaking point, I sometimes want to cry, because I know how happy my dad would have been if he could have seen the spectacle for himself.

At other moments, I feel like he's standing there beside me, like he used to when I was a little boy, mounting that inverted bucket to watch him do his thing, looking up at him, marveling at his perfect attention to his work, the pride he took in a job well done.

I look up to him still. For all my confidence, all my bravado, all my success, I have no illusions.

He'll always be the real Cake Boss.

10

Recipes from Mia Famiglia
Cookies, Pastries, Pies, Cakes, and Cupcakes

THESE RECIPES WILL ALLOW you to make the cookies, pastries, pies, cakes, and cupcakes described throughout the book, and on *Cake Boss*, the show. These are the most important recipes of my life. I hope that they bring you as much pleasure as they've brought me and my family and, of course, the customers of Carlo's Bake Shop.

At the bakery, we produce all these recipes, even the cakes, in enormous quantities but, for this book, I scaled down and tested them in a home kitchen. I used ingredients available in most supermarkets. In a few cases, I call for ingredients that might require that you make a trip to a baking shop or specialty store, or even for you to order something via the Internet. Please know that I only do this where I feel it's essential for the recipe, so that you can achieve a true, authentic flavor or texture, because I believe that baking should be easy and convenient, something you can do spontaneously, and as a family, creating your own memories to go with these treats.

BASIC TOOLS AND EQUIPMENT, TECHNIQUES, AND ADVICE

Before we dig into the recipes and get to the fun of baking, there are some suggestions I'd like to share with you. Having spent most of my life around a bakery, I've developed a number of strongly held opinions about what works and doesn't work. Some of what you're about to read might differ from other advice you've heard or read over the years. All I can tell you is that this is how we do it at Carlo's Bake Shop, or as close to it as is possible at home.

It's a good idea to have the following in your kitchen if you do, or plan to do, a lot of baking.

BAKING TRAYS

I suggest having one regular and one nonstick baking tray and, if possible, two of each to facilitate working in batches. Some companies sell the same half-sheet size professional trays we use, which measure 18 inches by 13 inches, but you can also use the more commonly available 9 inch x 13-inch baking tray, or 16 inch x 14-inch cookie sheet. I also recommend that you buy baking trays with rimmed sides to keep pastries from sliding off.

CAKE PANS

At home, I generally use a 9 inch x 2-inch round cake pan. Since many of the cake recipes in this book produce two 9-inch cakes, you'll want to have two of them. I like aluminum pans. (I know that Springform pans are popular, but I don't care for them because they're harder to clean and unnecessary. If you grease and flour a pan correctly [*see* page 208]—and let it cool, it will unmold just fine.)

CUPCAKE MOLD

The cake recipes in this book make 24 cupcakes, so I suggest having two 12-cupcake molds, preferably nonstick.

STAND MIXER

Baking begins with mixing. Many of the recipes in this section call for a stand mixer, and either the paddle or whip attachment. Invest in a good, sturdy stand mixer such as those made by Hobart. Where possible (with some cookie, pastry doughs, and frostings, for example), I indicate when a hand mixer (or just your hands) is a viable alternative.

KITCHEN THERMOMETER

You will need to check the temperature of some batters and when making buttercream. A kitchen thermometer is the only way to go.

MICROPLANE ZESTER

These little hand-held steel planks are the ultimate tool for grating citrus zest as fine as possible.

PASTRY BAG

There are two types of bag: polyurethane and canvas. The decision as to which bag to use is very important in piping and decorating cakes, but, for filling and frosting, you can use either. You will also need #6 and #7 plain tips for piping frosting. I suggest you purchase a complete set of pastry-bag tips, as you will surely want other tips on hand.

PASTRY BRUSH

A pastry bush is the best way to apply syrups and other soaking liquids to sponge cakes.

ROLLING PIN

A good, sturdy rolling pin is essential. Wood or marble pins are fine; weight and balance are more important than the material.

SPATULAS

A cake-icing spatula is the ideal tool for spreading fillings and frostings, while a rubber spatula is best for scraping dough and batter out of mixing bowls.

TURNTABLE

See page 209.

NOTES ON INGREDIENTS

CAKE FLOUR

I cannot urge you strongly enough to use cake flour in the cake recipes. It's more refined than all-purpose flour, and helps cakes achieve a smooth, superior mouthfeel. (Even in raw form, your hands can feel the pleasing density of cake flour; the color is a purer white as well.) If you want to ignore this plea, you can substitute all-purpose flour but the cakes won't have that elusive, almost creamy, texture.

COCOA

Cocoa is what gives chocolate cakes and other baked goods their chocolate flavor. I do not believe in skimping on cocoa. If at all possible, buy the best you can find. At Carlo's Bake Shop we use Callebaut. (If you feel like splurging, Valrhona is also terrific.) Regardless of brand, choose a cocoa that has a 22 to 24 percent fat content.

MILK

If you have a preference for low- or reduced-fat milks, I respect that, but encourage you to use whole milk in your baking if at all possible. The final product will taste better, and the fat helps bind the ingredients.

PASTRY FLOUR

Pastry flour can be a little tough to find in the supermarket, but you can order it easily via the Internet (*see* Sources, page 239). I like it for certain recipes because its relatively low protein content helps produce the desired texture in crusty cookies and pastry. You can substitute all-purpose flour, but you'll lose something.

VANILLA

Be sure to use pure vanilla extract in your baking; avoid any imitation or artificially flavored products. They don't fool the taste buds, and the chemical flavor can drag an entire cake down.

VEGETABLE OIL

A number of these recipes use vegetable oil. While you might be used to substituting canola or other neutral oils for vegetable oil, don't do that here. Vegetable oil has just the right viscosity and fat content for my cake recipes.

Cookies and Pastries

༄

COOKIES AND PASTRIES appeal to the little kid in all of us. For me, this is especially so, because they take me back to my very first days at Carlo's, when I marveled at my father's talent; making cookies to take home to my mom; and, later, in my first days on the job, learning to make cream puffs, cannoli, and St. Joseph's zeppole.

I may be the Cake Boss, but there's a special place in my heart for these desserts, because, while cakes are associated with special occasions, cookies and pastries are everyday treats. To that end, these recipes include advice on how to store, refrigerate, or even freeze pastries, so that you can always have some on hand.

Baking in Batches

Many of the cookie and pastry recipes in the book begin with my telling you to position a rack in the center of the oven. I strongly suggest that you bake *only* on your oven's central rack, even if that means baking in batches. Otherwise your cookies, pastries, and cakes won't all come out the same, and I'm a *big* believer in consistency. At Carlo's Bake Shop, our ovens are enormous, with shelves that rotate so that no pan blocks any other pan's heat and everything bakes evenly. That's impossible in a home oven, which is why I recommend the batch approach. It takes longer, but it's worth it. (If you don't have the time or patience for this, try to replicate our professional ovens by positioning the racks so there are several inches of space between them and switch the top and bottom tray midway through the baking process but, be quick about it, so you don't let too much heat out of the oven.)

Tarelles

(Vanilla Cookies)

When I was as a little kid, Dad brought home these little cookies in their glossy white box, and I used to dip them in milk. You can do the same, or enjoy them with coffee or espresso.

MAKES ABOUT 40 COOKIES

1¼ cups granulated sugar
2 extra large eggs
1 teaspoon pure vanilla extract
1¼ cups vegetable shortening
½ cup whole milk
2¼ cups all-purpose flour, plus more for flouring work surface
2¼ cups pastry flour (see page 157, and Sources, page 239), or
    additional all-purpose flour
2 teaspoons baking powder

1. Position a rack in the center of the oven and preheat to 350°F.
2. Put the sugar, eggs, and vanilla in the bowl of a stand mixer fitted with the paddle attachment and paddle at low-medium speed until combined, approximately 2 minutes. With the motor running, add the shortening and paddle for 30 seconds. Pour in the milk and paddle until it's thoroughly absorbed into the mixture, approximately 2 minutes.
3. Stop the motor and add the flours and baking powder. Paddle at medium-high speed until it comes together into a smooth ball of dough

and pulls away from the sides of the bowl, 3 to 5 minutes, then scrape down the bowl and paddle with a rubber spatula.

4. Lightly flour a work surface. Transfer the dough to the surface, and separate it into 2 equal pieces. Roll 1 piece into a ropelike shape, about 1 inch in diameter and 30 inches long. Cut the dough crosswise into about twenty 1½ inch pieces. Roll each piece into a ropelike shape, ½ inch in diameter, and bend to make a ring, pressing the ends together until they stick. Put as many as possible on a nonstick baking tray, about 1 inch apart, and bake until golden brown *on the bottom* (check by gently lifting an edge with a spatula), approximately 15 minutes. Meanwhile, roll out the remaining piece of dough and form about another 20 cookies.

5. When the first batch is done, remove the tray from the oven, carefully transfer the cookies to a wire rack to cool, let the tray cool, arrange another batch of cookies on the tray, and repeat. Continue to repeat until all the cookies have been baked and cooled, approximately 20 minutes after the last batch has come out of the oven. (If you have more than one baking tray, you can alternate, always having one tray ready to go.)

6. The cookies will keep in an airtight container at room temperature for at least 1 week.

Classic Biscotti

(Quaresimali)

This is one of the classic Italian biscotti, meant to be served alongside a freshly pulled espresso. Note that the amount of the flour in the batter is exact, but the amount used to dust the finished batter is approximate, because the batter is very moist. You might need to use more flour to make the dough easier to work with; think of it as a third hand, there to help you pick up and manipulate the batter.

MAKES ABOUT 36 BISCOTTI

1¾ cups (½ pound) roasted, peeled whole almonds
4 extra-large eggs
1½ cups pastry flour, all-purpose can be substituted, plus about 1½ cups
    flour for working with dough
1½ cups granulated sugar
¾ cup (¼ pound) pine nuts, preferably Spanish
1 tablespoon ground cinnamon
1 teaspoon pure vanilla extract
½ teaspoon baking ammonia (see *Safety Note*), optional

1. Position a rack in the center of the oven and preheat the oven to 350°F.
2. Put the almonds on a baking sheet in a single layer and toast in the oven, shaking the pan periodically to prevent scorching, until lightly toasted and fragrant, approximately 15 minutes. Remove the sheet from the oven and let cool.
3. Raise the oven temperature to 400°F.

4. Put the almonds, 2 of the eggs, the flour, sugar, pine nuts, cinnamon, vanilla, and baking ammonia in the bowl of a stand mixer fitted with the paddle attachment. Paddle at low-medium speed until the mixture comes together, approximately 30 seconds. Add another egg, making sure it lands in the bottom of the bowl (this will moisten the outside of the dough and pull any lingering dry ingredients from the sides). Paddle for another 30 seconds.

5. Mound ½ cup of flour on your work surface and transfer the dough from the bowl to the flour, using a rubber spatula to get as much as possible out of the bowl. Top with another ½ cup of flour to facilitate handling the dough. Separate the dough into 3 equal sections and, working with one at a time, roll by hand into 3 bars, pressing each down to about 16 inches long and ½ inch high. Transfer to a nonstick baking tray, leaving about 4 inches between each bar (you may need to do this in batches), and square the sides of the bars, gently tapping by hand. Coat each bar lightly with flour.

6. Beat the fourth egg in a small bowl and use a pastry brush to brush the bars with the egg.

7. Bake the bars until golden and firm, 25 to 30 minutes.

8. Remove the baking tray from the oven, let the bars cool on the tray for 20 to 30 minutes, then transfer to a cutting board. Bake the third bar if it did not fit on the baking tray with the first two. Cut off and discard (or snack on) an inch or so from each end and use a serrated knife to cut the remaining bar crosswise into 12 equal pieces.

9. The biscotti may be held in an airtight container at room temperature for up to 2 weeks.

Safety Note

This recipe calls for baker's ammonia, a classic leavener. *Do not confuse it with regular ammonia*, which is poison. Baker's ammonia has a strong smell in its raw state, but it bakes out.

Modern Biscotti

This is the basic formula for making modern, or designer, biscotti at Carlo's Bake Shop. You can adjust it to make any number of variations of your own design. There's no right or wrong, but my favorite is chocolate biscotti with pistachios, white chocolate, and dried cherries.

MAKES ABOUT 36 BISCOTTI

2½ cups whole nuts
1 cup granulated sugar
8 tablespoons (1 stick) unsalted butter, softened at room temperature
6 extra-large eggs
1½ teaspoons baking powder
1 teaspoon pure vanilla extract
4 cups all-purpose flour
1¾ cups nut flour (see Note), all-purpose flour can be substituted
1 cup semisweet chocolate chips

1. Position a rack in the center of the oven and preheat the oven to 350°F.
2. Put the nuts on a baking sheet in a single layer and toast in the oven, shaking the pan periodically to prevent scorching, until lightly toasted and fragrant, approximately 15 minutes. Remove the sheet from the oven and let cool.
3. Raise the oven temperature to 375°F.
4. Put the sugar, butter, 5 eggs, baking powder, and vanilla in the bowl of a stand mixer fitted with the paddle attachment. Paddle at medium speed until thoroughly mixed, approximately 2 minutes.

5. Stop the motor and add the all-purpose flour and nut flour. Paddle at medium speed for 1 minute. Lower the motor to low speed and add the almonds and chocolate chips. Paddle just until the mixture comes together in a ball, approximately 1 minute.

6. Separate the dough into 3 equal pieces.

7. Lightly flour a work surface, roll out each piece of batter into a log about 1½ inches in diameter and about 12 inches long. Transfer the pieces to a nonstick baking tray, placing them about 2 inches apart, and press down to about 16 inches long and ½ inch high. (You may need to do this in batches.)

8. Beat the remaining egg in a bowl and use a pastry brush to generously paint the bars.

9. Bake until solid and slightly rubbery, 25 to 30 minutes. Remove the tray from the oven and let the bars cool on the tray for 20 to 30 minutes. (If the third bar did not fit on the tray, transfer the baked bars to a cutting board and bake the third bar.) Lower the oven temperature to 325°F.

10. Cut off and discard (or snack on) the ends of each bar, then cut into ¾-inch diagonal cuts, about 12 per bar.

11. Return the pieces to the baking tray, open sides up (they will be slightly underdone), and bake until hardened, approximately 20 minutes. Remove from the oven and let the biscotti cool in the tray for 20 to 30 minutes.

10. The biscotti may be held in an airtight container at room temperature for up to 2 weeks.

(*Continued on next page*)

How To Make Nut Flours

To make nut flour, preheat the oven to 350°F. Put the nuts on a baking sheet in a single layer and toast in the oven, shaking the pan periodically to prevent scorching, until lightly toasted and fragrant, approximately 15 minutes. Remove the sheet from the oven and let cool. Transfer the nuts to the bowl of food processor fitted with the steel blade and pulse to a fine meal. Do not overprocess or they will become gummy.

Different nuts will yield different amounts of flour but, generally speaking, about 8 ounces of nuts will give you about 2½ cups of flour.

Modern Biscotti (*cont.*)

Biscotti Variations

To make almond biscotti, use whole, peeled almonds and almond flour.

To make pistachio biscotti, Use shelled, unsalted pistachios and pistachio flour. (Pistachio biscotti are especially delicious with dried sour cherries; replace ½ cup chocolate chips with ½ cup cherries.)

To make hazelnut biscotti, Use shelled hazelnuts (rub the skins off with a clean kitchen towel after toasting, or purchase already skinned and blanched hazelnuts and toast) and hazelnut flour.

To make chocolate biscotti, reduce all purpose flour to 3½ cups and add ½ cup cocoa.

You can use milk chocolate, semisweet chocolate, or white chocolate with any of these.

Chocolate-Chip Cookies

Chocolate-chip cookies are one of the most ubiquitous of all desserts, and are usually made with standard-issue chips. Do what we do, and seek out a high-quality chocolate. You will be amazed at how different the results are. For big impact, buy bars of chocolate and break or chop it into small chunks.

MAKES 24 COOKIES

1 cup (2 sticks) unsalted butter, softened at room temperature
1 cup granulated sugar
½ cup light-brown sugar
1 teaspoon baking soda
1 teaspoon fine sea salt
1 teaspoon pure vanilla extract
2 extra-large eggs
2¼ cups all-purpose flour
2½ cups semisweet chocolate chips

1. Position a rack in the center of the oven and preheat the oven to 350°F.
2. Put the butter, sugar, brown sugar, baking soda, salt, and vanilla in the bowl of a stand mixer fitted with the paddle attachment. (If you don't have a stand mixer, use a hand mixer fitted with the blending attachment.) Paddle at medium speed just until the ingredients come together in a uniform mass, approximately 2 minutes.
3. With the motor running, add the eggs, one at a time, adding the next

(Continued on next page)

Chocolate-Chip Cookies (*cont.*)

one only after the first one has been absorbed. Add the flour and mix until thoroughly integrated, approximately 30 seconds. Add the chips and mix just until they are blended in, approximately 30 seconds.

4. The dough can be wrapped in plastic wrap and refrigerated for up to 1 week or frozen for up to 2 months. Let come to room temperature before shaping and baking.

5. When ready to bake the cookies, break into small pieces and roll between the palms of your hands to form 24 meat-ball-sized balls. Place on two nonstick baking trays, about 2 inches apart.

6. Bake until flat and hot, 13 to 15 minutes. The cookies will look under-done, but will gently finish baking on the hot pan. Do not leave in the oven for more than 15 minutes, no matter what. Remove the baking trays from the oven and let the cookies cool completely on the trays, approximately 20 minutes.

7. Keep cookies in airtight container at room temperature for up to 3 days.

Pignoli Cookies

This is one of my favorite Sicilian cookie recipes. I recommend that you buy Spanish or Portuguese pine nuts, which have the best flavor. They are expensive, but you will not use all of them in the recipe. The 5 cups called for is to coat the cookies when you press them into the nuts. Alternately, you could buy just 2½ cups of nuts and press them into the cookies by hand, but that would be very time-consuming.

Note that the cookies need to rest overnight before baking.

MAKES ABOUT 48 COOKIES

2½ cups tightly packed almond paste (1 pound, 9 ounces)
1¼ cups granulated sugar
½ cup powdered (10x) sugar
1 heaping teaspoon cinnamon
1 tablespoon honey, preferably clover
1 teaspoon pure vanilla extract
5 extra-large egg whites
Five 12 inch x 12-inch (approximate) squares of parchment paper
5 cups pine nuts (about 1½ pounds)

1. Put the almond paste, granulated sugar, powdered sugar, cinnamon, honey, and vanilla in the bowl of a stand mixer fitted with the paddle attachment. Paddle at low-medium speed until the mixture is smooth with no lumps remaining, approximately 1 minute.

(Continued on next page)

Pignoli Cookies (*cont.*)

2. With the motor running, add the egg whites in 3 installments and paddle until absorbed, 30 seconds to 1 minute per addition.

3. Arrange a 12 inch x 12-inch piece of parchment paper on a work surface. Put the dough in a pastry bag fitted with a #6 plain tip and pipe the dough out into circles, 2 inches in diameter and about 1½ inches high, leaving about 2 inches of space between each circle. Repeat on 4 remaining pieces of parchment.

4. Spread the pine nuts out on a cookie sheet in a single layer. Take one of the cookie-dough covered parchment sheets in two hands and slowly invert it over the nuts. Press down so that nuts adhere to the dough and remove, very gently shaking the parchment to loosen any extra nuts. Set the nut-coated dough aside. Shake the cookie sheet to redistribute the pine nuts, and repeat with the remaining dough-covered sheets until all cookies are coated with pine nuts. Save any unused nuts for another use.

5. Leave the prepared cookies out, uncovered, at room temperature, overnight, to dry.

6. When ready to bake the cookies, position a rack in the center of the oven and preheat the oven to 350°F.

7. Set one of the parchment sheets on a baking tray and bake until the cookies are nicely golden, approximately 20 minutes. Remove the tray from the oven, carefully transfer the parchment to a heatproof surface to let the cookies cool, and bake the next sheet on the tray. Repeat until all cookies are baked, and let cool for approximately 20 minutes before serving. (The cookies can be held in an airtight container at room temperature for up to 1 week, or wrapped in plastic and frozen for up to 1 month.)

Tea Biscuits

These are the sconelike pastries that were the first mixing I ever did at Carlo's. The most important thing about making these is not to overmix the dough. Once you get all of the ingredients to just barely hold together, stop mixing, or it will become rubbery. The dough will look unfinished and flaky, but don't wait for those flakes to become incorporated. I encourage you to do what we do at Carlo's Bake Shop: Bake what you need right away, and freeze the remaining biscuits until you need them. You can bake them from the frozen state if you add five minutes to the baking time.

This recipe calls for cutting rectangle-shaped biscuits, but you may use different cutters to make circles or other shapes.

MAKES 12 BISCUITS

1¼ cups all-purpose flour, plus more for flouring work surface
1¼ cups pastry flour (see page 157), or an additional 1¼ cups all-purpose flour
½ cup vegetable shortening
¼ cup golden raisins
3 tablespoons granulated sugar
1 tablespoon baking powder
¾ teaspoon fine sea salt
¾ cup whole milk
2 tablespoons water
1 cup powdered (10x) sugar

(Continued on next page)

Tea Biscuits (*cont.*)

1. Position a rack in the center of the oven and preheat the oven to 375°F.
2. Put the all-purpose flour, pastry flour, shortening, raisins, sugar, baking powder, and salt into the bowl of a stand mixer fitted with the paddle. (If you do not have a stand mixer, you can also knead the ingredients by hand, working in a wide, deep bowl.) Paddle just until all of the ingredients come together, about 15 or 20 seconds. With the motor running, add the milk. As soon as the milk is blended in, mix for another 15 seconds, then stop.
3. Lightly flour a work surface. Roll the dough out to a ¾-inch to 1-inch thick rectangle, about 12 inches x 9 inches. Using a sturdy knife or pizza cutter, cut the dough into 12 rectangles. The rectangles can be wrapped in plastic wrap and frozen for up to 2 months.
4. Transfer the biscuits you plan to bake immediately to a nonstick baking tray, about 2 inches apart. Bake until golden brown and doubled in size and puffy, about 20 minutes. Remove the tray from the oven and let the biscuits cool on the tray for about 25 minutes.
5. Meanwhile, put the water and powdered sugar in a small bowl and use a rubber spatula to mix them into a pastry icing. (If baking fewer than 12 biscuits, adjust the quantities of water and sugar accordingly.) Smear some icing over the top of each biscuit with a cake icing spatula. These are best served warm, or on the day they are baked, but can be kept in airtight container at room temperature overnight.

Pecan Wedges

This is one of the desserts I made for sale in the Bergen Tech teacher's cafeteria, in exchange for my eating there. These are decadent little treats, with a number of textures and flavors packed into fairly tight quarters: the pastry itself, a caramel-pecan mixture that's poured into its center, and a chocolate shell.

MAKES 16 WEDGES

6 sticks (1½ pounds) unsalted butter, softened at room temperature
1 cup granulated sugar
2 extra-large eggs
¼ cup whole milk
4 cups pastry flour (see page 157), or all-purpose flour
1 cup light-brown sugar
3 tablespoons heavy cream
3 cups whole pecans
2 cups finely chopped semisweet high-quality chocolate

1. To make the dough, put 4 sticks of the butter and the granulated sugar in the bowl of a stand mixer fitted with the paddle, and paddle on low-medium speed until thoroughly mixed, approximately 1 minute. Add the eggs all at once and paddle until incorporated, approximately 1 minute. Add the milk and the pastry flour and mix until thoroughly blended, 30 seconds to 1 minute.

(Continued on next page)

Pecan Wedges (*cont.*)

2. Wrap the dough in plastic wrap and chill until stiff enough to be manipulated, about 30 minutes.
3. Position a rack in the center of the oven and preheat the oven to 400°F.
4. Divide the dough into four equal pieces. Lightly flour a work surface and roll out each piece of dough into an 18-inch log, 1½ to 2 inches high. Transfer to a baking tray and flatten the center of the log out so it looks like a ravine. It should be about 3 inches wide, fatter at the end than at the center. Crimp the edge on both sides. Repeat with all four pieces of dough, leaving about 2 inches between the logs (you may need to do this in batches), and set aside.
5. To make the caramel mixture, put the remaining 2 sticks of butter, the brown sugar, and cream in a saucepan and bring to a boil over high heat. Immediately remove from the heat and stir in the pecans. Spoon the pecan-caramel mixture into the ravine in the center of the logs. Bake until golden brown, about 20 minutes.
6. Remove trays from the oven, transfer the bars to a cutting board, and cut each bar crosswise into 4 or 5 wedges.
7. Meanwhile, melt the chocolate in a double boiler set over medium-high heat. Dip half of each wedge into the chocolate and let cool and dry on a wire rack or parchment paper for 30 minutes. These are best enjoyed the same day, but can be refrigerated in an airtight container for up to 3 days.

Lobster Tails

This is the recipe for lobster tails, the cornerstone of which is the sfogliatelle *dough. I want to be honest with you: Unless you are a professional baker, and an accomplished one at that, you probably shouldn't try to make these. I've seen grown men brought to the brink of tears trying to make* sfogliatelle*. However, I thought it was important to include this recipe because I want you to see what goes into making this classic of Italian baking. If you can make these and they come out well, please move to Hoboken and apply for a job at Carlo's!*

If you decide to try these, you will need a number of things: a sturdy stand mixer, along the lines of a Hobart home model, because the dough becomes very thick when mixed and can break a lesser machine (seriously). You will also need a pasta machine or roller, and a long, wide wood or marble work surface, at least 6 feet by 4 feet.

MAKES ABOUT 32 LOBSTER TAILS

8¾ cups all-purpose flour, plus more for flouring
2½ cups water
1 tablespoon fine sea salt
3 to 4 cups vegetable shortening
Cream Puff Dough (page 181)
Lobster Tail Cream (page 178)
Powdered (10x) sugar, for dusting lobster tails

(Continued on next page)

Lobster Tails (*cont.*)

1. Put the flour, water, and salt into a stand mixer fitted with the hook attachment and mix at low speed until it pulls together into a dense, uniform dough, 15 to 20 minutes.
2. Lightly flour your work surface and transfer the dough to it.
3. Roll the dough out as thin as possible. You can use a pasta machine to start, but the dough must be fed through by a second person so that one person can keep extending the dough along the length of the table; you want to end up with one unbroken piece of dough, about 6 feet long. If using a rolling pin, periodically flip the dough over to ensure even rolling.
4. Once the dough is rolled out, work it from beneath, massaging it outward from the center with your fingers until it's as close to see-through as possible. It's okay if it tears *very* slightly here and there, but excessive tearing will ruin the layers in the final pastry.
5. Beginning at one end, smear shortening over the dough. Roll the dough toward you as thin as possible, pulling it taut between each turn. Smear shortening over the next section before you roll it up. As the roll gains in diameter, you will need to pull and roll in sections, starting at one edge, then pulling the center, then the other end.
6. Continue to grease, roll, and pull like this until you reach the end. You should have a roll about 2 inches in diameter and about 4 feet long. Grease the outside with shortening, set it on a baking tray, and refrigerate overnight, at least 8 hours, uncovered.
7. The next day, remove the roll from the refrigerator and let come to room temperature for 1 hour.
8. Stretch the roll by hand to even it out. Use a serrated knife to cut 4 inches of the roll off each end (the layers are too loose at the sides) and discard. Then cut the remaining roll crosswise into about thirty-two ¾-inch pieces.

9. Using the balls of your hands to avoid marring them, lightly grease each piece on top and bottom with shortening, gathering them on a tray.

10. One by one, open each disc, starting with the ball of your hand. Use your thumb, index finger, and middle finger to coax the dough open from below. The layers will extend like a telescope into a cone shape. (It might be helpful to imagine an upside-down pottery wheel.)

11. Fill each cone with a heaping tablespoon of Cream Puff Dough. Flap the shell closed and return to the tray.

12. Position a rack in the center of the oven and preheat the oven to 400°F.

13. Stack 2 baking trays (to prevent direct heat from scorching the bottom of the pastries) and arrange as many cones as you can on the top tray, leaving 4 inches between them.

14. Bake until expanded, flaky, lightly browned, and crispy, 30 to 35 minutes. Remove from the oven, transfer to a wire rack, and let cool to room temperature. Repeat until all cones have been baked and cooled, about 30 minutes after the last batch has come out of the oven. (The finished shells can be placed in Ziploc bags and frozen for up to 2 months. Let thaw before filling and serving.)

15. Put the Lobster Tail Cream in a pastry bag fitted with the #4 plain tip. Make a hole in the back of each shell with your index finger. Shove the tip into the hole and pipe, squeezing hard, to force the cream into the center of the cavity.

16. Dust the lobster tails with powdered sugar and serve, or refrigerate in an airtight container for up to 2 days.

Lobster Tail Cream

In addition to lobster tails, this decadent cream can be used to fill and/or frost cakes; it's especially delicious on our Vanilla Cake; see page 214 for suggestions. The amount of Bailey's Irish Cream is negligible, but it adds a subtle elegance.

MAKES 5½ CUPS

Italian Custard Cream (page 234)
Italian Whipped Cream (page 205)
2 tablespoons Bailey's Irish Cream liqueur, plus more to taste, optional

1. Put the custard cream in a mixing bowl. Add the whipped cream, a little at a time, folding it in with a rubber spatula.
2. Drizzle the Bailey's Irish Cream, if using, over the mixture, gently mixing it in. Add more to taste, if desired, but do not overmix the cream.
3. The cream can be refrigerated in an airtight container for up to 4 days. Whip briefly by hand to refresh before using.

Cream Puffs

Is there a better example of truth in advertising than the name cream puffs? *A light, flaky, cloudlike pastry is filled with a rich, fluffy custard cream. The combination is compulsively enjoyable and a perennial favorite at Carlo's.*

You have two options for filling these cream puffs: halve them and fill them like a sandwich, or load them from the bottom. Filling from the bottom limits the exposure of the cream to the elements and will buy you another day or two of longevity. At Carlo's Bake Shop, we continue Old Man Carlo's tradition of cutting the puffs and filling them, but we only sell fresh ones; any that don't get sold on a given day are donated to a local homeless shelter.

MAKES 24 CREAM PUFFS

Cream Puff Dough (recipe follows)
3 cups Italian Custard Cream (page 234)

1. Position a rack in the center of the oven and preheat the oven to 450°F.
2. Transfer the dough into a pastry bag fitted with the #6 plain tip. Pipe rounds on 2 nonstick baking trays, about 2 inches in diameter by about ½ inch high, leaving 2 inches between each puff. You should be able to make 24 puffs.
3. Bake the puffs in the oven, in batches if necessary, until golden brown, 15 to 20 minutes.
4. Remove the tray from the oven and let the puffs cool on the tray for 20 minutes.

(Continued on next page)

Cream Puffs (*cont.*)

5. Fill the puffs one of the following ways:

     Option 1: Cut in them in half horizontally with a serrated knife. Use a pastry bag fitted with the #7 star tip to pipe filling onto each bottom piece (you can rinse out, dry, and reuse the same bag you used for the dough, or you can use a spoon if you'd like). Top with the top pieces.

     Option 2: Use your pinkie to hollow out the puffs from the bottom. Use a pastry bag fitted with the #7 star tip (you can rinse out, dry, and reuse the same bag you used for the dough) to pipe cream into the puffs from the bottom.

6. Serve the cream puffs right away or refrigerate in an airtight container. Cream puffs that have been halved and filled will last for 1 day; those filled from the bottom will last for 2 to 3 days.

Cream Puff Dough

In addition to making cream puffs, this dough is one of the great secrets of sfogli-atelle *(page 175).*

MAKES ENOUGH FOR 24 CREAM PUFFS

1 cup water
6 tablespoons unsalted butter
⅛ teaspoon fine sea salt
1 cup all-purpose flour
4 extra-large eggs

1. Put the water, butter, and salt in a heavy saucepan and bring to a boil over high heat. Add the flour and stir with a wooden spoon until the ingredients come together into a smooth, uniform dough, approximately 2 minutes.

2. Transfer the mixture to the bowl of a stand mixer fitted with the paddle attachment. (If you don't have a stand mixer you can use a hand mixer fitted with the blending attachments.) Start paddling on low speed, then add the eggs, one at a time, until thoroughly absorbed, mixing for 1 minute between each egg, and stopping the motor periodically to scrape down the sides and bottom of the bowl with a rubber spatula. Finish with the final egg and mix for an additional 2 minutes.

3. Use the dough immediately. It does not refrigerate well.

Cannoli

These are authentic cannoli, made according to the recipe my dad picked up at his grandfather's bakery when he was growing up in Sicily. Consider making these in large batches; because of the way the shells are fried in the lard they are able to stay preserved, so can be saved for a long time and filled when you're ready to serve them.

A few notes: The best, most authentic cannoli are made with lard and fried in lard. You can use vegetable shortening instead but, if you want that resilient crunch and classic flavor that you associate with cannoli from Carlo's or another true Italian bakery, you need lard.

You will also need a 6-inch, ¾-inch to 1 diameter, wooden dowel.

If all of this seems like too much trouble, you can purchase cannoli shells (see Sources, page 239) and fill them with the Cannoli Cream (page 185).

MAKES 10 CANNOLI

1 cup all-purpose flour, plus more for flouring dough and work surface
3 tablespoons granulated sugar
2 tablespoons leaf lard (see Sources, page 239), plus several cups for frying; may be replaced with vegetable shortening, exact amount will depend on size of your pot
2 tablespoons distilled white vinegar
2 extra-large eggs
¼ teaspoon cinnamon
¼ teaspoon fine sea salt
3 cups Cannoli Cream (recipe follows)
Powdered (10x) sugar for dusting cannolis

1. Put the flour, granulated sugar, 2 tablespoons of the lard, vinegar, 1 egg, cinnamon, and salt into a stand mixer fitted with the hook attachment and mix on low-medium speed until well combined, approximately 10 minutes. (There is no need to stop the motor to scrape the sides because this dough will pull together into a ball when it's ready.)

2. Remove the dough from the bowl, wrap it in plastic wrap and let rest at room temperature for at least 30 minutes or up to 3 hours, to soften the dough and make it less elastic.

3. Lightly coat the dough with flour and roll it through a pasta machine set to the thickest setting (usually number 1). If you do not have a pasta machine, use a rolling pin to roll the dough out as thin as possible on a lightly floured surface, to no more than $\frac{1}{8}$-inch thick. Cut 5-inch-long ovals from the dough (*see* How To). Gather up the excess dough, knead it together, roll it out, and cut ovals again. You should have 10 ovals.

4. Wrap 1 oval lengthwise around the dowel. Be very careful to wrap it loosely, leaving a little space between the dowel and the pastry dough so that, when fried, the inside will be cooked as well.

5. Beat the remaining egg in a small bowl and use a pastry brush to paint one end of the shell with the egg. Pull the egg-brushed end over the opposite end, and press them together, sealing the shell around the dowel.

6. Line a large plate or platter with paper towels.

7. Fill a wide, deep, heavy pot two-thirds full of lard and set over medium-high heat. Heat the lard to a temperature of 350°F to 375°F.

8. Carefully lower the dowel into the oil and let shell fry until golden brown, turning it with a slotted spoon as it fries, approximately 10 minutes. Use the spoon to carefully remove the dowel from the lard and transfer to the paper-towel-lined plate to cool.

9. When the shell is cool enough to touch, approximately 10 minutes, pull the dowel out.

(*Continued on next page*)

Cannoli (*cont.*)

10. Repeat steps 8 and 9 until all shells have been fried and removed from the dowel. (The shells may be held in an airtight container at room temperature for up to 3 months; I urge you to not fill the cannoli more than 1 hour before serving: They may become soggy.)

11. When ready to fill and serve the cannoli, put the pastry cream into a pastry bag fitted with the #7 plain tip. Pipe filling into each shell until it is filled and the cream sticks out both ends.

12. Dust the finished cannoli with powdered sugar and serve.

How to make the trademark cannoli shape: Use a 4-inch round cookie cutter (or the mouth of a 4-inch bowl) to punch circles out of the dough, and press the circles in from the sides with your hands to squish them into ovals.

Cannoli Cream

This is the classic ricotta-based filling for cannoli. It's also wonderful as a cake filling (see page 212).

If you can find cocoa drops, replace the chocolate chips with them; they are made specifically for cannoli cream.

MAKES ABOUT 3 CUPS

2 cups fresh ricotta
⅔ cup granulated sugar
¼ teaspoon cinnamon
⅓ cup semisweet chocolate chips

1. Put the ricotta, sugar, and cinnamon in the bowl of a stand mixer fitted with the paddle attachment. (If you don't have a stand mixer you can use a hand blender fitted with the blending attachments.) Paddle on low to medium speed until the sugar is completely dissolved, 2 to 3 minutes. (The best way to tell if it's dissolved is to taste the mixture until you don't detect any graininess.) Take care not to overmix, or the mixture will become soft and runny.
2. Add the chips and paddle just until evenly distributed, approximately 30 seconds. Stop to keep from breaking up the chips.
3. Use the cream immediately or refrigerate in an airtight container for up to 5 days.

St. Joseph's Zeppole

(Sfingi)

This seasonal specialty was, and still is, offered at Carlo's from mid-January until St. Joseph's Day, on March 19. (In Italy, they are known as bignè di S. Giuseppe and are prepared in the same way that we make them at Carlo's.) I used to help my father make them, manning the fryer while he piped the zeppole. (These St. Joseph's Zeppole are related to the popular street-fair treats in name only; street-fair zeppole are fried dough dusted with powdered sugar and served piping hot.)

Making these requires a two-step frying process: a cold pot, with the oil at a relatively cold 225°F, and a hot pot, with the oil at 350°F to 375°F. When working with my father, I would lower the piped-out dough into the cold oil by first arranging them on a split-open sugar bag, then lowering the bag, and knocking the zeppole off with a stick. After about ten minutes, they would puff up to twice their size, at which point I'd fish them out with a spider (straining wand), drain them, and transfer them to the hot pot, where they fried again. Then we'd drain them again, cut them in half, and pipe them full of Cannoli Cream.

These are never better than when they are right out of the fryer, so fill them and eat them as soon as they are cool enough to handle. They are also delicious filled with Italian Custard Cream (page 234).

MAKES 12 ZEPPOLE

1 cup water
6 tablespoons leaf lard (see Sources, page 239), plus several cups for
    frying, and greasing wax paper (vegetable shortening can be sub-

stituted, but I believe you should try to use lard for zeppole and cannoli)
⅛ teaspoon fine sea salt
1¼ cups all-purpose flour
4 extra-large eggs
3 cups Cannoli Cream (page 185)
Powdered (10x) sugar, for dusting zeppole
12 maraschino cherries, optional

1. Put the water, 6 tablespoons of the lard, and salt in a heavy saucepan and bring to a boil over high heat. Add the flour and stir with a wooden spoon until the ingredients come together into a smooth, uniform dough, approximately 2 minutes.

2. Transfer the mixture to the bowl of a stand mixer fitted with the paddle attachment. (If you don't have a stand mixer you can use a hand mixer fitted with the blending attachments.) Start paddling on low speed, then add the eggs, one at a time, until thoroughly absorbed, mixing for 1 minute between each egg, stopping the motor periodically to scrape down the sides and bottom of the bowl with a rubber spatula. Finish with the final egg and mix for an additional 2 minutes.

3. Grease three 8 inch-x-8-inch pieces of wax paper lightly with lard.

4. Transfer the dough to a pastry bag fitted with the #7 star tip. Pipe 4 circles, each about 2 inches in diameter, a few inches apart on each sheet of wax paper. If using a reusable bag, wash out and dry it, fit it with a #7 star tip again, and fill with the Cannoli Cream. Otherwise, fit a new bag with the #7 star tip and fill with Cannoli Cream.

5. Put enough lard into a wide, heavy pot to fill it about 8 inches high, set it over medium-high heat and heat until the lard melts and reaches a tem-

(Continued on next page)

St. Joseph's Zeppole (*cont.*)

perature of 225°F. (This is the cold pot.) In another wide, heavy pot, add enough lard to fill the pot about 8 inches high. Set over medium-high heat until the lard melts and reaches a temperature of 350°F to 375°F. (This is the hot pot.)

6. Working with one piece of wax paper at a time, carefully lower the zeppole from one piece into the cold pot (they will stick to the lard) and gently knock them off with a wooden spoon, taking care not to splash hot oil. Fry until they puff up to about double their size, approximately 10 minutes. Use a straining wand or slotted spoon to lift them out one at a time, letting any excess oil return to the pot, and transfer to the hot pot. Let fry in the hot pot until they are golden brown and crispy, 4 to 5 minutes per side, turning them over carefully with the slotted spoon after the first side is done.

7. Remove the zeppole from the oil with a slotted spoon and drain on paper towels. As soon as they are cool enough to handle, approximately 5 minutes, cut them in half horizontally with a serrated knife. Pipe Cannoli Cream over the bottom half, set the top half on top. Pipe some cream into the hole. Dust with powdered sugar and set a cherry on top of the cream in the center, if desired.

8. These will never be as good as they are when eaten right away, but they can be kept in an airtight container in the refrigerator for up to 2 days.

Tiramisu

This popular Italian dessert was a standard offering at most of the Venetian hours we catered at the halls and country clubs in the area. In the Valastro family, we refer to it as the Italian pick-me-up because it has such huge quantities of sugar and caffeine.

SERVES 6 TO 8

1 cup brewed espresso
1 cup granulated sugar
¼ cup plus 1 tablespoon coffee liqueur
4 extra-large egg yolks
1 pound mascarpone cheese
2 tablespoons sweet marsala
1 cup heavy cream
40 store-bought ladyfingers
¼ cup cocoa powder (see page 157)

1. Put the espresso, ½ cup of the sugar, and ¼ cup of the coffee liqueur into a heavy saucepan, and bring to a simmer over medium-high heat. Whisk until the sugar dissolves, 3 to 4 minutes. Remove the pan from the heat and let the syrup cool.

2. Put the yolks, marscapone, marsala, remaining ½ cup sugar, and remaining 1 tablespoon of coffee liqueur in the bowl of a stand mixer fitted with the whip attachment and whip on medium speed until light and

(Continued on next page)

Tiramisu (*cont.*)

airy, approximately 7 minutes. (If you don't have a stand mixer, you can use a hand mixer fitted with the whip attachments.) Transfer the mixture to another bowl and clean and dry the stand mixer bowl and the whip attachment, returning them both to the mixer.

3. Put the cream in the bowl of the stand mixer and whip until stiff peaks form. Gently fold the cream mixture into the marsala mixture.

4. One by one, dip the ladyfingers in the espresso syrup and arrange a layer in the bottom of a 12 inch-x 8-inch pan. Spoon a layer of cream over the ladyfingers. Dip and arrange another layer of ladyfingers over the cream, with the second layer perpendicular to the first. Spoon the remaining cream over the top.

5. Dust the tiramisu with cocoa powder. Cover loosely with plastic wrap and refrigerate for at least 2 hours, or up to 3 days. To serve, use a kitchen spoon to scoop out portions into small bowls or glass dishes.

Pies

∾

IN TERMS OF BOTH baking and eating, pies fall somewhere between pastry and cake. They are meant to be sliced and shared, so are ideal for get-togethers, but aren't quite as special or rarefied as a cake. They're also relatively simple to make: Once you master the dough, you can pretty much make any pie that strikes your fancy.

I've heard from a number of home cooks that they find pie-making intimidating, usually because of the crust. There's really nothing to fear. Baking's like anything else; the more you do of it, the better you get. If you just can't get your pies to come out right, you can always—even for the recipes in this book—use a store-bought pie shell.

I've tried in this chapter to share some of my favorite American and Italian pies, bringing both sides of my heritage, and that of Carlo's, to your kitchen.

Crostata

As Lisa and I fell in love, I realized that she loved something else as well: Nutella, the chocolate-hazelnut spread. I devised this adaptation of a crostata, *one of the traditional desserts we used to offer in our original location on Adams Street, for her, filling it with Nutella.*

You can also blind bake the Pasta Frolla *and fill it with jams such as apricot or raspberry. If you do that, use only all-purpose flour in the dough.*

You will need a 10-inch fluted tart from with a removable bottom.

MAKES ONE 10-INCH PIE

*Pasta Frolla (page 197), made by replacing the pistachio flour with
    hazelnut flour, or with only all-purpose flour
All-purpose flour, for flouring a work surface
One 26½ ounce jar Nutella
Few tablespoons of coarse crystal or rock sugar, for dusting the top of the
    crostata*

1. Position a rack in the center of the oven and preheat the oven to 350°F.
2. If the *Pasta Frolla* has been refrigerated, remove it from the refrigerator. Lightly flour a work surface. Set aside about one-quarter of the dough for lattice, and roll out the remaining dough in a circle, about ½ inch thick and 16 inches in diameter. (*See* Note, page 193.)
3. Roll the dough up onto the rolling pin (*see* How To, page 196), and transfer to a 10-inch fluted tart pan with a removable bottom, unspooling it over the top. Tap the pan on the counter and the dough will fall into place. Put your hands at the 2 o'clock and 10 o'clock positions on

the side of the pan, and rotate from just under the lip to cause the excess dough to fall away; add it to the dough you set aside for lattice.

4. Fill the shell with Nutella, using a rubber spatula to spread it evenly.

5. Roll the remaining dough out into to a rectangle 12 inches x 8 inches, and ¼ inch thick. Cut into six ¾-inch-wide strips using a pizza cutter or sharp knife. Make a lattice pattern on the pie starting in the center. Put the next strip midway between the center and one outer edge, and repeat on the other side. Turn the pie about one-third around and lay the remaining 3 strips at even intervals at a slight angle.

6. Put water in a spray bottle and spray it lightly over the top of the *crostata*. Sprinkle the sugar over the top; the water will help it to adhere.

7. Bake the *crostata* in the oven until the lattice strips are golden brown and the Nutella has risen slightly and feels dense to the touch in the center, 25 to 30 minutes.

8. Remove the pan from the oven and let cool for 1 to 2 hours. Slice into pieces and serve, or keep in an airtight container at room temperature for up to 4 days.

Note: You can also use this recipe to make 12 small *crostata* (2 inches in diameter). If doing this, skip the lattice and bake for 15 to 20 minutes.

Ricotta Pie
(Torta di Ricotta)

This classic Italian dessert is made by filling Pasta Frolla *(Italian short dough) with a rich, ricotta filling that gets a nice, citrus lift from lemon zest and orange-blossom water. The recipe goes back to Old Man Carlo, and it came with the bakery, handed down to my dad, along with the keys to the door. In Italy, the dessert is especially popular at Easter and Christmas.*

The quality of the ricotta in this pie is very important. At the bakery, we still get fresh ricotta delivered from a farm in Lebanon, New Jersey, in three-pound tin cans packed on ice, the same way they used to come to the bakery years ago. You can get away with a supermarket brand (no light or low-fat ricotta, please), but if there's an Italian market in your town or a Little Italy, it's worth a trip to procure some creamy, freshly prepared, ricotta to make this right.

Orange-blossom water is also crucial; along with the ricotta, it really gives this pie its essence and subtly relieves the richness of the cheese.

MAKES ONE 9-INCH PIE, ENOUGH TO SERVE 8 TO 10

1 pound fresh ricotta
1 cup granulated sugar
3 tablespoons orange-blossom water (see Sources, page 239)
½ teaspoon finely grated lemon zest
3 extra-large eggs, at room temperature
Pasta Frolla *(Italian short dough), recipe follows*
All-purpose flour, for flouring work surface

1. Position a rack in the center of the oven and preheat the oven to 365°F.

2. To make the filling, put the ricotta, sugar, orange-blossom water, and lemon zest in a mixing bowl. Wash and dry your hands. With immaculately clean hands, work the ingredients together until you feel all the sugar evaporate into the ricotta (the graininess will disappear). Add 1 egg at a time and work in with your fingers until thoroughly absorbed and the mixture is smooth. Wash and dry your hands again.

3. If the *Pasta Frolla* has been refrigerated, remove it from the refrigerator. Lightly flour a work surface. Set aside about one-quarter of the dough for the lattice, and roll out the remaining dough in a circle, about 14 inches in diameter (*see* How To, page 196) and about ¼ inch thick. Roll it up onto the rolling pin (*see* How To, page 196), and transfer to a 9-inch pie pan, unspooling it over the top. Tap the pan gently on the counter and the dough will fall into place. Put your hands at the 2 o'clock and 10 o'clock positions on the side of the pan, and rotate the pan from just under the lip to cause the excess dough to fall away; add it to the dough you set aside for the lattice.

4. Pour the filling into the center of the *Pasta Frolla*–lined pan, using a rubber spatula to get as much filling as possible out of the bowl.

5. Roll the remaining dough out into to a rectangle 12 inches x 8 inches, and ¼ inch thick. Cut into six ¾-inch-wide strips using a pizza cutter or sharp knife. Make a lattice pattern on the pie starting in the center. Put the next strip midway between the center and one outer edge, and repeat on the other side. Rotate the pan about 120 degrees and lay the remaining 3 strips at even intervals at a slight angle.

6. Bake the pie until the lattice strips are golden brown and the filling has risen slightly and feels dense to the touch in the center, 45 minutes to 1 hour.

(Continued on next page)

Ricotta Pie (*cont.*)

7. Remove the pan from the oven, and let cool for 1 to 2 hours. Serve right away or refrigerate, covered loosely with plastic wrap. The pie can be refrigerated for 4 to 5 days, and served cold or at room temperature.

How to Roll Pastry onto a Rolling Pin: Put the rolling pin at the far side of the dough and use your fingers to coil it around the pin, then simply roll it up onto the pin.

How to Measure for a Pie Tin without a Ruler: If you don't have a ruler in the kitchen, invert your pie pan over the dough, centering it, making sure you have a 2-inch border of dough around the pan. (You can eyeball 2 inches much more accurately than the 14 inches mentioned in the recipe.)

Pasta Frolla

(Italian Short Dough)

This is the Italian short dough, used to make a variety of pastries including pasticiotti *(small custard-filled tarts) and* Crostata *(page 192).*

MAKES 2 TARTS OR 2 CROSTATA

1 cup (2 sticks) unsalted butter, softened at room temperature
1 cup granulated sugar
1/2 teaspoon finely grated lemon zest
1/2 teaspoon pure vanilla extract
1/2 teaspoon honey, preferably clover
1/8 teaspoon baker's ammonia (see Safety Note, page 163, and Sources, page 239)
1/4 cup room-temperature water
1 1/2 cups all-purpose flour, plus more for flouring work surface
1/2 cup pistachio flour (page 165), or additional 1/2 cup all-purpose flour

1. Put the butter, sugar, lemon zest, vanilla, honey, and baker's ammonia in the bowl of a stand mixer fitted with the paddle attachment and paddle on low speed just until the ingredients are coated in butter, a few seconds, then raise the speed to low-medium and continue to mix until smooth, approximately 1 minute.

(Continued on next page)

Pasta Frolla (*cont.*)

2. With the motor running, pour in the water in a thin stream and paddle until thoroughly combined, approximately 1 minute.
3. Stop the motor, and pour the all-purpose flour and pistachio flour into the center of the bowl. Paddle on low speed for about 10 rotations. Stop the motor, scrape down the sides of the bowl with a rubber spatula, then paddle until the ingredients come together into a uniform dough, 30 seconds to 1 minute.
4. Scrape the dough onto a piece of plastic wrap, bundle, and refrigerate until ready to use. (You can refrigerate the dough for up to 1 week, or freeze for up to 2 months.)

Pumpkin Pie

This is the pumpkin pie that was sold at Carlo's Bakery on Adams Street. It seemed out of place among the Italian specialties but, every Thanksgiving, the store sold an incredible number of them; a touching sign that, while most of our customers held fast to their cultural roots back in Italy, they also embraced the traditions of their adopted country.

MAKES ONE 9-INCH PIE, ENOUGH TO SERVE 10 TO 12

1 can (15 ounces) pumpkin puree (I like Libby's Pure Pumpkin)
¾ cup granulated sugar
1½ teaspoons cornstarch
½ teaspoon fine sea salt
1 teaspoon ground cinnamon
¼ teaspoon ground cloves
¼ teaspoon ground ginger
¼ teaspoon ground nutmeg
¼ teaspoon ground allspice
¼ teaspoon ground mace
1 teaspoon pure vanilla extract
1½ cups whole milk
2 extra-large eggs, at room temperature
1 unbaked 9-inch pie crust, store bought or homemade (page 201)

1. Position a rack in the center of the oven and preheat the oven to 450°F.

(Continued on next page)

Pumpkin Pie (*cont.*)

2. Put the pumpkin, sugar, cornstarch, salt, cinnamon, cloves, ginger, nut-meg, allspice, mace, and vanilla in the bowl of a stand mixer fitted with the paddle attachment. Paddle at low-medium speed for approximately 2 minutes.

3. With the motor running, pour in the milk in 2 additions. Stop the motor, scrape the sides of the bowl with a wooden spatula, restart, and paddle for and additional 2 minutes. Add the eggs and paddle until absorbed, approximately 2 additional minutes.

4. Pour the mixture into a 9-inch pie crust in a pan, and bake for 15 min-utes, then the lower heat to 375°F, and bake until a finger dabbed onto the surface emerges clean, 30 to 40 minutes.

5. Remove the pie from the oven and let cool for 1 to 2 hours. Slice and serve right away, or cover with plastic and refrigerate for up to 3 days.

Pie Crust

There's nothing wrong with buying a prepared pie crust, but it's so easy to make your own, that I urge you to do so whenever possible.

MAKES ONE 9-INCH PIE CRUST

2 cups all-purpose flour, plus more for flouring work surface
¾ cup vegetable shortening
1 tablespoon granulated sugar
1 teaspoon fine sea salt
7 tablespoons ice-cold water (if making in the summer, use 6 table-
  spoons to account for increased humidity affecting the moisture
  content of the flour)

1. Put the flour, shortening, sugar, and salt in the bowl of a stand mixer fitted with the paddle attachment and paddle at lowest speed just until the mixture holds together, approximately 30 seconds. (If you don't have a stand mixer, you can put the ingredients in a bowl and blend with a hand mixer fitted with the blending attachments.) Add 6 tablespoons water, and paddle until absorbed, approximately 30 seconds.
2. Transfer the dough to a piece of plastic wrap and refrigerate for 30 to 60 minutes.
3. Lightly flour a work surface, and roll out the dough in a circle, about 14 inches in diameter (*see* How To, page 196) and about ¼ inch thick. Roll it up onto the rolling pin (*see* How To, page 196), and transfer

(*Continued on next page*)

Pie Crust (*cont.*)

to a 9-inch pie pan, unspooling it over the top. Tap the pan gently on the counter and the dough will fall into place. Put your hands at the 2 o'clock and 10 o'clock positions on the side of the pan, and rotate the pan from just under the lip to cause the excess dough to fall away. (If molded to an aluminum pie pan, the dough can be wrapped in plastic and frozen for up to 2 months. Let thaw to room temperature before filling and baking.)

How to blind bake: If you need to bake the crust with no filling, fill the pie with dry beans or rice, or set another pie pan in the well, invert, and bake on the center rack of an oven preheated to 350°F until the crust is firm and golden, approximately 25 minutes.

Banana Cream Pie

This is one of the classics of American baking that we began to offer after moving to Washington Street. By all means express yourself by how you slice and arrange the bananas and pipe the whipped cream; there are not a lot of ingredients in this recipe, so you should make the most out of each of them.

MAKES ONE 9-INCH PIE

Italian Custard Cream (page 234)
Italian Whipped Cream (page 205)
3 large bananas
1 baked 9-inch pie shell (page 201), or store-bought pie shell, blind baked
Juice of 1 large lemon
1 large strawberry, optional

1. Put the custard in a mixing bowl and use a rubber spatula to fold in half the whipped cream, making a French cream.
2. Peel 2 of the bananas and slice them crosswise over the French cream, so the slices fall into the cream.
3. Transfer the banana cream to the shell, using a rubber spatula to scrape as much cream out of the bowl as possible and then level it off in the pie crust.
4. Transfer the remaining whipped cream into a pastry bag fitted with the #7 star tip and pipe blobs of cream all over the pie. Peel the remaining

(*Continued on next page*)

Banana Cream Pie (*cont.*)

banana and slice it crosswise on an angle into 8 pieces. Put the pieces in a bowl, drizzle the lemon juice over them, and gently toss to coat them with lemon juice and prevent them from oxidizing. Arrange the banana slices at even intervals around the perimeter of the pie.

5. If using the strawberry, slice decoratively position it in the center of the pie.

How to hide oxidized bananas: The lemon juice in this recipe will keep the bananas from oxidizing, but for good measure (and more flavor), consider topping the pie with chocolate cake crumbs (page 213), processed chocolate cookies, or by grating a few ounces of semisweet chocolate over it. You can also pour warm Chocolate Ganache (page 237) over each banana.

Italian Whipped Cream

MAKES ABOUT 2½ CUPS

1½ cups heavy cream
¼ cup plus 2 tablespoons granulated sugar

1. Put the cream and sugar in a bowl and whip with on high speed with a hand mixer fitted with the blending attachments. Do not overmix or you'll end up with butter.
2. The cream can be refrigerated in an airtight container for up to 3 days. Whip by hand to refresh before using.

Chocolate Cream Pie

This is the other all-American dessert that was offered at Carlo's Bakery on Adams Street, although it was made with the shop's distinctly Italian-style custard cream.

MAKES ONE 9-INCH PIE

One 9-inch pie shell, homemade (page 201) or store bought
Chocolate Custard Cream (page 234)
Italian Whipped Cream (page 205)

1. Blind bake the pie crust according to the instructions on page 202, finishing by baking the crust with nothing inside it for an additional 10 minutes, or until golden brown. Let cool thoroughly at room temperature for 2 to 3 hours.
2. Pour the Chocolate Custard Cream into the pie shell, smoothing it with a rubber spatula.
3. Put the whipped cream in a pastry bag fitted with the #7 star tip and make a tic-tac-to pattern over the top of the pie, then pipe a loop border around the perimeter. (If you don't want to use a pastry bag, you can skip the pattern and border and simply apply whipped cream over the top with a spatula.)
4. Slice into portions and serve at once or cover loosely with plastic wrap and refrigerate. It will keep for up to 3 days, after which the pie will become soggy.

Carlo's Cakes and Cupcakes

YOU MAY NEVER USE a cake mix again!

My goal with the following recipes is to show you how easy it can be to make great cakes from scratch. I've selected a few simple recipes for this chapter—Carlo's Bake Shop's Greatest Hits. Many of them are the ones you've read about in this book, and the ones we have customers choose from in our now-famous consultations.

You'll also find a handful of the most popular frostings and an adaptable recipe for making syrups for soaking sponge cakes, as well as my tips for trimming, filling, and frosting cakes. As for which frostings and fillings to use with which cakes, let your imagination be your guide: Mix and match these recipes as you like and create your own signature cakes at home.

GENERAL CAKE-MAKING TIPS
AND TECHNIQUES

Here are my tips for executing steps called for repeatedly in the cake recipes, and some general advice you should follow or keep in mind when baking and working with cakes.

TO GREASE AND FLOUR A CAKE PAN

To flour a cake pan, first grease with a thin, even layer of unsalted butter, nonstick cooking spray, or vegetable oil, just to lightly coat it. Add a small fistful of flour (about ¼ cup) to the center of the pan, tip the pan on its side, and rotate the pan to coat the inside with flour. Tap the pan gently on your work surface to loosen the excess flour, and return the excess to your flour container. Tap again and discard any lingering flour into the sink or garbage can.

FREEZING CAKES

Freezing sometimes gets a bad rap in the food world because people associate it with TV dinners and frozen pizzas. However, there are times when a freezer can be your best friend. I don't insist on it in the recipes, but freezing a freshly baked and cooled cake is one of the best things you can do. It seals in all the moisture, whereas cakes tend to dry out in the refrigerator. Also, if you plan to ice and/or decorate a cake, it will be firmer when it emerges from the freezer, and you'll have an easier time trimming, halving, and icing it. Cakes should be frozen for one to two hours for optimum trimming texture. You can freeze them for longer, but they will become very hard and should be allowed to thaw slightly before you try to cut into them; do not try to trim a cake that's hard as a rock because the knife can slip, which is dangerous. Be sure the cake has a little give to it before trimming.

WHEN IN DOUBT, *SCRAPE*

Bakers have a saying: "Bakers scrape." By that, I mean that when you're mixing in a stand mixer, some ingredients can collect at the bottom and sides of the bowl and not be fully incorporated into whatever it is that you're mixing. Many of the recipes in this section include instructions to stop the motor and scrape the bowl, but if you're ever in doubt, don't wait for me to give you permission—stop that motor and scrape those sides.

TRIMMING AND CUTTING THE CAKE

All cakes must be trimmed before decorating them. Use a serrated knife to remove the top layer of discolored "skin." Because it makes the cake easier to cut evenly, I like to work with a frozen cake (*see* page 208).

If the cake you're making requires you to cut the cake in half horizontally, first set the cake on your work surface. Kneel or bend so that the cake is at eye level and get a good, accurate look at it. Keep your eye fixed on the point where the knife enters the cake, and applying pressure with your free hand to the top, rotate the cake against the knife, keeping it straight to get a nice, even cut. If you will be filling a cake, try to make the layers level with each other, trimming if necessary so that they rest straight when stacked.

The Turntable: A Decorator's Best Friend

If you plan to pipe cakes or cupcakes, a turntable is an absolutely essential piece of equipment. You need a good, sturdy, stainless-steel professional-caliber turntable, such as those manufactured by Bakery Crafts (*see* Sources, page 239). The reason a turntable is so important is that when using a pastry bag on a cake, your arm doesn't move. Turn clockwise or counterclockwise, whichever is easier.

FILLING AND ICING CAKES

I like to use a pastry bag to fill cakes because it's the right tool no matter what filling or frosting you are using. If you're using a thick cream for a filling, using a spatula might cause the cake to break. Similarly, a soaked sponge cake will come apart with very little provocation. Using a pastry bag minimizes the amount of spreading and scraping required to neatly fill and ice a cake.

FILLING CAKES

To fill a cake using a pastry bag, fit the bag with the #6 plain tip. Set the first layer of cake on the turntable. Apply steady pressure to pipe the filling in

The Hand of the Bag: Piping Fillings and Frostings

When you use a pastry bag, you should fill it about two-thirds full, being sure to squeeze the contents as far down into the bag as possible so they can be forced out of the tip with just the slightest pressure.

Try to develop the ability to use a pastry bag with one hand, resting the weighty, full part of the bag on your forearm and leaning the back of the bag against your upper arm or shoulder. This will keep one hand free for turning a turntable or performing other tasks.

Using a pastry bag effectively is all about pressure. Generally speaking, when you use

the bag, you will use either apply steady pressure, for long lines, or piping filling and/or frosting, or a pulsating pressure for creating borders and shapes.

There are four main pressure techniques for decorating with a pastry bag: squeeze and pull, steady pressure, steady pressure and movement, and pulse. For filling and frosting cakes, the technique called for is steady pressure, which involves squeezing the bag for a sustained period of a few seconds to produce a continuous line or circle of frosting or cream, such as the filling for an éclair.

concentric circles, stopping to lift the bag after completing each circle. After the layer is covered with frosting circles, use your cake icing spatula to gently smooth it out into an even layer. Carefully set the next layer on top, gently pressing down to ensure it's nice and level, then lay down the next layer of filling in the same manner.

ICING (FROSTING) CAKES

Before icing a cake, double check to be sure the layers are nice and straight and aligned, and be sure the cake is centered on your turntable. Even a four-layer cake should have the same shape as an uncut cake. If necessary, trim the layers to level them, or use a little extra icing under uneven layers to straighten them. As Jimmy Lee used to say to me, "If the cake already looks even before you've touched it, that's half the battle."

Put the frosting in a pastry bag fitted with a #7 star tip.

Not Filling, Soaking

As their name suggests, Italian sponge cakes are made to be soaked with a syrup (*see* page 236), which they drink up . . . well, like a sponge. They are dense, dry cakes that really aren't complete until they've been soaked.

To soak a sponge cake, use a pastry brush to generously apply the syrup to the cake, pausing periodically to let the cake soak it up. You might be surprised how much syrup a cake can take on. The vanilla sponge recipe in this chapter can absorb the entire syrup recipe on page 236.

If layering a sponge cake do not apply the syrup to the layers until the layers are on the cake; they will break if you try to lift them after soaking.

A sponge cake will deepen in flavor during a day or two in the refrigerator. Store it there, on a plate, covered loosely with plastic wrap.

Spinning the turntable, apply steady pressure to the bag to pipe concentric circles on top of the cake, stopping and lifting the bag between circles. Then, also spinning the table, pipe frosting around the sides, starting at the top and working your way down.

Use a cake-icing spatula to smooth the circles on top of the cake together, by holding the spatula parallel to the cake top, and spinning the turntable, gradually lowering the surface of the spatula close to the cake. Turn your knife perpendicular to the cake and smooth the sides, again gradually moving the spatula closer to the cake.

Finally, while spinning the turntable, hold the spatula parallel to the top of the cake and lower it just to smooth the top one final time, leaving it nice and straight and ready to be decorated.

Ratios of Cake to Filling

The appropriate balance of flavors and textures varies from cake to cake, but there are some guidelines that apply most of the time.

Chocolate Ganache (page 237), Italian Buttercream (page 232), Vanilla Frosting (page 230), Chocolate Fudge Frosting (page 231), and Cream Cheese Frosting (page 235) are all rather dense and rich, so the proper ratio is of filling to cake is 1:2, meaning a layer of filling should be approximately half the height of a layer of cake.

Italian Custard Cream (page 234), Cannoli Cream (page 185), Italian Whipped Cream (page 205), Lobster Tail Cream (page 178), and My Dad's Chocolate Mousse (page 236) are relatively airy and do not threaten to overwhelm the flavor or texture of the cake, so the proper ratio filling to cake is 1:1, meaning a layer of filling should be approximately the same height as a layer of cake.

Cake, Cupcake, Filling, and Frosting Recipes

❧

MANY OF THESE RECIPES feature a yield for cupcakes as well. Bake cupcakes at 360°F to prevent them from crowning.

Why Two Cakes?

Note that many of the cake recipes produce two 9-inch cakes. This is because you will generally want to use the cakes as layers, and this will provide you with two layers while saving you the need to halve the cakes. (To produce three-layer cakes, cut both cakes in half. This will leave you with an extra half cake; pulse it in a food processor to make crumbs for coating the outside of a frosted cake, or save it for snacking.)

Because it is not generally layered, the recipe for sponge cake produces a single cake.

Vanilla Cake

This is a home-cook-friendly version of the recipe I adapted from my father's old formula for an American-style vanilla cake. At home, as at Carlo's Bake Shop, it will produce the same moist cake and perfect grain every time.

The custard cream is optional. If you want the cake to be supermoist and dense, you need it, but it will be delicious without it. (It doesn't affect the yield very much because the custard itself doesn't rise.) You might be surprised to learn that I use vegetable oil to take the place of the liquid shortening we use at the bakery, but it replicates the effects better than I ever could have imagined before testing recipes for this book.

Use this cake as the basis for everything from birthday cakes to strawberry shortcake.

Be sure the batter is at the indicated temperature before baking or the cake will crown and crack.

MAKES TWO 9-INCH CAKES OR 24 CUPCAKES

2½ cups cake flour, plus more for flouring the cake pans
2 cups sugar, plus more for unmolding cake
2 cups Italian Custard Cream (page 234), optional
¾ cup vegetable oil
2¼ teaspoons baking powder
1 teaspoon pure vanilla extract
½ teaspoon fine sea salt
4 extra-large eggs, at room temperature
1 cup whole milk

Unsalted butter, for greasing two cake pans (about 2 tablespoons); non-stick cooking spray or vegetable oil may be substituted

1. Position a rack in the center of the oven, and preheat the oven to 350°F.

2. Put the flour, sugar, custard cream, if using, vegetable oil, baking powder, vanilla, and salt in the bowl of a stand mixer fitted with the paddle attachment. (If you don't have a stand mixer, you can put the ingredients in a bowl, and use a hand mixer with the blending attachments, but take extra care to not overmix.) Mix on slow just until the ingredients are blended together, a few seconds, then raise the speed to low-medium and continue to mix until smooth, approximately 1 additional minute.

3. With the motor running, add 1 egg at a time, adding the next one after the previous one has been absorbed into the mixture. Stop the motor periodically and scrape the bowl from the bottom with a rubber spatula to integrate the ingredients, and return the mixer to low-medium speed. After all the eggs are added, continue to mix for an additional minute to ensure the eggs have been thoroughly mixed in. This will help guarantee that the sugar is dissolved and that the flour has been thoroughly mixed in, which will help produce a luxurious mouthfeel in the final cake.

4. With the motor running, add the milk, ½ cup at a time, stopping the motor to scrape the sides and bottom between the two additions. Continue to mix for another minute or until the mixture appears smooth. Before baking, be sure the batter is at 70°F to 73°F, or the cake will crown. (Test by plunging a kitchen thermometer into the center of the batter; if it is too warm, put the bowl in the refrigerator for a few minutes; if too cool, let it rest at room temperature.)

5. Grease two 9-inch cake pans (2 inches high) with the butter, and flour them (*see* page 208).

(*Continued on next page*)

Vanilla Cake (*cont.*)

6. Divide the batter evenly between the two cake pans, using a rubber spatula to scrape down the bowl and get as much batter as possible out. Bake until the cake begins to pull from the sides of the pan and is springy to the touch, 25 to 30 minutes.

7. Remove the cakes from the oven and let cool for at least 30 minutes, preferably an hour. The cakes should be at room temperature before you remove them from the pan. Put a piece of parchment paper on a cookie sheet, top with sugar, and one at a time, turn the pans over and turn the cakes out onto parchment; the sugar will keep it from sticking. Refrigerate or freeze (*see* page 208) until ready to decorate.

Crumb Cake

Our crumb cake is legendary, but I have to give credit where it's due: Just like the ricotta pie recipe was handed down to my dad by Old Man Carlo, this recipe was inherited from the original owners of Schoning's. It has a number of loyal fans. Perhaps the most passionate aficionado was a New Jersey native who, hospitalized with cancer in California, asked his daughter to have our crumb cake delivered cross country as a pick-me-up. Mauro personally saw to the request, FedExing the cake, and the story became the subject of a newspaper article that's mounted and hangs next to the counter at Carlo's, a constant reminder of the special place our baked goods hold in the lives of our customers.

MAKES TWO 9-INCH CRUMB CAKES

2½ cups vegetable shortening
1¼ cups light-brown sugar
¼ cup plus 1 tablespoon granulated sugar
1½ teaspoons fine sea salt
1½ teaspoons ground cinnamon
1½ teaspoons baking powder
2¾ cups all-purpose flour
1 recipe Vanilla Cake (page 214), in two pans, ready to bake

1. Position a rack in the center of the oven and preheat the oven to 350°F.
2. Put the shortening, light brown sugar, granulated sugar, salt, cinnamon, and baking powder in the bowl of a stand mixer fitted with the paddle

(Continued on next page)

Crumb Cake (*cont.*)

attachment. Paddle until the ingredients come together, approximately 3 minutes. With the motor running, add the flour and mix until the flour has been absorbed into the mixture and is thoroughly moistened but the mixture remains chunky, 3 to 4 minutes. The mixture will look like a crumb topping.

3. Top the cake with the crumb mixture and bake until the crumbs are golden and the cake is spongy, 20 to 25 minutes.

4. Remove from the oven and let cool slightly, approximately 10 minutes. Serve warm or at room temperature. The can be held in an airtight container at room temperature for 2 to 3 days.

Chocolate Cake

This is adapted from our house chocolate cake recipe at Carlo's, which is also our devil's food cake. The buttermilk is the key to its texture, a secret shared with us by Old Man Mike.

MAKES TWO 9-INCH CAKES, OR 24 CUPCAKES

1½ cups cake flour, plus more for flouring the cake pans
1½ cups sugar
8 tablespoons (1 stick) unsalted butter, softened at room temperature
⅓ cup cocoa
1 teaspoon baking soda
¼ teaspoon baking powder
⅓ cup melted unsweetened Baker's chocolate
½ cup hot water
2 extra-large eggs, at room temperature
½ cup buttermilk
Unsalted butter, for greasing two cake pans (about 2 tablespoons);
   nonstick cooking spray or vegetable oil may be substituted

1. Position a rack in the center of the oven, and preheat the oven to 350°F.
2. Put the flour, sugar, butter, cocoa, baking soda, and baking powder in the bowl of a stand mixer fitted with the paddle attachment. (If you don't have a stand mixer, you can put the ingredients in a bowl, and use a hand mixer with the blending attachments, but take extra care to not

(Continued on next page)

Chocolate Cake (*cont.*)

overmix.) Mix on slow just until the ingredients are blended together, a few seconds, then raise the speed to low-medium and continue to mix until smooth, approximately 1 additional minute.

3. Stop the motor and pour in the chocolate. Mix for 1 minute, then, with the motor running, pour in the hot water. Then add the eggs, 1 egg at a time, adding the next one after the previous one has been absorbed. With the motor still running, pour in the buttermilk. Stop the motor periodically and scrape from the bottom with a rubber spatula to be sure all the ingredients are fully integrated, and return the mixer to low-medium speed. Continue to mix for an additional minute to ensure the eggs are fully absorbed. This will help insure that all the sugar is dissolved and the flour is thoroughly mixed in, which will help produce a luxurious mouthfeel in the final cake. Before baking, be sure the batter is at 70°F to 73°F, or the cake will crown. (If it is too warm, put it in the refrigerator for a few minutes; if too cool, let it rest at room temperature.)

4. Grease two 9-inch cake pans (2 inches high) with the butter, and flour them (*see* page 208).

5. Divide the batter evenly between the two cake pans, using a rubber spatula to scrape down the bowl and get as much batter as possible out. Bake until the cakes begin to pull from the sides of the pan and is springy to the touch, 25 to 30 minutes.

6. Remove from the oven and let cool for at least 30 minutes, preferably an hour. The cake should be at room temperature before you remove it from the pan. Put a piece of parchment paper on a cookie sheet, top with sugar, and turn the cake out onto parchment; the sugar will keep it from sticking. Refrigerate or freeze (*see* page 208) until ready to decorate.

Italian Sponge Cake
(Pan di Spagna)

Sponge cake got its name because it's a cake that's meant to be soaked, which is the purpose of many classic European cakes. On its own, it's dry, but when you spoon or brush a liqueur or syrup over it, it drinks it in and is transformed. This recipe only produces one cake because, conventionally, you cut this cake in half, usually filling it with a cream infused with the same liqueur you used to soak it.

Generally, you will make this cake with layers that are equal in height to the layers of cake, but if you use a rich filling like Chocolate Ganache (page 235) or Chocolate Fudge Frosting (page 229), you should use half as much, because the filling may overwhelm the cake.

MAKES ONE 9-INCH CAKE

1½ cups sugar, plus more for lining parchment paper
5 extra-large eggs at room temperature
1 teaspoon pure vanilla extract
Drop of lemon oil, optional (see Sources, page 239)
1½ cups cake flour, sifted, plus more for flouring the cake pan
⅓ cup vegetable oil
Unsalted butter, for greasing cake pan (about 1 tablespoon); nonstick cooking spray or vegetable may can be substituted

1. Position a rack in the center of the oven, and preheat the oven to 350°F.

(Continued on next page)

Italian Sponge Cake (*cont.*)

2. Put the sugar, eggs, vanilla, and lemon oil, if using, in the bowl of a standing mixer fitted with the whisk attachment. (If you don't have a stand mixer, you can put the ingredients in a bowl, and use a hand mixer with the blending attachments.) Beat starting on low and raise to medium and whip until the mixture is thick, shiny, and ivory in color, and has multiplied several times in volume, approximately 15 minutes (*see* How To). Remove the bowl from the mixer and use a rubber spatula to scrape as much mixture as possible off the whisk attachment and into the bowl.
3. Add the flour and patiently fold it in with a rubber spatula, then pour in the oil, and fold in until fully absorbed into the mixture.
4. Grease and flour a 9-inch cake pan (page 208). Pour the batter into the pan, scraping down the sides with a rubber spatula.
5. Bake until the cake begins to pull from the sides of the pan and is springy to the touch, 30 to 40 minutes.
6. Remove from the oven and let cool for at least 30 minutes, preferably an hour. The cake should be at room temperature before you remove it from the pan. Put a piece of parchment paper on a cookie sheet, top with sugar, turn the cake out onto the parchment; the sugar will keep it from sticking. Refrigerate or freeze (*see* page 208) until ready to decorate.

How to whip eggs: I remember making Italian sponge in the winter with my dad. We used to put electric heaters next to the mixer to speed up the process (warmer eggs volumize faster). If you're in a hurry, you can apply hot air to the outside of your mixer's bowl with a hair dryer to pull off the same trick.

Carrot Cake

Our carrot cake is supermoist, with a heightened flavor of cinnamon. This is also one cake where you should ignore my suggestion to try different frostings: Cream Cheese Frosting (page 235) is the only way to go with carrot cake.

MAKES TWO 9-INCH CAKES, OR 24 CUPCAKES

3 cups finely grated carrots (from about 5 large carrots)
2½ cups cake flour, plus more for flouring the cake pans
2 cups granulated sugar
2 cups Italian Custard Cream (page 234), optional
¾ cup vegetable oil
2¼ teaspoons baking powder
2 teaspoons ground cinnamon
1 teaspoon baking soda
1 teaspoon pure vanilla extract
½ teaspoon fine sea salt
4 extra-large eggs, at room temperature
1 cup whole milk
½ cup chopped walnuts, optional
¼ cup golden raisins, optional
Unsalted butter, for greasing 2 cake pans (about 2 tablespoons),
    nonstick cooking spray or vegetable oil may be substituted

1. Position a rack in the center of the oven and preheat the oven to 350°F.

(Continued on next page)

Carrot Cake (*cont.*)

2. Put the carrots, flour, sugar, custard, if using, oil, baking powder, cinnamon, baking soda, vanilla, and salt in the bowl of a stand mixer fitted with the paddle attachment. (If you don't have a stand mixer, you can put the ingredients in a bowl, and use a hand mixer with the blending attachments.) Mix on low just until the ingredients are tossed together well, a few seconds, then raise the speed to low-medium and continue to mix until the mixture is smooth, approximately 1 additional minute.

3. With the motor running, add 1 egg at a time, adding the next one after the previous one has been absorbed. Stop the motor periodically and scrape from the bottom of the bowl with a rubber spatula to incorporate, and return the mixer to low-medium speed.

4. Continue to mix for an additional minute to ensure that the eggs are fully absorbed. This will help insure that all the sugar is dissolved and the flour is incorporated, which will help produce a luxurious mouthfeel in the final cake.

5. With the motor running, pour in the milk, ½ cup at a time, stopping the motor to scrape the sides and bottom of the bowl between the two additions. Continue to mix for another minute or until the mixture appears smooth. Add the walnuts and raisins and mix just to integrate them.

6. Grease two 9-inch cake pans with the butter, and flour them (*see* page 208).

7. Divide the batter evenly between the two cake pans, using a rubber spatula to scrape down the bowl and get as much batter as possible out. Before baking, be sure the batter is at 70°F and 73°F, or the cake will crown. (Test by plunging a kitchen thermometer into the center of the batter; if it is too warm, put the bowl in the refrigerator for a few minutes; if too cool, let it rest at room temperature.)

8. Bake until the cake begins to pull from the sides of the form and is springy to the touch, 25 to 30 minutes.

9. Remove from the oven and let cool for at least 30 minutes, preferably an hour. The cake should be at room temperature before you remove it from the pan. Put a piece of parchment paper on a cookie sheet, top with sugar, dump onto parchment; the sugar will keep it from sticking. Refrigerate or freeze until ready to decorate (see page 208).

Red Velvet Cake

This is a classic of American baking that originated in the South and made its way up North. As with Carrot Cake (page 223), I am strict classicist with Red Velvet Cake, only frosting it with the traditional Cream Cheese Frosting (page 235).

MAKES TWO 9-INCH CAKES OR 24 CUPCAKES

1¼ cups vegetable shortening
2 cups granulated sugar
1 tablespoon cocoa powder
4½ teaspoons (2 tubes) red food-coloring gel
3 cups cake flour, plus more for dusting the cake pans
1¼ teaspoons fine sea salt
1¼ teaspoons pure vanilla extract
1¼ teaspoons baking soda
1¼ teaspoons distilled white vinegar
3 extra-large eggs
1¼ cups buttermilk
Unsalted butter, for greasing 2 cake pans (about 2 tablespoons); non-stick cooking spray or vegetable oil may be substituted

1. Position a rack in the center of the oven and preheat the oven to 350°F.
2. Put the shortening, sugar, cocoa powder, food coloring, cake flour, salt, vanilla, baking soda, and vinegar in the bowl of a stand mixer fitted with the paddle attachment. Paddle, starting at low spend, then raise the speed to low-medium and mix for about 1 minute. Add the eggs, 1 at a

time, mixing for 1 minute after each is absorbed into the mixture. Add the buttermilk in two portions, stopping to scrape the sides of the bowl between additions.

3. Grease two 9-inch cake pans (2 inches high) with the butter, and flour them (see page 208).

4. Divide the batter evenly between the two cake pans, using a rubber spatula to scrape down the bowl and get as much batter as possible out.

5. Bake until the cake begins to pull from the sides of the pan and is springy to the touch, 35 to 40 minutes.

6. Remove from the oven and let cool for at least 30 minutes, preferably an hour. The cake should be at room temperature before you remove it from the pan. Put a piece of parchment paper on a cookie sheet, top with sugar, dump onto parchment; the sugar will keep it from sticking. Refrigerate or freeze until ready to decorate (see page 208).

Frostings and Filling

Vanilla Frosting

For a creamier frosting, use milk instead of water, but note that you must refrigerate it, as well as any cakes filled or iced with it. Let it come to room temperature before using, and whip briefly by hand to refresh it.

MAKES ABOUT 4 CUPS, ENOUGH TO
FILL AND ICE ONE 9-INCH CAKE

2½ cups (5 sticks) unsalted butter, softened at room temperature
5 cups powdered (10x) sugar
1 tablespoon pure vanilla extract
¼ teaspoon fine sea salt
3 tablespoons lukewarm water

1. Put the butter in the bowl of a stand mixer fitted with the paddle attachment and mix on low speed until butter is smooth with no lumps. With the motor running, add the sugar, 1 cup at a time, only adding the next cup after the first addition has been integrated into the mixture.
2. Stop the machine and add the vanilla and salt. Paddle on low-medium speed until completely smooth, approximately 2 minutes. Add the water and continue to mix until light and fluffy, 2 to 3 minutes.
3. The frosting can be kept in an airtight container at room temperature for up to 2 days.

Chocolate Fudge Frosting

For a creamier frosting, use milk instead of water, but note that you must refriger-
ate it, as well as any cakes filled or iced with it. Let it come to room temperature
before using, and whip briefly by hand to refresh it.

MAKES ABOUT 4 CUPS, ENOUGH TO
FILL AND ICE ONE 9-INCH CAKE

2½ cups (5 sticks) unsalted butter, softened at room temperature
5 cups powdered (10x) sugar
⅔ cup cocoa
1 tablespoon pure vanilla extract
¼ teaspoon fine sea salt
3 tablespoons lukewarm water

1. Put the butter in the bowl of a stand mixer fitted with the paddle attachment and paddle on low speed until smooth, with no lumps, approximately 3 minutes. With the motor running, add the sugar, one cup at a
   time, only adding the next cup after the first addition is absorbed.
2. Stop the machine and add the cocoa, vanilla, and salt. Paddle on low-
   medium speed until completely smooth, approximately 2 minutes. Add
   the water and continue to paddle until light and fluffy, 2 to 3 minutes.
3. The frosting will keep for up to 2 days in an airtight container at room
   temperature.

Italian Buttercream

I adapted this recipe from one used at the Culinary Institute of America, shown to me by a group of students for whom I did a demonstration.

MAKES ABOUT 7 CUPS

8 extra-large egg whites
2 cups granulated sugar
½ cup water
4 cups (8 sticks) unsalted butter, at room temperature, cut into small
  cubes
1 tablespoon pure vanilla extract

1. Put the whites in the bowl of a stand mixer fitted with the whisk attachment.
2. Put 1½ cups of the sugar and the water in a heavy saucepan and bring to a boil over medium-high heat, stirring with a wooden spoon to dissolve the sugar. Continue to cook, without stirring, and bring to the softball stage (240°F).
3. Meanwhile, whip the whites at high speed until soft peaks form, approximately 5 minutes. With the motor running, add the remaining ½ cup sugar gradually, continuing to whip until medium peaks form.
4. When the sugar reaches 240°F, with the motor running, pour it into the egg whites, very slowly, in a thin stream, to avoid cooking the eggs. Raise the speed to high, and continue to whip until the mixture has cooled to room temperature, 10 to 15 minutes.
5. Stopping the motor between additions, add the butter in 5 increments,

scraping the bowl with a rubber spatula before adding each addition of butter. With the motor running, add the vanilla, and whip just until it is blended in.

6. The buttercream can be refrigerated in an airtight container for up to 1 week.

Italian Custard Cream

This cream is a mainstay of Carlo's, used in many cakes and pastries. The longer you cook it, the thicker it will become, so feel free to adjust the texture to suit your taste.

MAKES ABOUT 3 CUPS, ENOUGH TO
FILL AND ICE ONE 9-INCH CAKE

2½ cups whole milk
1 tablespoon pure vanilla extract
1 cup granulated sugar
⅔ cup cake flour, sifted
5 extra-large egg yolks
2 teaspoons salted butter

1. Put the milk and vanilla in a saucepan and bring to a simmer over medium heat.
2. In a bowl, whip together the sugar, flour, and egg yolks with a hand mixer. Ladle a cup of the milk-vanilla mixture into the bowl and beat to temper the yolks—as you are whisking the yolks move the pot on and off the flame so that you don't scramble the eggs.
3. Add the yolk mixture to the pot and beat with the hand mixer until thick and creamy, about 1 minute. Remove the pot from the heat, add the butter, and whip for 2 minutes to thicken the cream. Transfer to a bowl. Refrigerate at least 6 hours. Will keep for up to 1 week.

Note: To make chocolate custard cream, add 1½ ounces of melted, cooled unsweetened baker's chocolate along with the butter. For a richer chocolate flavor, add a little more.

Cream Cheese Frosting

This is the traditional frosting for Carrot Cake (page 223) and Red Velvet Cake (page 226). For my money, nothing compares to Philadelphia cream cheese, which I suggest you use for this. It's best to use this as soon as you make it because it gets very stiff in the refrigerator; if you have to refrigerate it, do not microwave it to freshen it. Instead, let it rest at room temperature for 4 hours to soften.

MAKES ABOUT 3 CUPS, ENOUGH TO
FILL AND ICE ONE 9-INCH CAKE

16 ounces cream cheese
8 tablespoons (1 stick) unsalted butter, softened at room temperature
1 teaspoon pure vanilla extract
2 cups powdered (10x) sugar, sifted

1. Put the cream cheese and butter in the bowl of a stand mixer fitted with the paddle attachment and paddle at medium speed until creamy, approximately 30 seconds.
2. With the motor running, pour in the vanilla and paddle for 30 seconds. Add the sugar, a little at a time, and mix until smooth, approximately 1 minute after the last addition.
3. Use right away, or refrigerate in an airtight container for up to 2 days.

My Dad's Chocolate Mousse

This was the recipe my dad used for chocolate mousse, which is, essentially, chocolate whipped cream. Just as he did back in the day, we use it for mousse layers on cakes and to fill mousse rings. It's light and rich at the same time, and is very easy to make.

This chocolate whipped cream is fluffy and rich, and gets along with a wide range of cakes and fillings.

MAKES ABOUT 3½ CUPS, ENOUGH TO
FILL AND ICE ONE 9-INCH CAKE

2 cups heavy cream
½ cup granulated sugar
3 tablespoons cocoa powder
1 tablespoon Kahlúa or coffee liqueur

1. Put the cream, sugar, cocoa powder, and Kahlúa ingredients in a stainless-steel mixing bowl.
2. Blend with a hand mixer at high speed until fluffy, about 1 minute. Use immediately or refrigerate in an airtight container for up to 3 days.

Chocolate Ganache

This ganache can be used in two ways, as a filling and/or poured over a cake.

To use it as a filling, refrigerate it, transfer it to a pastry bag, and pipe it out following the directions on page 210.

To pour ganache over a cake, melt it in a double boiler and simply pour it over a cake or layer. To top layers of pastry cream or chocolate mousse with ganache, pour it on and smooth it with a cake icing spatula.

MAKES ABOUT 2 CUPS

1 cup heavy cream
9 ounces semisweet chocolate, coarsely chopped
1 tablespoon light corn syrup

1. Put the heavy cream in a saucepan and set over medium-high heat. As soon as it begins to simmer, remove the pot from the heat. Add the chocolate and stir with a wooden spoon to melt the chocolate. Stir in the corn syrup.
2. Transfer to a bowl and refrigerate for about 1 hour. If using for filling, soften until pourable in a double boiler over medium heat.

Syrups

This is the recipe I use to make syrups for soaking sponge cakes, such as the one on page 221. I have listed the liqueurs called for in this book but you can also use it to make syrups of your own creation using others.

For a stronger flavor, increase the amount of liqueur up to ½ cup.

As for which brands to select for the liqueurs, I generally recommend staying away from the cheap stuff (what bartenders call well spirits), and choosing what you like to drink.

MAKES ABOUT 1⅓ CUPS

1 cup water
1 cup granulated sugar
¼ cup liqueur, such as Rosolio, Strega, or rum

1. Put the water, sugar, and liqueur into a saucepan, bring to a simmer over medium-high heat.
2. Whisk until the sugar dissolves, approximately 3 to 4 minutes. Let cool before using. The syrup may be refrigerated in an airtight container for up to 2 weeks.

Sources

Basic tools and equipment, as well as some hard-to-find ingredients used in the recipes in this book, can be found at the Web sites listed here.

AMAZON: WWW.AMAZON.COM
Baking supplies, kitchen utensils, cannoli shells, lard, nut flours, orange-blossom water, turntables.

KING ARTHUR FLOUR: WWW.KINGARTHURFLOUR.COM
Baking supplies and equipment, baker's ammonia, cake flour, lemon oil, pastry flour, nut flours.

WILLIAMS SONOMA: WWW.WILLIAMS-SONOMA.COM
Baking supplies and equipment.

Acknowledgments

I would like to thank the following people for their special support of this project, of *Cake Boss*, the show; of Carlo's Bake Shop; and of me.

My wife, Lisa. Thank you for all of your incredible support over the years, for being my rock, and for always believing in my crazy schemes and being the first (and sometimes *only*) person to say, "Yeah! You're going to do it!" You're my biggest fan and my biggest constructive critic. I know my schedule doesn't always give us as much time together as we'd like, but you are on my mind, and in my heart, always.

My Sofia Bear, Buddy, and Marco, my three kids. You are the joys of my life, and all that I do, I do for you. Whether you all end up in the baking trade or not, I know you'll carry on the best traditions of the Valastro family.

Mary Valastro, Mama. Thank you for being such a fantastic mother and for helping to instill such good values in me. You helped make me the man I am today and I am forever grateful.

My four big sisters, or maybe I should say "my second mothers": Grace, Madeline, Mary, and Lisa. You guys aren't just *mia famiglia*; you're also some of my best friends. Thank you for always believing in me, and for always, *always* being there for me, and for all the great memories, many of them yet to come, that we share.

My brothers-in-law, Mauro, Joey, and Joe. You've always helped me achieve my goals. God gave me great sisters, but it's also like he gave me great

241

brothers because you aren't like in-laws to me; you're the brothers I never had, my real brothers.

My crew, Frankie, Danny, Sal, and the rest of the Carlo's staff. Without you guys I couldn't do what I do. You are like my second family, and I appreciate all your hard work. You've helped me turn Carlo's Bake Shop into a household name. I also have to give a special shout-out to Adam Bourcier: Thank you for all the help on the book, and for helping me achieve bigger and better things. It's a big boat we're driving these days, and I couldn't keep it on course without you as my first mate. It's official: You're family, too!

My collaborator, Andrew Friedman. We became very close while writing this book, didn't we? I poured out my soul, and you made it sound like it went right from my heart to the page. You are the unsung hero of this book; I couldn't have done it without you. So many late nights we worked like animals at my house and I couldn't be happier with what we accomplished. You are truly gifted in what you do and you are with me for life—a made man in the Cake Boss's *famiglia*.

The team at my publisher, Free Press. Our editor, Leslie Meredith, for her great passion for her work (and for food!); Publisher Martha Levin for her belief in the project; Assistant Editor Donna Loffredo for her help during the editing and production stage; Publicist Christine Donnelly and Director of Publicity Carisa Hays, for getting the word out. And to Editor-in-Chief Dominick Anfuso and Associate Publisher Suzanne Donahue for their very special support of this project.

Jon Rosen and the team at William Morris Endeavor Entertainment. Thanks for helping me elevate my career to the next level, for believing in me, and for being my good friends. Onward and upward!

Erin Niumata of Folio Literary Management, who was the agent for this book. I greatly appreciate your friendship and all your help shaping this project and getting it set up right. Maura Teitelbaum at Abrams Artists Agency, thanks for all your help getting my career started off in the right way, and for your early efforts on this project.

My extended family—my aunts and uncles, cousins and second cousins—and all my friends (you know who you are). Thanks for your belief, even during the hard times, and most of all for all the good times. I could've filled ten more books telling all our great stories. I'm glad to have so many fond memories and that you've shared the journey with me.

The loyal customers of Carlo's Bake Shop. Thank you for making us what we are today. Not many businesses make it one hundred years, and without you we'd be nothing. I hope we have another century together.

I'm very proud to say that I'm a son of both Hoboken and Little Ferry, and of the great state of New Jersey, the only place I would ever want to live. I'm glad I've been able to shed some good light on the Garden State and show off what we have to offer.

Without my fans, I'd be nothing. I never tire of hearing how *Cake Boss* brings families together. The expressions on your faces and the stories you guys tell me when I have a chance to meet you bring tears to my eyes. I promise to always work as hard as I can to give you 100 percent, to never turn my back on you, and to always be ready to stop and sign an autograph or take a picture. You are all the best. Thank you and I love you.

I have to also thank God, for giving me a blessed life, even before I became the Cake Boss, just having such wonderful family and friends and all these wonderful stories to share with the world has brought tremendous meaning to my life.

Art Edwards at High Noon Entertainment. Thank-you for sharing my vision, understanding my goals, and helping me put it all in motion. I trusted my family story with you and knew that you would do the right thing. You did that, and more. I am eternally grateful.

Nick Budabin and the Hoboken High Noon Crew. You guys are in the trenches with me every single day and I can honestly say that you are among the few people I've ever met who work as hard as bakers! Sometimes we yell. Sometimes we joke. Sometimes we cry. It's all because we want the best for the show, and I never forget that. You guys are the best crew that any "talent" could ask for. I consider you all family and I love feeding you those cake scraps. You're the best.

Jim Berger and the Denver High Noon Crew. Although we don't see each other that often, thanks for believing in me, and my vision, working hard, spending hours going over footage, and, most important, for being my friends.

Andy Strauser, director of Talent Development and Casting at Discovery, the man who discovered me. Thank you for taking a chance on a baker from Hoboken, New Jersey. I will always be grateful for that.

To Jon Sechrist, my wonderfully creative producer at TLC. You have no idea how much I look forward to our Tuesday conversations about *Cake Boss* episodes. Over the past year I really feel that we've become family, and I appreciate all your hard work and effort to help make *Cake Boss* what it is today.

The rest of my extended family at TLC and Discovery. David Zaslav, president and CEO of Discovery Communications; Eileen O'Neill, president and general manager of TLC; Joe Abruzzese, president of Advertising Sales for Discovery; Nancy Daniels, vice president of Development and Production for Discovery; Howard Lee, vice president East Coast Development and Production for Discovery; Dustin Smith, director of Publicity for TLC; and John Paul Stoops, director of licensing for Discovery. Thanks to you all for believing in me and my family and portraying us in such a great light. Thank you for giving us a chance to make Carlo's Bake Shop into a household name and for working as hard as you do to make *Cake Boss* a success. I appreciate everyone's hard work and hope you all know that I consider you all part of *mia famiglia*.

Index

Page numbers in *italics* refer to illustrations.

Abruzzese, Joe, 145

Ace of Cakes, 140, 141

Almond Biscotti, 166

Almonds, 112, 166

Altamura, Italy, 14, 15, 53–56

Amato, Little Frankie, 6, 18, 126, 127, 139, 144, 146

Amato, Maria, 126

Amato, Nickie, 18

Amato, Nicoletta, 126

Ammonia, baker's, 163

Anthony, Saint, 11–12, 22, 74, 76, 85 bread, 73, *73*

Artisanal cooking movement, 96, 97

Assembly line system, 66, 131

Azzinaro, Gary, 138

Baker's ammonia, 163

Bakery Crafts, 209

Baking powder, 45, 93

Baking trays, 154

Banana Cream Pie, 203–204

Bari, Italy, 14, 15

Basic tools and equipment, 154–56, *154–56*

Batches, baking in, 159

Bayonne, New Jersey, 15

Belgiovine, Gloria, 120, 122

Belgiovine, Mauro, 120, 121

Bench work, 47–48, *48,* 49

Bergen County Technical School, 51–52

Berger, Jim, 144, 145

Birthday cakes, 3, *29,* 34, 35, 36 decorating, 59, 104–105

Biscotti, 112, 162, 164

    Classic Biscotti (*Quaresimali*), 162–63

    Modern Biscotti, 164–65

    recipe improvements, 112

    Variations, 166

Biscuits, Tea, 171–72
Bow and Dots, 124
Bows, 108
Bread, 12, 13
    bruschetta, 97
    St. Anthony's, 73, *73*
Bridal magazines, 66–67, 108,
    125–26, 146
Brides, 126, 146
Brooklyn, New York, 14
Bruschetta, 97
Brush, pastry, 155, 211
Budadin, Nick, 138, 139
Buddy Delight cake, 61–62
Butter, 48, 96, 129
Buttercream, 59, 81, 91, 108, 109,
    232
    flowers, 105
    piping, 105–106
    science of, 91
Buttercream, Italian, 232–33
Buttermilk, 219

Cacciavillani, Tony, 137, 141, 142
Cake(s), 207–226
    consultation, 109–111, 112,
        140–41
    birthday, 3, *29,* 34, 35, 36, 59,
        104–105
    Carrot Cake, 223–25
    Chocolate Cake, 219–20
    Crumb Cake, 217–18
    decorating, *see* Decorating cakes
    filling and icing tips, 210–12
    fondant, 107–109, *109,* 113,
        124–26

freezing, 208, 209
frostings and fillings, 229–38
general cake-making tips and
    techniques, 208–209
Italian Sponge Cake, 221–22
orders, 102–103, 106–107
ratio of filling to, 212
recipe improvements and updates,
    90–100
Red Velvet Cake, 226–27
science of, 92–96
theme, 112–13, *113,* 115, 142,
    146–47, 148–51
three-layer, 213
trimming and cutting, 209
two-layer, 213
Vanilla Cake, 214–16
wedding, *see* Wedding cakes
Cake Boss (TV show), 6–7, 135, 138,
    144–52, 153
    Bridezilla episode, 111
    debut episode, 145–46
    filming of, 138–39, 142, 144–47,
        149
    Leaning Tower of Pisa cake, 150
    NASCAR cake episode, 142
    Sesame Street episode, 150
Cake flour, 157
Cake pans, 154
    greasing and flouring, 208
California cheesecake, 59
Callebaut cocoa, 96, 157
Cannoli, 56, 96, 100, 182
Cannoli (recipe), 182–84
Cannoli Cream, 185
Capreto, 56

Carlo's Bake Shop, Hoboken, New
    Jersey, 3–4, *4,* 5, *5,* 6–7, *10,* 16,
    73, 146, 149, 153
  assembly line system, 66, 131
  beginnings of, 16
  Buddy Jr. becomes boss of, 89–100
  Buddy Sr. as boss of, 16–19, 21–26,
    33–37, 41–49, 57–58, 82–83,
    96, 108, 116, 151–52
  Cake Boss and, 138–39, 144–52
  consultations, 109–111, 112, 141
  cupcakes, 128–31
  customers, 102–103, 106–111,
    126, 141
  death of Buddy Sr. and, 76, *76,*
    77–80, 87, 148
  equipment, 23–25
  factory, 151
  fondant cakes, 107–109, *109,* 113,
    124–26
  logo, 42, *42*
  of mid-late 1990s, 101–116
  moves locations, 41–43
  operations, 23–26
  ordering cakes at, 102–103, 106–107
  recipe improvements and updates,
    90–100, 112
  "slip" system, 98
  theme cakes, 112–13, *113,* 115,
    146–47, 148–51
  thirtieth-anniversary celebration of,
    65, *65*
  wedding cakes, *see* Wedding cakes
  weekly ingredients used at, 129
  See also specific products and employees
Carrot Cake, 223–25

Cassata cake, 56
Castano, Madeline, *4,* 5, 18, *19,* 31,
    43, *82*
Castano, Mauro, 5, 43, 101–102, 106,
    112, 136, 141, 143, 150
Catholicism, 11–12, 15, 73–74
Cheesecakes, 59, 63
Cheese Frosting, Cream, 235
Chocolate, 96, 166
Chocolate Biscotti, 166
Chocolate cake, 96, 219
  recipe improvements, 96
Chocolate Cake, 219–10
Chocolate-Chip Cookies, 167–68
Chocolate Cream Pie, 206
Chocolate Fudge Frosting, 231
Chocolate Ganache, 237
Chocolate Mousse, My Dad's, 236
Chocolate volcano mousse, 59
Christmas, 25, 37, 117, 118
Church cakes, 34
Classic Biscotti (*Quaresimali*), 162–63
Cocoa, 96, 157
Coffee, 112
  Tiramisu, 189–90
Columbia Presbyterian Hospital, New
    York City, 69
Computers, 147
Coney Island, 14, 56–57
Consultations, cake, 109–111, 112,
    140–41
Cookies and pastries, 96, 112, 116,
    159–90
  baking in batches, 159
  Biscotti Variations, 166
  Cannoli, 182–84

Cookies and pastries (*cont.*)
    Chocolate-Chip Cookies, 167–68
    Classic Biscotti (*Quaresimali*),
       162–63
    Cream Puffs, 179–80
    Lobster Tails, 175–77
    Modern Biscotti, 164–65
    Pecan Wedges, 175–76
    Pignoli Cookies, 169–70
    St. Joseph's Zeppole (*Sfingi*),
       186–88
    Tarelles (Vanilla Cookies), 160–61
    Tea Biscuits, 171–72
    Tiramisu, 189–90
Copacabana nightclub, *17*
Cream, Cannoli, 185
Cream, Italian Custard, 234
Cream, Italian Whipped, 205
Cream, Lobster Tail, 178
Cream cheese, 55, 129, 235
Cream Cheese Frosting, 235
Cream Pie, Banana, 203–204
Cream Pie, Chocolate, 206
Cream puff cake, 34–35, 59
Cream puff dough, 83, 181
Cream Puff Dough, 181
Cream puff log, 59
Cream puffs, 36, 37, 179
Cream Puffs, 179–80
Crostata, 192–93
Crumb Cake, 217–18
Crust, Pie, 201–202
Cupcake(s), 128–31, 207–227
    Carrot Cake, 223–25
    Chocolate Cake, 219–20
    decoration, 129, 131

    flower, 129, 131
    general cake-making tips and
       techniques, 208–209
    Red Velvet Cake, 226–27
    science of, 131
    towers, 129
    Vanilla Cake, 214–16
Cupcake Café, New York City, 129
Cupcake mold, 155
Custard cream, 93, 96, 214, 234
Custard Cream, Italian, 234
Customers, 102–103, 106–111, 126,
    141
    consultations, 109–111, 112,
       140–41
Cutouts, 108

Daniels, Nancy, 144
Danish, 48
    dough, 45, 46
Decorating cakes, 57–64, 66, 81, 90,
    102, 104–106
    birthday cakes, 59, 104–105
    cupcakes, 129, 131
    fondant, 107–109, *109,* 113,
       124–26
    theme cakes, 112–13, *113,* 115,
       142, 146–47, 148–51
    wedding cakes, 59, *60,* 63, *64,*
       106–111
    See also Frostings and fillings;
       Piping; *specific decorations*
Depression, 16
Discovery Communications, 145
Dishwasher, 98–100
Dough, 1–2, 25, 140

cream puff, 83, 181
mixing, 43–47
pasta frolla, 25, 47, 96, 197–98
rolling, 24–25, 47–48
sfogliatelle, 1–2, 25, 48, 82–87, 89,
90–91, 148, 175–77
Dough, Cream Puff, 181
Dough, Italian Short (*Pasta Frolla*),
197–98
Dove wedding cake, 148
Dragone, Danny, 6, 24, 29, 34, 59–61,
90, 91, 141, 148
Drapes, 108
Drop line, 105
Duncan Hines, 93

Éclairs, 36, 37
Edrick, Rick, 143–44
Edwards, Art, 139–40, 141, 144, 145,
147
Eggs, 23, 45, 47
Entenmann's, 93, 94
Equipment, 98
basic, 154–56, *154–56*
See also specific equipment
Espresso, 112

Fashionista cake, 148
Fats, 45, 48, 93, 96, 157, 158, 182
Faugno, Bartolina, 86
Faugno, Giovana, 54–55
Faugno, Grace, *4,* 5, 6, 18, *18, 19,* 31,
43, *82,* 86, *86*
Faugno, Joey, 6, 43, 78, 80, 86, *112,*
144, 146
Faugno, Robert, 86

Fernandez, Stephanie "Sunshine," 6
Filling cakes, tips for, 210–11, 212
Fillings. *See* Frostings and fillings
Finklestein, Arnold, 138
Fire-truck cake, 148
Flour, 45, 129
cake, 157
greasing and flouring cake pans,
208
nut, 112
pastry, 157
Flowers, 105–106, 108, 129
cupcake, 129, 131
sugar, 107, 123–24, 126, 141
Fondant cakes, 107–109, *109,* 113,
124–26
Food coloring, 124
Food Network, 135, 139–40, 141
Food Network Challenge, 135–37, 139,
140–41, 143, 144
For the Bride, 126
Freezing cakes, 208, 209
French cream, 35
Frostings and fillings, 58–64, 66, 104–
105, 111, 210–12, 229–38
Chocolate Fudge Frosting, 231
Chocolate Ganache, 237
Cream Cheese Frosting, 235
fondant, 107–109, *109,* 113,
124–26
Italian Buttercream, 232–33
Italian Custard Cream, 234
My Dad's Chocolate Mousse, 236
piping, 210–12
ratios of cake to filling, 212
Syrups, 238

Frostings and fillings (*cont.*)
   tips for, 210–12
   Vanilla Frosting, 230
Fruit log, 59
Fudge Frosting, Chocolate, 231

Ganache, Chocolate, 237
Gelatin, 108
German-American bakeries, 41, 42
Glycerine, 108
Goldman, "Duff," 140, 141
Good Morning America, 143
Greasing and flouring cake pans, 208
Groovy Girl, 124
Grucci family, 148
Guastaffero, Carlo, 16

Hands, used in baking, 38–39, *47,* 84,
   116, 130, 133
Hazelnut Biscotti, 166
Hazelnuts, 112
Hearst, Linda, 125–26
High Noon Productions, 139, 141, 144
Hobart mixer, 23, 92, 175
Hobart whipped-cream machine, 98
Hoboken, New Jersey, 3, 13, 15, 19, 31,
   35, 41, 57, 73, 112, *128,* 137, 149

Icing. *See* Frostings and fillings
Icing cakes, tips for, 211–12
Indricotherium cake, 150
Ingredients, notes on, 157–58
Italian Buttercream, 232–33
Italian Custard Cream, 234
Italian Short Dough (*Pasta Frolla*),
   197–98

Italian Sponge Cake (*Pan di Spagna*),
   221–22
Italian Whipped Cream, 205
Italy, 9–12, 13, 14, 15, 53–56, 112
   bakeries, 55–56
   traditions, 23, 55–56, 97, 122,
     139

Johnson & Wales College of Culinary
   Arts, 142

Kathleen, Richard, 138
Kitchen thermometer, 155

Lard, 96, 182
Las Vegas, 115
Leaning Tower of Pisa cake, 150
Lee, Howard, 144
Lee, Jimmy, 57–58
Lion's Club, 53
Lipari, Sicily, 10–12, 13
Liqueur, 238
Little Ferry, New Jersey, 26–29, 31, 76,
   78
Lobster Tail Cream, 178
Lobster tails, *77,* 82–87, 89, 100, 175
   sfogliatelle dough for, 82–87, 90–91,
     175
Lobster Tails, 175–77
Logo, Carlo's Bake Shop, 42, *42*

Macaluso, Joe, 59–62, 103
Magazines, bridal, 66–67, 108,
   125–26, 146
Magnolia Café, New York City, 129
"Majestic Dreams," 137

Margarine, European, 96
McBride, Maria, 146
Microplane zester, 156
Milk, 45, 46, 47, 157
    types of, 157, 219
Mixer, 23–24, 45–47, 83, 85, 92
    Hobart, 23, 92, 175
    stand, 155
Mixing, 43–47, 92
    science of, 92–95
    scraping sides of bowl, 209
    times, 94
Mob, 51, 64
Modern Biscotti, 164–65
Modern Bride, 125–26
Mold, cupcake, 155
Mother's Day, 129, 131
Mousse, My Dad's Chocolate, 236
My Dad's Chocolate Mousse, 236

Naples, 56
NASCAR cake, 142
New York City, 31, *128,* 129
    bakeries, 129
Nutella, 192
    Crostata, 192–93
Nutex, 93
Nut flour, 112
Nuts, 112, 166

Oil, vegetable, 158
O'Neill, Eileen, 145
Orders, cake, 102–103, 106–107
Orecchio, Joe, 34–35
Ortiz, Steve, 75, 76
Oven, 159

Pagnotta, Father, 73, 74
Pan di Spagna (Italian Sponge Cake),
    221–22
Pans, cake, 154
    greasing and flouring, 208
Pasta frolla, 25, 47, 96
Pasta Frolla (Italian Short Dough),
    197–98
Pasticiotti, 24, 37
Pastries. *See* Cookies and pastries
Pastry bag, 36–37, 81, 131, 155, 210
    piping fillings and frostings,
        210–12
    pressure techniques, 210
    types of, 155
Pastry brush, 155, 211
Pastry flour, 157
Pecan Wedges, 173–74
Philadelphia Cream Cheese, 235
Pies, 191–206
    Banana Cream Pie, 203–204
    Chocolate Cream Pie, 206
    Crostata, 192–93
    Italian Whipped Cream, 205
    Pasta Frolla (Italian Short Dough),
        197–98
    Pie Crust, 201–202
    Pumpkin Pie, 199–200
    Ricotta Pie (*Torta di Ricotta*),
        194–96
Pignoli cookies, 56, 169
Pignoli Cookies, 169–70
Pine nuts, 169
    Pignoli Cookies, 169–70
Pininch, Lucille, 18
Pininch, Sal, 6, 18, 24, 85, 148

Piping, 36–37, 63, 104–105, 131, 209, 210
  fillings and frostings, 210–12
  tips for, 210–12
Pistachio Biscotti, 166
Pistachios, 112, 166
Pumpkin Pie, 199–200

Quaresimali, 112, 162
Quaresimali (Classic Biscotti), 162–63

Raisins, 45
Recipes, 153–238
  cake and cupcake, 213–27
  cookies and pastries, 159–60
  frostings and fillings, 229–38
  pies, 191–206
  See also specific recipes
Red velvet cake, 124, 226
Red Velvet Cake, 226–27
Refrigerators, 151
Religion, 11–12, 73–74, 77, 85
Ricotta, 185, 194
Ricotta Pie (*Torta di Ricotta*), 194–96
Ridgefield Park Junior Senior High School, 64, 71
Rockleigh Country Club, 126
Rolling dough, 24–25, 47–48
Rolling pin, 24–25, 47, 48, 155
Rondo sheeter, 98
Russom, Chris, 136

Saint Francis Church, Hoboken, New Jersey, 73
Saint Joseph's Church, Jersey City, New Jersey, 73, 74

St. Joseph's Day, 186
St. Joseph's zeppole, 96, 186
St. Joseph's Zeppole (*Sfingi*), 186–88
Salt, 45
Saltz, Joanna, 125–26
San Marzano liqueur, 148
Schlueter, Steven, 138
Schoning's City Hall Bake Shop, Hoboken, New Jersey, 41–42
Science of baking, 91–96, 131
Scraping the sides of bowl, 209
Sea urchins, 55
Sechrist, Jon, 144
September 11 terrorist attacks, 126
Sesame Street, 150
Sfingi (St. Joseph's Zeppole), 186–88
Sfogliatelle, 25, 82, 82–87
  dough, 1–2, 25, 48, 82–87, 89, 90–91, 148, 175–77
  Lobster Tails, 175–77
Sheeter, 85, 91, 98
Shortening, 45, 93, 96, 129
Sicily, 10–12, 13, 53–56
Sienkiewicz, Rafael, 138
"Slip," 98
Soaking a sponge cake, 211
Sopranos, The, 137–39
Sources, 239
Spatula, 156, 212
Sponge cake, 35, 211, 221
  soaking in syrup, 211, 238
Sponge Cake, Italian (*Pan di Spagna*), 221–22
Sports, 48–50
Spot Creative, 143
Stand mixer, 155

Starbucks, 112

Steinfeld, Sarah, 138

Strauser, Andy, 143, 144

Strawberry cheesecake, 59, 63

Stretch, 138–39

Sugar, 45, 129
   flowers, 107, 123–24, 126, 141

Sunday dinner, 23

Syrups, 212, 238
   soaking sponge cake in, 212, 238

Syrups (recipe), 238

Tarelles, 21, 160

Tarelles (Vanilla Cookies), 160–61

Tea biscuits, 45, 171

Tea Biscuits, 171–72

Television, 6–7, 66, 135–52
   Cake Boss, 6–7, 135, 138, 144–52
   Food Network Challenge, 135–37,
      139, 140–41, 143, 144

Temperature control, 94–95

Teterboro High School, 64

Thanksgiving, 199

Theme cakes, 112–13, *113,* 115, 142,
      146–47, 148–51
   on *Cake Boss,* 146–51
   See also specific themes

Thermometer, kitchen, 155

Times Square, New York City, *128*

Tiramisu, 59, 189

Tiramisu (recipe), 189–90

TLC, 6, 143–44, 145

Today Show, 137

Tomato sauce, 122

Tools and equipment, basic, 154–56,
      154–56

Torta di Ricotta (Ricotta Pie), 194–96

Trays, baking, 154

Trimming and cutting cake, 209

Tubito, Madeline, 15–16, 22, *22,* 23

Tubito, Nicolas, 15–16, 22

Turntable, 156, 209
   filling and icing cakes on, 210–12

Upfronts, 145

Valastro, Anna, 10, 12, 13

Valastro, Antonio, 10, 11, 12–14

Valastro, Bartolo, Jr. (Buddy Jr.), *4, 5,
      20, 29, 30, 39, 44, 47, 48, 49,
      51, 52, 54, 64, 83, 112, 121,
      127, 128, 133*
   becomes boss of Carlo's Bake Shop,
      89–100
   birth of, 19–20, *20*
   as a businessman, 72–73, 79, 90,
      106–112, 129, 143–45
   on *Cake Boss,* 144–52
   childhood of, 21–39
   cake decorating and, 57–64, *64, 66*
   cupcakes and, 128–31
   customers and, 102–103, 106–111,
      126, 141
   death of his father, 70–76, *76,*
      77–79, 148
   education as a cake boss, 36–38,
      41–67, 84–85
   as a father, 127–28, 130, 131–33
   fondant cakes and, 107–109, *109*
   hands of, 38–39, *47,* 84, 116, 130,
      133
   marriage of, 121, *121,* 122–28, 129

Valastro, Bartolo, Jr. (Buddy Jr.) (*cont.*)
    recipe improvements and updates,
        90–100, 112
    in school, 31–32, 49, 51–52, 64, 71
    sfogliatelle dough mastered by,
        82–87, 89, 90–91
    television career of, 135–52
    theme cakes and, 112–13, *113,*
        115, 142, 146–47, 148–51
    trip to Italy, 53–56
    wedding of, 126–27, *127*
Valastro, Bartolo, Sr. (Buddy Sr.),
        9–20, *17–19,* 28–29, *29, 30,*
        52, 54, 65, 123, 130, 146, 148,
        151–52
    as boss of Carlo's Bake Shop, 16–19,
        21–26, 33–37, 41–49, 57–58,
        82–83, 96, 108, 116, 151–52
    buys Carlo's Bakery, 16–17
    childhood of, 10–14
    death and funeral of, 74–76, *76,*
        77–79, 148
    ill health of, 50–51, 63, 69–76
    marriage of, 16–17, *17,* 18–20,
        52, 70–74
    relationship with son Buddy Jr.,
        31, 33–39, 49–57, 65, 69–76,
        84–85, 89–90, 123, 127, 128,
        130, 146, 148, 151–52
Valastro, Buddy (son of Buddy Jr.),
        99, *128,* 130, 131–33, *133*
Valastro, Franny, 10, 12, 13
Valastro, Grace, 10–14, 17–18, *19,*
        22, 26, 44, *44,* 54, 57, 76, 86,
        114
    death of, 114

Valastro, Josie, 10, 12, 13
Valastro, Lisa, *4,* 5, 6, 18, *19,* 31, 32,
        38, *38, 39,* 43, *82,* 92
Valastro, Lisa Belgiovine, 117, 118–21,
        121, 127, 128, 133, *133,* 139
    marriage of, 121, *121,* 122–28,
        129
    wedding of, 126–27, *127*
Valastro, Marco, 133, *133*
Valastro, Mary (mother of Buddy Jr.),
        14–20, *17–19,* 22–23, 27–29,
        29, 30, 49, 52, 69, *73, 82, 83,*
        114, *114,* 120, 138
    at Carlo's Bake Shop, 16–19,
        41–49, 99, 101, 144, 148
    death of her husband, 70–76, *76,*
        77–79, 148
    marriage of, 16–17, *17,* 18–20, *52,*
        70–74
    retirement of, 148
Valastro, Mary (sister of Buddy Jr.), *4,*
        5, 18, *19,* 31, *82,* 99, *99*
Valastro, Sofia, 99, 127–28, *128,* 130,
        133
Valenti, Dominic, 34, 80, 85
Valentine's Day, 120–21
Valrhona cocoa, 157
Vanilla, 158
Vanilla cake, 46, 92–93, 124, 129, 214
    recipe improvements, 92–96
    science of, 92–96
Vanilla Cake, 214–16
Vanilla Cookies (*Tarelles*), 160–61
Vanilla Frosting, 228
Van Nordstrom, Betty, 123
Vegetable oil, 158

Venetian Hour, 59, 61, 62, 126, 189

Vermil, John, 42, 47–48

Vernola, Mike, 42, 95–96, 97

Verspohl, Greg, 137, 141, 142

VFW, 107

Wedding cakes, 3, 4, 34, 35, 36, *60,* 106–111, 115, 136, 137, 140–41
    in bridal magazines, 66–67, 108, 125–26, 146
    cancellations, 107, 111
    consultation, 109–111, 140–41
    cost of, 107
    decorating, 59, 160, 63, *64,* 106–111
    fondant, 107–109, *109,* 124–26

orders, 106–112
    on television, 136, 137, 140–41, 148, 149

Wedges, Pecan, 173–74

Whipped cream, 35, 104
    piping, 104–105

Whipped Cream, Italian, 205

Whipped-cream machine, 98

Winter cakes, 125

World War II, 11

Zabaglione, 126

Zaslav, David, 145

Zeppole, 96, 186

Zeppole, St. Joseph's (*Sfingi*), 186–88

Zester, microplane, 155

ABOUT THE AUTHOR

Buddy Valastro is an accomplished fourth-generation baker born in Hoboken, New Jersey. At an early age, it was clear that he was a natural baker and would go into the family business. He loved spending time with his father, also called Buddy, a master baker, as his apprentice, spending countless hours in the bakery learning the Old World secrets of baking. They dreamed that together they would make Carlo's Bakery a household name. Since his father's passing when Buddy was seventeen, and with the help of his family, his father's recipes, and his own innovative decorating and sugar-art techniques, Buddy has taken Carlo's Bakery to new heights.

Today, Buddy is a master baker and cake decorator who is often asked to demonstrate, compete, and teach his craft around the country. In his traditional, old-school Italian bakery, Buddy and his staff turn out thousands of wedding cakes, specialty cakes, and pastries weekly. His award-winning designs have been featured numerous times in different bridal and baking magazines. Carlo's Bakery has also been featured in books, newspapers, such as the *New York Times*, and television, mostly TLC's hit *Cake Boss*, although he and his cakes have also been featured on *The Today Show*, *Good Morning America*, *The View*, and HBO's hit series, *The Sopranos*.

PHOTO CREDITS

Bronx Zoo Cake: Jay King
Buddy's Wedding Cakes: Studio Uno
Sugar Flowers: Theresa Mercado
All other images: Tina Rupp

AVAILABLE IN NOVEMBER 2011!

LEARN HOW TO BAKE
FROM THE

HIMSELF!

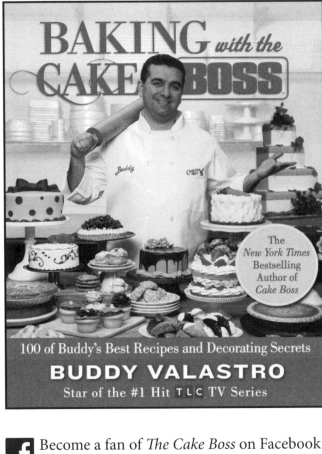

Learn how to bake the way Buddy learned—old school! This cookbook takes you from basic cookies to delicious pastries to the beautifully decorated cakes for which Buddy is famous, following the learning curve of everyone who comes to work at Carlo's Bake Shop. Starting with the basics of baking, this is the Buddy System, perfect for learning to bake like the Boss.

Includes step-by-step instructional photos and more than 100 recipes!

f Become a fan of *The Cake Boss* on Facebook at www.facebook.com/CakeBoss.

For more information about *The Cake Boss*, please visit www.SimonandSchuster.com or www.tlc.howstuffworks.com/tv/cake-boss.

*f*P **FREE PRESS**
A Division of Simon & A CBS COMPANY